THE ART OF THE ZOMBIE MOVIE

A HISTORY OF ZOMBIE MOVIES, FROM THE SILENT ERA TO TODAY

LISA MORTON

FOREWORD BY JOHN A. RUSSO

Published by

APPLAUSE
THEATRE & CINEMA BOOKS

An Imprint of Globe Pequot, the trade division of
The Rowman & Littlefield Publishing Group, Inc

Copyright © Elephant Book Company Limited 2023

www.elephantbookcompany.com

Applause Books
An imprint of Globe Pequot, the trade division of
The Rowman & Littlefield Publishing Group, Inc.
4501 Forbes Blvd., Ste. 200, Lanham, MD 20706

www.rowman.com

Distributed by NATIONAL BOOK NETWORK

Trade Book Division Editorial Offices
64 South Main Street, Essex, Connecticut 06426

Editorial director: Will Steeds
Project manager: Tom Seabrook
Book design: Paul Palmer-Edwards
Picture researcher: Sally Claxton
Indexer: Paula Clarke Bain

Printed in China

Library of Congress Cataloging-in-Publication Data is available upon request.

ISBN 978-1-4930-6970-5

www.applausebooks.com

FRONTISPIECE: "Official Portrait" of the conquistador (affectionately known as "Wormface" and portrayed by Ottaviano Dell'Acqua) from Lucio Fulci's *Zombi 2* (1979), by the British artist Jolyon Yates. This ink-and-digital work was done for the November 2015 issue of *Monster!* magazine. In a nod to *Zombi 2*'s famous shark vs. zombie fight, the zombie is wearing a shark-tooth necklace.

BACKGROUND THIS SPREAD: Original artwork by the American artist Basil Gogos (1929–2017) for director Sergio Martino's 1972 giallo (an Italian strand of horror movie) *All the Colors of the Dark*. This artwork appeared on an American one-sheet poster under the title *They're Coming to Get You*; the film would later be re-released as *Day of the Maniac*. On the one-sheet, the artwork was tinted blood-red.

CONTENTS

FOREWORD
IT ALL STARTS WITH THE SCRIPT

John A. Russo

When I met Quentin Tarantino for the first time at the premiere of George A. Romero's *Land of the Dead* in Pittsburgh, we were having a couple of beers at the bar, and he said, "I made a movie I didn't finish, then I read your books and took notes and made charts, and that's what guided me through my first complete movie."

Needless to say, I was flattered. He was talking about my three nonfiction books on moviemaking, which have come to be known as "Bibles of Independent Filmmaking." (These have since been updated and republished as one book under the title *How to Make Exciting Money-Making Movies*.) I'm not trying to sell my book, I'm merely emphasizing a key point for anyone who aspires to be a writer, producer, or director, not just of horror films but of any type of film.

When George A. Romero was featured on a television show called *Iconoclasts*, he said, "You know, when you say that you want to be a filmmaker, you don't say you just want to be a *horror* filmmaker, you say that you want to be a *filmmaker*."

An excellent point. Because the same theme, plot, and character considerations apply to *all* films as well as horror films. A genuine and deep understanding of the art and craft of moviemaking should not vary from one genre to another. A script for an outstanding horror movie must have unity, coherence, and emphasis. It should deal with an important theme, and that theme should be explored through the eyes of intriguing characters facing some form of life-or-death jeopardy. It is not enough to just come up with a weird, frightening monster or serial killer who goes around butchering one victim after another. It worked in *Friday the 13th*—but it generally fails. Cardboard characters who make dumb decisions will be laughed at by sophisticated audiences—as was pointed out in a series of Geico commercials.

When Russ Streiner, Rudy Ricci, and I first wrote our script for a *Night of the Living Dead* sequel we called *The Return of the Living Dead*, we weren't able to finance it after shopping it for ten years to potential investors and distributors. At first I was pitched as the director, and next I brought in Tobe Hooper—and even still, no one would come up with any money. Then Tom Fox bought us out so he could hire Dan O'Bannon, who was bankable due to his work on *Alien* and *Blue Thunder*. But even with Dan's topnotch credentials, the studio guys at Orion and Hemdale said, "You can't make straight horror anymore. Straight horror is dead. You have to turn it into a comedy."

Dan O'Bannon totally rewrote our existing script—and the rest is history! The movie was a smash hit and has spawned about a dozen sequels. The plot is exciting, the zombies are an intriguing departure from the original kinds of zombies that populated *Night of the Living Dead*, and the main characters are not "cardboard" or "cannon fodder." They have depth to them, and they harbor human frailties and conflicts that lead to their self-destruction. It works off of the universal theme of whether or not we human beings, with all our imperfections, can learn to get along with one another and survive a desperate situation, or whether our egos, our petty jealousies, or even our greed, will cause us to destroy each other.

To be a top writer or filmmaker, you have to focus on a theme that intrigues and excites you and decide what types of characters can best help you to explore that theme. After we made *Night of the Living Dead* and it became a great success, it occurred to me that it could be thought of as *Stagecoach* with zombies instead of Indians. *Stagecoach* had John Wayne as the gunslinger/hero, the prostitute he was smitten with, and the drunken doctor whose skills would be put to the test under dire jeopardy. *Night of the Living Dead* had the hero, Ben; the naive young couple, Tom and Judy; Barbara, who is nearly catatonic; and the hardheaded guy, Harry Cooper, in the basement with his nearly estranged wife and his ghoul-bitten daughter. Both pictures have a perfect assortment of characters to explore their universal theme and carry their stories forward.

As far as zombies are concerned, I am not a purist. I'm not hung up on slow zombies versus fast zombies. I don't care if they eat brains or just human flesh. Make it work. If you can come up with a brand-new kind of zombie or a brand-new kind of plot, more power to you! Make me want to watch your movie!

This fabulously illustrated book will evoke scary but happy memories of the entertaining movies of your youth and beyond. It makes full use of the artwork and iconic images of those films to bring to life a compelling history of the stars, the creators, and the marketers of zombie movies from when they first began and through the modern era when they were turned into ghouls and flesh-eaters.

Every movie has to be sold, and that's where the great poster art that fills this book is vitally essential. Thrills, chills, and vivid memories will leap out at you from hundreds of full-color pages. They will enable you to spend hours and hours going back and reliving the horror movies that have always thrilled you.

Welcome to the world of Lisa Morton and *The Art of the Zombie Movie*!

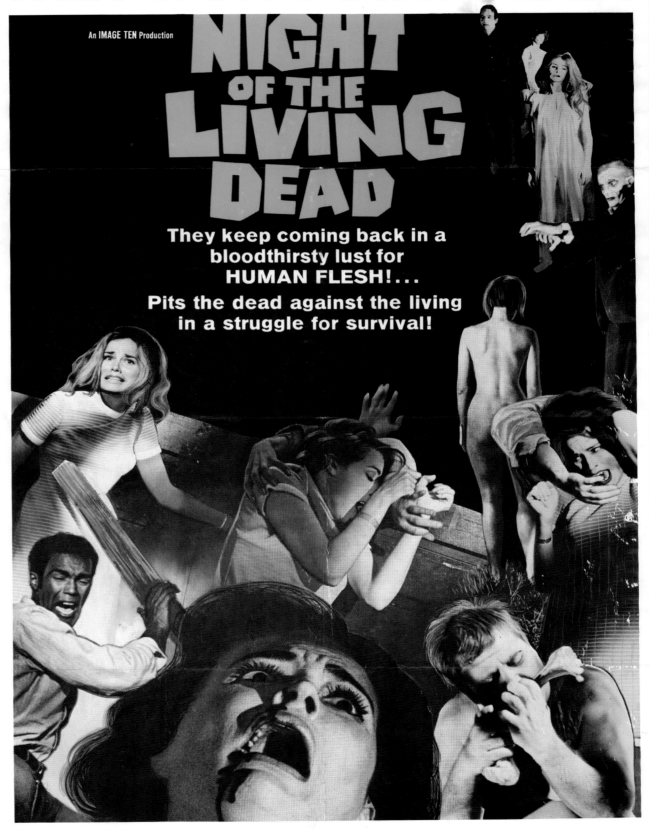

RIGHT: One-sheet poster for *Night of the Living Dead.* When Black actor Duane Jones was cast in the lead role of "Ben" in *Night of the Living Dead,* the choice wasn't motivated to make a statement on race, but rather because Jones was the best actor who was considered for the part.

INTRODUCTION

"They're coming to get you, Barbara . . ."

Johnny in *Night of the Living Dead* (1968)

In the late eighteenth century, English readers first began to encounter strange creatures called "zombies" (the word derives from the French Creole *zombi*, a kind of malevolent spirit). These mentions came in travelogues—published mainly in magazines like *The Universal*—and initially they described something akin to ghosts: "They are supposed to be the spirits of dead wicked men, that are permitted to wander, and torment the living," reads one 1788 account of a trip to St. Domingo in the Caribbean.

Over the next century, references to zombies changed slightly, occasionally noting (more accurately) that they were corpses resurrected by Vodou magicians called *bokors* in order to labor in the fields; they had no will but that of the *bokor* and could toil without the need for much sustenance or rest. Since those who planted, harvested, and milled the sugar had originally been seized from their African homelands and brought to the Caribbean by the French and Spanish, it's easy to read the zombie (then) as a metaphor for the horrors of slavery.

It wasn't until the 1920s, however, that zombies came to wider attention in popular culture. That happened thanks to the work of a journalist and travel writer named William Seabrook. Seabrook roamed the world, spending time with indigenous peoples in South America, Arabia, and Haiti, chiefly pursuing his interest in occult practices; he even had a passing acquaintance with the "Great Beast" himself, Aleister Crowley. In 1929, Seabrook published a book called *The Magic Island*, recounting his experiences living in Haiti and studying Vodou. In a chapter entitled ". . . Dead Men Working in the Cane Fields," Seabrook wrote that he was interested in zombies because—unlike the vampires and werewolves also found in local legends—the soulless, risen dead seemed unique in world folklore. He described zombies in far more depth than anything previously released:

"It seemed . . . that while the *zombie* came from the grave, it was neither a ghost, nor yet a person who had been raised like Lazarus from the dead. The *zombie*, they say, is a soulless human corpse, still dead, but taken from the grave and endowed by sorcery with a mechanical semblance of life—it is a dead body which is made to walk and act and move as if it were alive. People who have the power to do this go to a fresh grave, dig up the body before it has had time to rot, galvanize it into movement, and then make of it a servant or slave, occasionally for the commission of some crime, more often simply as a drudge around the habitation or the farm, setting it dull heavy tasks, and beating it like a dumb beast if it slackens."

Seabrook's guide, a local named Polynice, told him that zombies did require food, but it couldn't contain salt or meat; were either of those to be consumed, the zombies would immediately regain awareness and seek to return to their graves. Polynice pointed out four laborers whom he claimed were zombies, but when Seabrook later discussed the encounter with a learned Haitian doctor, the man showed him a section of the Haitian penal code that addressed the crime of using "substances which, without causing actual death, produce a lethargic coma." Nearly sixty years later, anthropologist Wade Davis would also put forth the theory that zombies were actually the drugged living in his book *The Serpent and the Rainbow*.

The Magic Island found an immediate audience, and voodoo soon became a profitable commodity in American popular culture. On February 10, 1932, a play called *Zombie*,

---

"The *zombie*, they say, is a soulless human corpse, still dead, but taken from the grave and endowed by sorcery with a mechanical semblance of life—it is a dead body which is made to walk and act and move as if it were alive."

William Seabrook, *The Magic Island* (1929)

---

by Kenneth Webb, opened at the Biltmore Theatre on Broadway. Although it closed less than three weeks later, it inspired filmmakers Victor and Edward Halperin to create the film *White Zombie*, which opened later that same year. Lifting heavily from *The Magic Island*, *White Zombie*—the first major zombie movie—stars Bela Lugosi as "Murder" Legendre, a voodoo master who has resurrected both laborers for the local sugar mill and his former enemies to serve as his personal servants.

How, then, did corpses—mainly those of Black laborers—brought to undead life via magic to constitute free labor transform into hordes of shambling, mindless flesh-eaters? Throughout the twentieth-century, the word "zombie" continued to change and be applied to new concepts in everything from philosophy to computers. But it took a 1968 film—one that, ironically, never actually uses the Z word—to complete the zombie's transformation.

George A. Romero's *Night of the Living Dead*, with its depiction of an apocalypse of slow-moving monsters bent only on consumption, calls its risen dead "ghouls," and

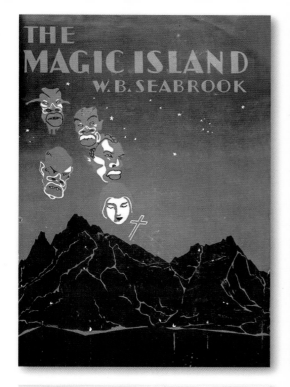

See page 20

"Here are deep matters, not easily to be dismissed by crying blasphemy."

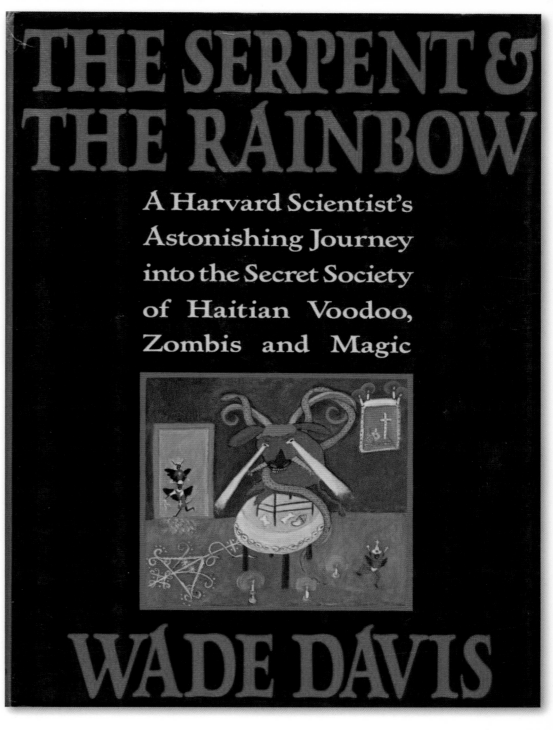

TOP LEFT: Original dust-jacket cover for the first edition of William Seabrook's *The Magic Island*, published by Harcourt, Brace & Company in 1929. In his introduction to a 2016 reissue of the book, George A. Romero noted that the brief chapter on zombies "was enough to elevate the 'zombie' into the ranks of pop-culture stardom."

BOTTOM LEFT: Frontispiece from *The Magic Island* by Alexander King (1899–1965), an Austrian-born artist and writer who became known in the 1950s for his appearances on talk shows. The voodoo bocor's hat in this illustration probably inspired part of the costume for Bela Lugosi's character, "Murder" Legendre, in *White Zombie*.

ABOVE RIGHT: Dust-jacket art for the first edition of Wade Davis's *The Serpent and the Rainbow*, published by Simon and Schuster in 1985. The illustration by American artist Susan McCaslin is based on Haitian artworks. The *vèvè* symbol at lower left corresponds with the *loa* (Vodou spirit) Loco, a patron of healers and plants.

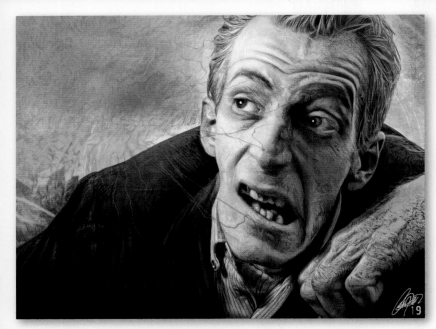

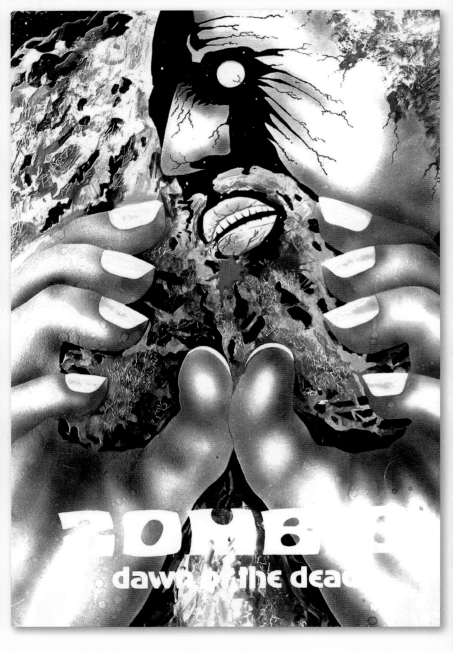

TOP LEFT: Portrait by the American artist Frederick Cooper of *Night of the Living Dead*'s iconic first zombie. Actor Bill Hinzman was part of the investment group Image Ten, and was originally invited to appear as a zombie in a crowd shot; when the cemetery scenes were filmed near the end of principal photography, George Romero asked Hinzman to play the "cemetery ghoul."

BOTTOM LEFT: British quad poster for George A. Romero's *Creepshow* (1982), written by Stephen King. Although Bernie Wrightson illustrated the *Creepshow* comic book, this poster features art by British artist Tom Chantrell (1916–2001), whose other works include the famed British quad for *Star Wars*.

ABOVE RIGHT: German poster for Romero's *Dawn of the Dead* (1978). Note the European title, *Zombie*; its release in some territories as *Zombi* led to a chain of Italian "sequels" that have little to do with Romero's film. German exhibitors so disliked this poster that most copies of it were destroyed.

Romero has noted that he never thought of them in 1968 as "zombies," which were still associated with Caribbean Vodou practices. *Night*'s masterful 1978 sequel, *Dawn of the Dead*, uses the word "zombie" only once; but when that film was released in Europe under the title *Zombi*, imitations would soon appear on movie screens around the world, and from then on the hungry walking dead were forever imprinted on the cultural consciousness as *zombies* (a name Romero said he embraced "eagerly and gratefully").

Because "zombie" has had a shifting meaning and flexibility across time, the term is frequently applied to everything from the silent classic *The Cabinet of Doctor Caligari* (1920) to…well, whenever the dead are resurrected. However, the zombie—in either its original Vodou form or the later Romero transmogrification—has certain distinct characteristics that separate it from other supernatural entities. In both classic and modern form, the zombie is a corpse that has risen to walk again; this resurrection has been accomplished via supernatural means, although science is occasionally brought to play (see, for example, Edward L. Cahn's 1955 entry *Creature with the Atom Brain*). These dead creatures are without will and intelligence, driven only to obey or consume.

"No one can stay in Haiti long without hearing Zombies mentioned in one way or another, and the fear of this thing and all that it means seeps over the country like a ground current of cold air."

Zora Neale Hurston, *Tell My Horse: Voodoo and Life in Haiti and Jamaica* (1938)

This definition rules out ghosts, which have no physical body; and vampires, which usually retain personality and some free will in their undead state. *Caligari*'s "somnambulist," Cesare, may have inspired some of the later look of zombies, with his pale, gaunt visage, but he is quite alive, and thus not truly a zombie. Horror films about cannibals, like the infamous 1980 *Cannibal Holocaust*, may coopt the gore of zombie films, but zombies can't technically be called cannibals since they don't eat their own kind (nor are the flesh-eaters in movies like *Cannibal Holocaust* dead). The zombie is a form of revenant—a being returned from the grave in a physical body, not as a spirit—but not all revenants are zombies; think, for example, of the undead from another Romero film, *Creepshow* (1982), who return with sinister purpose.

Now that zombies have been concretely defined, we can ask: why have these monsters infiltrated the mass consciousness of the last half-century in a way that no other has? Zombies seem to be everywhere these days—in movies, on television, in literature and games and comics, even in music. Why? They aren't glamorous or erotic, like vampires;

they don't express our fears of technology; they don't materialize in old buildings to reveal our unease at our shared past; and, despite the popularity of live festivals that draw thousands dressed as zombies, most of us have no secret desire to become one—as we might have with, say, the powerful and rage-fueled werewolf.

It's perhaps no surprise that the popularity of zombies began to accelerate in the 1970s. In response to the affluent conformity (and McCarthyism) of the 1950s, the '60s had been the growth of anti-establishment counterculture groups and the passage of the Civil Rights Act in 1968; after Richard Nixon was elected and then forced to resign as a result of the Watergate Scandal, the nation lost much of its earlier idealism. Self-help gurus and psychics populated the bestseller lists, offering serenity in an increasingly confused time. Turning away from earlier goals of pursuing the status quo, the idea of attaining individuality was expressed in everything from fashion to television commercials. "Conformity," the beloved President John F. Kennedy once said, "is the jailer of freedom and the enemy of growth."

The zombie is the ultimate expression of our terror of conformity. The soulless, purposeless walking dead is stripped of everything that makes us individual; there's a reason that a group of zombies is often described as a "horde," a mass that is uniform and implacable. The mythology surrounding the zombie further reduces the living to little more than meat; survivors fight to retain life (and the survivor's rugged persona is undeniably part of the appeal), but to the zombies (and possibly to audiences as well) they are the next meal, the next gore effect.

Why do we love watching these films? Partly because they provide a thrill ride, with their emphasis on violence, combat, and blood; but mainly because they poke at our fears about the failure of both our deepest selves and our broader society. The best zombie films also offer the possibility of winning the battle, albeit that the new world created in the aftermath may be something very different.

Zombie films also address other societal ills as well. Look at both 1932's *White Zombie* and 1968's *Night of the Living Dead*, the two films that perfectly define the range of zombie cinema: race figures prominently in both, as the cruelly used laborers in the first film and the valiant protagonist who is shot by a white mob in the second are Black. Zombie movies also address our unease about disease, our uncertainties about science, medicine, and government (which seem to fail in the face of a zombie plague), and our fears for the future.

The last question, and the one that pertains to this book, is: why should we enjoy looking at images that capture these films in all their messy splendor? Because the films thrill us, horrify us, make us laugh and scream…and the art extends the experience, capturing individual moments that allow us to relive them. One could say that the art reminds us that we are still alive enough, still *us* enough, to feel something.

Here's to the zombie film, then, with all of its random splatter, both physical and mental.

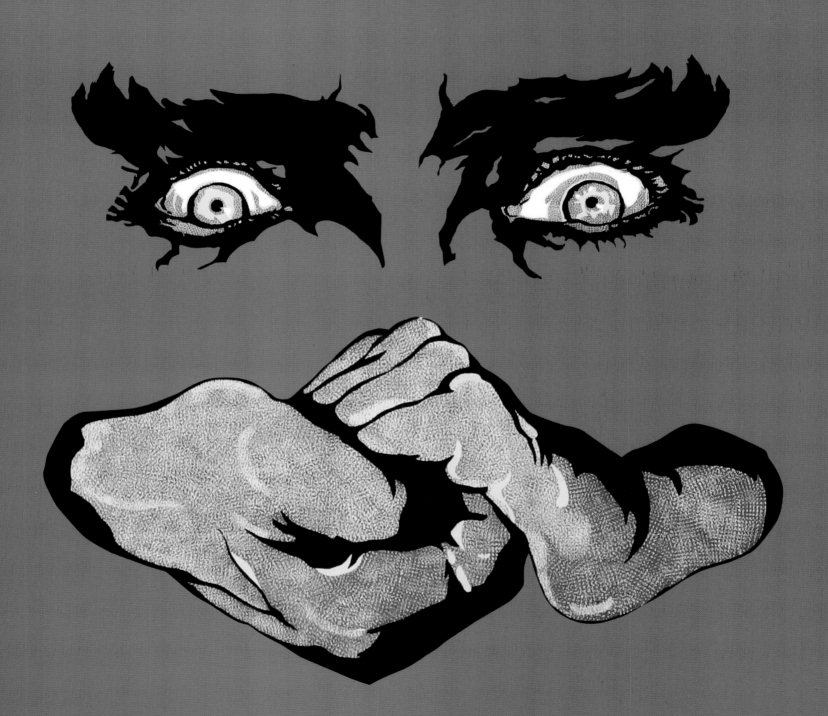

1
THE FIRST ZOMBIES

"THEY ARE NOT MEN, MONSIEUR
—THEY ARE DEAD BODIES."

THE COACH DRIVER IN *WHITE ZOMBIE* (1932)

> ## "Cinema should be an escape ... people need magic. We all seek it."
>
> Jacques Tourneur, director of *I Walked with a Zombie*, from a 1979 video interview

In 1927, the first sound motion picture (*The Jazz Singer*) appeared and effectively put an end to the silent era. Since the word "zombie" didn't enter the greater public discourse until two years later, when William Seabrook's *The Magic Island* was published, zombies are missing from the entire silent-film era. Vodou (or, in its more popular alternate spelling, voodoo) featured in only one significant silent film, 1917's *Unconquered,* and that centered on human sacrifice.

The closest any of the silents edged toward zombie territory was the classic 1920 German film *The Cabinet of Dr. Caligari* (*Das Cabinet des Dr. Caligari*). Directed by Robert Wiene, featuring stylized sets and characters, Dr. Caligari is considered the finest example of German Expressionism and a comment on how immoral authority can dominate and control. Its story of the "somnambulist" Cesare (Conrad Veidt)—a man unable to awaken from his lifelong sleep unless directed to by the malevolent sideshow performer Dr. Caligari, portrayed by Werner Krauss—is not technically a zombie movie, since Cesare is alive. However, its depiction of the deathly pale, hollow-eyed Cesare moving mechanically and without his own will (his actions are all dictated by Caligari) can be seen as an influence on later zombie movies, especially *Night of the Living Dead.*

The ideas presented in *The Magic Island* took a few years to spread. Zombies appeared first in short pulp-horror stories like G. W. Hutter's "Salt Is Not for Slaves" (from the August/September 1931 issue of *Ghost Stories*). Hutter was actually Garnett Wilson, who a year later would write the screenplay for the first real zombie film, *White Zombie.*

Directed by Victor Halperin and starring Bela Lugosi and Madge Bellamy, *White Zombie* draws liberally from *The Magic Island,* even costuming its characters in garb similar to that shown in illustrations by Alexander King that appear in the book. The film, which Lugosi shot a year after starring in Universal's *Dracula,* is centered on a young couple, Madeline and Philip (Bellamy and John Harron), who are about to be married at the Haitian estate of their mutual acquaintance Beaumont (Robert Frazer); Beaumont, however, is secretly in love with Madeline, and he engages the services of the amoral and conniving voodoo master "Murder" Legendre (Lugosi) to make Madeline his (entranced) bride instead. The film does contain moments of genuine horror—namely the scene in a sugar mill operated completely by zombies, and the climax set in Legendre's cliff-side "Castle of the Living Dead"—but *White Zombie* was dismissed by critics at the time because of its bad acting and cheap production values. The film, which was produced independently on a budget of less than $100,000, was shot in eleven days, mainly on the Universal lot, even using sets from *Dracula.* (Universal's great makeup artist Jack Pierce, who had created the look of the studio's most iconic monsters, also devised Lugosi's makeup as Legendre.)

> ## "She's Alive ... Yet Dead! She's Dead ... Yet Alive!"
>
> Original newspaper ad for *I Walked with a Zombie* (1943)

Despite the reviews, *White Zombie* generated sizable box-office numbers, so it could be thought of as the first hit indie horror film; and, despite lawsuits that even attempted to prevent the producers from using the word "zombie," it did generate a sequel, 1936's *Revolt of the Zombies,* which—oddly—is set in Cambodia, not Haiti. *Revolt,* which stars Dean Jagger and Dorothy Stone (and frequently uses closeups of Lugosi's eyes from *White Zombie*), is technically not even a zombie film, since it involves the use of ancient Asian magic to hypnotize the living in an effort to create invincible soldiers during World War I.

White Zombie also accomplished one other feat: it created a template for the next twenty years of zombie films, which nearly all revolved around visitors or adventurers to a Caribbean isle who discover a white zombie master; that master may be using either occult ritual or science (or a combination) to create zombies, all of whom either are the white ingénue or Black zombies threatening her. Although a few of the films (like Jean Yarbrough's *King of the Zombies* and Jacques Tourneur's *I Walked with a Zombie*) included Black actors in more interesting roles, most were plainly designed for white audiences at a time when Jim Crow laws and segregation were in active use throughout the United States.

Just as Bela Lugosi left Universal briefly to make *White*

PREVIOUS SPREAD: Art from the 1938 re-release of *White Zombie,* emphasizing—as much of the promotional material for the film did—Bela Lugosi's "zombie grip" and hypnotic eyes.

ABOVE LEFT: Window card for *White Zombie*, emphasizing Bela Lugosi as "Murder" Legendre. Lugosi must have been hurt by some of the reviews he received for his performance; the *Pittsburgh Post-Gazette*, for example, remarked, "you're supposed to squirm around in your seat [but] laughing out loud seems like a better idea."

TOP RIGHT: This illustration by Alexander King appears in the chapter of William Seabrook's *The Magic Island* (1929) entitled ". . . Dead Men Working in the Cane Fields," which focuses on the voodoo practice of returning the dead to life (to serve as slave labor), and which introduced zombies to popular culture.

BOTTOM RIGHT: Original lobby card (with UFA studio stamp in the lower left corner) for *The Cabinet of Dr. Caligari* (1920), showing Cesare (Conrad Veidt) rising from his cabinet while Dr. Caligari (Werner Krauss, right) stands by. Caligari's appearance was based in part on the philosopher Arthur Schopenhauer.

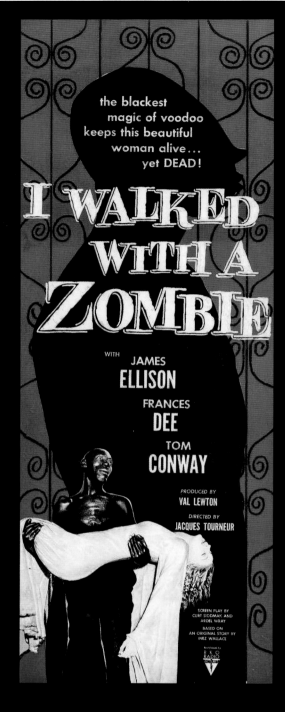

TOP LEFT: Lobby card for *The Devil's Daughter* (1939). An alternative title for the film was *Pocomania!*, which is a branch of the Afro-Jamaican spirituality Myal (distinct from Obeah, the practice depicted in the film). Star Nina Mae McKinney, who was sometimes referred to as "the Black Garbo," was posthumously recognized by the Black Filmmakers Hall of Fame.

BOTTOM LEFT: An 11×14 lobby card for *King of the Zombies* (1941). Black actor Mantan Moreland's screen career was supernatural right from the start: he debuted in *That's the Spirit* (1933) as a security guard in a haunted pawnshop. Besides his run as chauffeur Birmingham Brown in the Charlie Chan films, he was also famed for a series of comedic mysteries that paired him with Frankie Darro.

ABOVE RIGHT: Insert poster for a 1956 re-release of *I Walked with a Zombie* (originally released in 1943). Although Carrefour, the zombie played by Darby Jones and featured prominently on this poster, is the film's most recognizable Black character, of equal importance is the singer Sir Lancelot, whose songs director Jacques Tourneur compared to a Greek chorus.

Zombie, the studio's other horror star, Boris Karloff, returned to his native Great Britain in 1933 to make a feature about the walking dead. However, *The Ghoul*, directed by T. Hayes Hunter, is not a zombie movie because the eponymous character (played by Karloff) is a wealthy man who attains immortality via a priceless jewel called "Eternal Light"; when he returns from death (which he does to exact revenge), he retains his personality and will. The film contains some atmosphere and an interesting performance from Karloff (despite being hidden behind an odd makeup of shaggy brows), but it's now notable chiefly for having been considered a lost film until the original negative was discovered in a forgotten film vault at Shepperton Studios in the UK at some point in the 1980s.

Probably the oddest zombie film to come from this period was *Ouanga* (also known as *The Love Wanga*), directed and written by George Terwilliger, shot in Haiti and Jamaica, and originally intended for release in 1935 but ultimately held back until 1942. A mix of melodrama and horror film, *Ouanga* is about a mixed-race plantation owner, Klili Gordon (Fredi Washington, a well-known member of the Harlem Renaissance who starred in the 1934 *Imitation of Life*), who falls in love with her neighbor, Adam Maynard (Philip

---

By 1945, the voodoo zombie had run its course, just as the other classic monsters had, due to a real-life horror that caused vampires, werewolves, and the walking dead to pale in comparison: the atom bomb.

Brandon); when Adam rejects Klili in favor of Eve (Marie Paxton), Klili turns to her skills as a voodoo high priestess, eventually calling on two zombies to kidnap Eve. The film, which in 2021 was restored by the UCLA Film and Television Archive, addresses head-on the Black/white tensions between Klili and Adam, but is (with the exception of Washington) badly acted, and limns voodoo as a primitive spectacle. *Ouanga* was remade with an entirely Black cast in 1939 as *The Devil's Daughter* (also known as *Pocomania!*); voodoo, however, was replaced with Obeah, and although zombies are never mentioned, the climax centers on a ritual to turn the Obeah priestess Isabelle's rival into a controlled, soulless creature. The ritual turns out to be an elaborate con.

Ten years later, director Jacques Tourneur, producer Val Lewton, and writers Curt Siodmak and Ardel Wray would make what is inarguably the finest zombie film from the first half of the twentieth century: *I Walked with a Zombie* (1943). This eerie tale of a Canadian nurse (Frances Dee) who arrives at a remote Caribbean island to care for the paralyzed wife of a plantation owner is the only film of the voodoo-zombie cycle to deal with the history of slavery in

the Caribbean (and the roles played by colonial plantation owners); it also looks more realistically at voodoo as a religion, and suggests zombification as an illness. Although the film received mixed reviews upon its release, it was successful at the box office, and it has since come to be regarded as one of the best horror films of the 1940s.

The influence of both *White Zombie* and *I Walked with a Zombie* is plainly visible in 1944's *Voodoo Man*, in which Bela Lugosi and George Zucco bizarrely play voodoo priests in decorated velvet cloaks who have control of a bevy of white-robe-clad, blank-eyed female zombies. The film is perhaps notable for being the first *meta* zombie movie, since the young protagonist (played by Michael Ames) is a screenwriter who ends up handing his producer (whose initials are the same as the film's real producer Sam Katzman) a script entitled *Voodoo Man* and suggesting that Bela Lugosi should star in it.

The '40s also saw the rise of comic zombie movies, beginning in 1940 with *The Ghost Breakers*. Starring Bob Hope and Paulette Goddard in a plot that has Goddard's character inheriting an old South Seas mansion, this enjoyable romp includes both ghosts and zombies, and the latter are genuinely unnerving.

Released a year later, *King of the Zombies* has two heroic American spies (played by Dick Purcell and John Archer) who crash on an isolated Caribbean island while searching for a missing admiral; there, they encounter the mysterious Dr. Sangre (Henry Victor), who claims to be an Austrian refugee but is actually a German spy trying to use voodoo to obtain information from the captured admiral. With the inclusion of Black comedian Mantan Moreland as a third lead, *King of the Zombies* manages to remain light, fast, and zany. It also trailblazes the way for decades of zombie movies about Nazis either creating zombies or returning as them, which would continue on through films like *The Frozen Dead* (1966) and *Dead Snow* (2009).

Less successful was *Zombies on Broadway*, a 1945 vehicle for RKO's Abbott and Costello knockoff team, Wally Brown and Alan Carney. The plot puts these two hams in the service of a mobster (Sheldon Leonard) who's trying to open a Broadway night club called "The Zombie Hut" and tasks the duo with finding a real zombie for opening night. Their search takes them to the Caribbean island of San Sebastian (the same island where *I Walked with a Zombie* took place), where they encounter a mad doctor (Bela Lugosi) creating zombies with a serum he's invented. The ensuing hijinks tend more toward embarrassment than amusement.

By 1945, the voodoo zombie had run its course, just as the other classic monsters had, due to a real-life horror that caused vampires, werewolves, and the walking dead to pale in comparison: the atom bomb. The next decade would see all of the old favorites resurrected in new, atomic-powered versions. Zombies, not yet ready to return to their graves, would soon be controlled by aliens and scientists instead of voodoo masters.

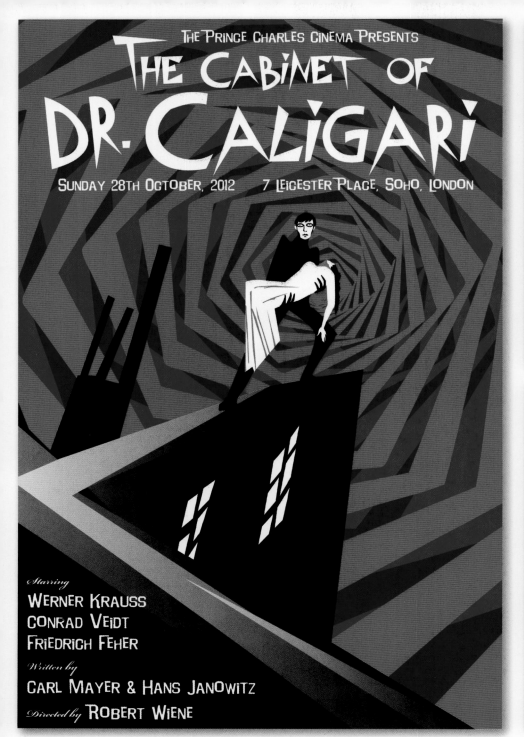

ABOVE LEFT: This silkscreened print by the Mexican artist Rodolfo Reyes was created for a 2012 screening of *The Cabinet of Dr. Caligari* at the Prince Charles Cinema in London. "The twisting spiral and the angled buildings," he says, "are a representation of the unbalanced nature of the Doctor and Cesare."

TOP RIGHT: Three-color screen print by the American artist Kevin Tong, created for exhibition at the Mondo Gallery during the 2014 SXSW festival. There was also a gold variant of this work, released in a run of 150 signed and numbered prints; this, the silver colorway, was limited to 300.

BOTTOM RIGHT: Alternative German poster for *The Cabinet of Dr. Caligari*, using the German spelling of "Kabinett." The film's writers, Hans Janowitz and Carl Mayer, actually titled their script using the English spelling, "Cabinet."

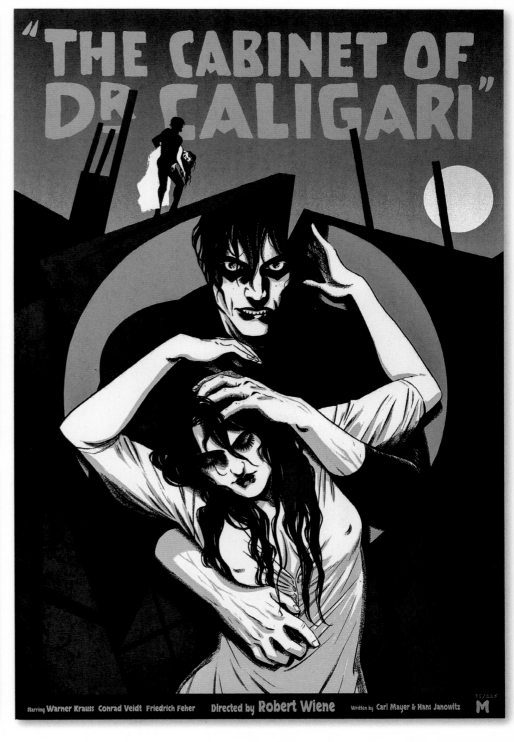

TOP LEFT: Poster for the 1923 UK release of *The Cabinet of Dr. Caligari*. The distributor, Phillips Film Company, put out dozens of silent films during the period 1919 to 1925.

BOTTOM LEFT: Original Austrian poster for *The Cabinet of Dr. Caligari* created by Atelier Ledl Bernhard (the studio of Rudolf Ledl and Fritz Bernhard), who also supplied art for beer and liquor posters as well as other films. Their style was characteristic of the art from Germany's Weimar period.

ABOVE RIGHT: A limited-edition screen-print poster from 2015 by the artist Becky Cloonan, known chiefly as a comic book artist. In 2012, Cloonan became the first woman to draw DC Comics' main *Batman* title. She has also worked with Dark Horse, Marvel, and Tokyopop.

ABOVE LEFT: An alternative poster for *White Zombie* by the artist Doug P'Gosh that employs part of the slogan used by United Artists for its 1938 re-release of the film. "Lugosi's role in *Dracula* may be more famous," P'Gosh says, "but I find his portrayal of Legendre in *White Zombie* more interesting, and the film itself better. Many scenes scream out (no pun intended) to be turned into paintings."

TOP RIGHT: *White Zombie* art from 2008 by Francesco Francavilla, an American artist who also illustrated the macabre 2010s reboot of the *Archie* comics. Actor Clarence Muse (shown here on the right), who has the small but pivotal part of the coachman who explains zombies, claimed that Lugosi had a hand in *White Zombie*'s script and direction, but this has been questioned by later scholars.

BOTTOM RIGHT: Alternative poster for *White Zombie* by the artist Elvisdead (Mathieu Pequignot), featuring Lugosi as Legendre. Strangely, although it appeared in press materials related to the film, the name Legendre is never spoken in the film, although Lugosi's character is referred to once as "Murder."

OPPOSITE: Portrait of Lugosi as Legendre by the American artist Frederick Cooper. Lugosi would become somewhat bitter about *White Zombie*, expressing a belief that while it was profitable enough to make a tremendous amount of money for the producers (somewhat true), he himself was underpaid. He may have taken on the role due to money problems of his own, as he filed for bankruptcy in October 1932.

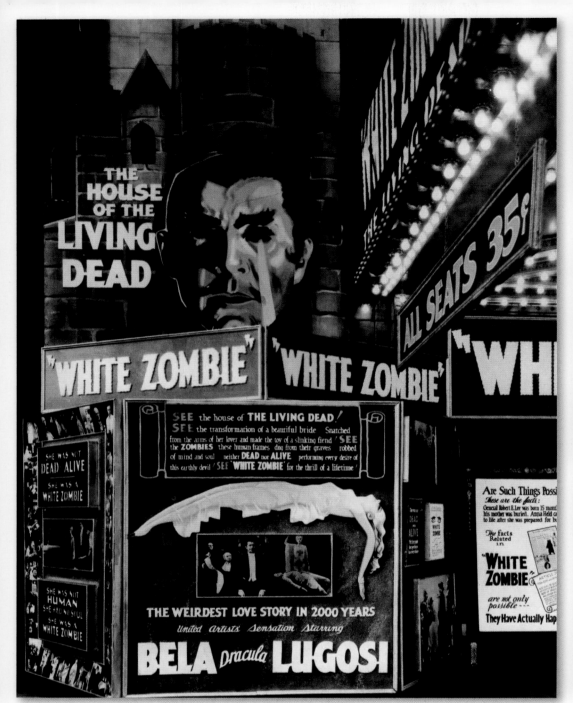

ABOVE LEFT: Theatrical promotional ad for *White Zombie*. During the Great Depression, theater owners often engaged in ballyhoo to draw in audiences; some even used real costumed performers or piped sound effects out into the street (drums, chanting, bird calls) to promote the film.

TOP RIGHT: Half-sheet poster from the original 1932 release of *White Zombie*. As well as its fine portrait of Lugosi, this artwork also shows Frederick Peters as Chauvin, the former executioner who becomes one of Legendre's zombie servants. At six foot three and 250lbs, Peters's Chauvin is the largest and most frightening of the film's zombies.

MIDDLE RIGHT: A lobby card from the 1932 release of *White Zombie*. Although young lovers Neil (John Harron) and Madeline (Madge Bellamy) feature prominently here, the more dynamic image shows Legendre surrounded by his zombie servants (all former enemies) and, at far left, Beaumont (Robert Frazer), who hires Legendre to zombify Madeline.

BOTTOM RIGHT: Hand-tinted lobby card from the 1932 release of the film showing the romantic leads surrounded by Legendre and his zombies inside his cliffside castle. The castle was likely inspired by the real Palace of Sans-Souci in Milot, Haiti, which was built in 1813 for Haitian king Henry I.

TOP LEFT: This Legendre figure was released by Hong Kong collectibles company Star Ace Toys in 2022 in three formats: a standard ⅙ scale figure with hat, knife, small crow, wax doll, and a separate pair of "hypnotic gesture" hands; a deluxe version with light-up lamppost, tombstone, and flying crow; and a limited-edition black-and-white version.

BOTTOM LEFT: A Murder Legendre mask produced by Retro-a-go-go! Both mask and box were designed by Doug P'Gosh. The company and artist have also produced masks of Lugosi's Dracula, as well as his Igor from *Son of Frankenstein*. There is also a black-and-white variant of this mask.

ABOVE RIGHT: One-sheet poster art from the 1938 re-release of *White Zombie*. First released in 1932, the film was independently produced, with financing put together by producer Phil Goldstone, and then distributed by United Artists.

FROM VAMPIRES TO VOODOO: BELA LUGOSI

"There is something of a mysterious, hypnotic quality about the man himself, particularly about his deep-set eyes, and the reason appears to be that he has probed life too deeply."

Description of Bela Lugosi, from the pressbook for *White Zombie*

By the time Bela Lugosi made *White Zombie*, he was already well on his way to becoming a horror icon, thanks to his performance in Universal's *Dracula* (1931), directed by Tod Browning.

Born Béla Ferenc Dezső Blaskó in Lugos, Hungary, in 1882, Lugosi was a popular performer in the National Theatre of Hungary, served in the Austro-Hungarian Army during World War I, and arrived in the United States in 1920. He soon found acting work in New York, where in 1927 he was cast in the Broadway production of *Dracula*. After playing the vampire count in hundreds of stage performances, he was cast by director Tod Browning in the film version, which proved to be hugely successful. With *Murders in the Rue Morgue* and *White Zombie* (both in 1932), Lugosi was forever typecast as a horror actor. He went on to appear in dozens of films, including *Island of Lost Souls* (1932), *The Black Cat* (1934), *The Raven* (1935), *The Invisible Ray* (1936), *Son of Frankenstein* (1939), *Black Friday* (1940), *You'll Find Out* (1940), *The Wolf Man* (1941), and *The Body Snatcher* (1945). Toward the end of his life, as he struggled with addictions and money problems, Lugosi worked principally with the notorious schlockmeister Edward D. Wood, Jr.; their relationship would be chronicled by Tim Burton in his 1994 film *Ed Wood*, for which Martin Landau won an Academy Award for his performance as Lugosi.

Lugosi viewed *White Zombie* with both bitterness and pride. His salary on the film was a sore spot; he claimed it was only $500, although it was likely more. Later in life, he called the film one of his favorites, even stating in a 1952 article that he hoped to soon be appearing in a sequel called *Return of the White Zombie* (which was completely untrue). Critics in 1932 were divided on his performance: Richard Watts, Jr. in the *New York Herald Tribune* stated that "good makeup cannot conceal a bad actor"; conversely, *Film Daily noted* that "Bela Lugosi is very impressive." However, the passing of time has brought a critical re-evaluation to both the film and Lugosi's portrayal of Legendre, with most modern film scholars considering it

Lugosi, who was married five times, was often desperate for money; although he'd famously turned down the role of Frankenstein's monster (the role of course made Boris Karloff a star), by the mid-'30s he was accepting virtually any role that was offered to him, resulting in a string of largely forgettable pictures (with an occasionally small part

With *Murders in the Rue Morgue* and *White Zombie*, Lugosi was forever typecast as a horror actor.

in a classic like *The Wolf Man* in 1941). He made several other zombie films, including *Bowery at Midnight* (1942), *Voodoo Man* (1944), and *Zombies on Broadway* (1945), an especially bad zombie comedy that casts him as a mad scientist in Haiti, creating zombies via a serum.

Zombies on Broadway essentially ended the trend of voodoo zombies in 1940s cinema, but Lugosi made one more zombie movie: Ed Wood's notorious *Plan 9 from Outer Space* (1957), about aliens creating zombies in an effort to conquer earth. It was to be his final film appearance. He died of a heart attack on August 16, 1956, at the age of seventy-three, and was buried wearing one of his Dracula capes and his Dracula ring.

As an actor, Lugosi was a true artist who once said, "Whenever an actor gets satisfied with his work, he's done—he's through." Although he is now chiefly remembered for his portrayal of the bloodthirsty count, his performance as "Murder" Legendre has become iconic in its own way, engendering posters, collectible figures, and analysis. Lugosi has also influenced such diverse arts as music (the 1979 goth-rock classic "Bela Lugosi's Dead" by Bauhaus), fine art (Andy Warhol's 1963 silkscreen print "The Kiss," which depicts Lugosi leaning into the neck of *Dracula* costar Helen Chandler), and even manga (Paru Itagaki's long-running

RIGHT: Lugosi poses as Legendre in the main hall of his "Castle of the Living Dead" in this promotional still from *White Zombie*. His performance, arriving on the heels of his work in *Dracula* and *Murders in the Rue Morgue*, cemented his stereotyping as a horror actor. Director Victor Halperin noted of working with him, "He never got tired of closeups."

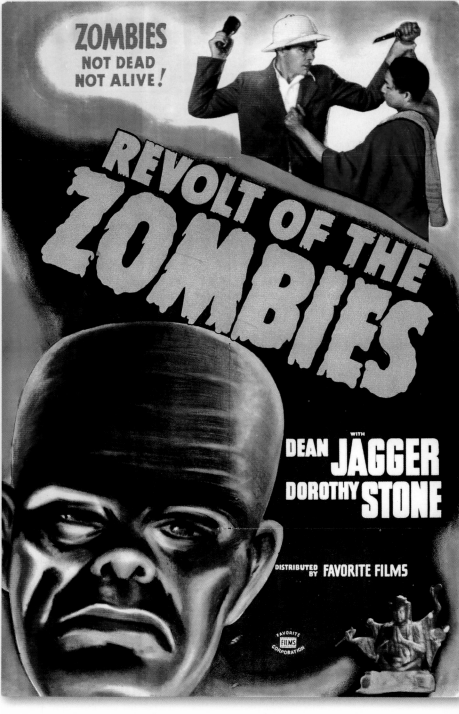

ABOVE LEFT: One-sheet poster for *Revolt of the Zombies* (1936). In director Victor Halperin's unofficial sequel to *White Zombie*, Dean Jagger takes on the role of the magician; it's possible that Lugosi's contract with Universal wouldn't allow him to work for another company in 1936.

ABOVE RIGHT: One-sheet poster for the 1947 re-release of *Revolt of the Zombies*, featuring a zombie that looks considerably more like Noble Johnson's zombie from *The Ghost Breakers* (1940) than any of the spellbound soldiers in *Revolt*.

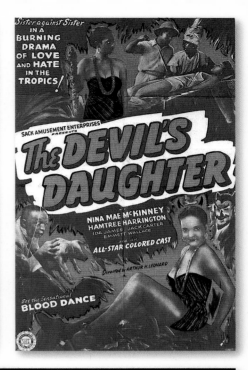

ABOVE LEFT: This silkscreened three-sheet for *Revolt of the Zombies* was made even rarer by the comparison to *White Zombie*, since *Revolt* endured a lengthy court case continuing past its initial release that restricted any promotional materials from mentioning the earlier film.

TOP MIDDLE: 1942 poster for *Ouanga*, here billed as *The Love Wanga*. Originally intended for release in 1935 (and issued in Great Britain in 1936), *Ouanga* was beset by problems from the beginning; director George Terwilliger was supposedly even cursed with a "ouanga" after attempting to film Haitian voodoo followers.

TOP RIGHT: Poster for *The Devil's Daughter* (1939), a remake of *Ouanga* that was actually released in the U.S. before the first film. Made with an entirely Black cast, it replaces voodoo with Obeah, a West Indies religion that incorporates deities known as the Abosom and the Abonsam and is similar to Vodou and Myal.

BOTTOM RIGHT: Mexican lobby card from a 1960 release of *Revolt of the Zombies* that also uses the Noble Johnson–like zombie face. This one is signed by the artist Aguirre Tinoco, who produced art for a number of horror, science fiction, and *luchador* (wrestler) films from the 1950s onward.

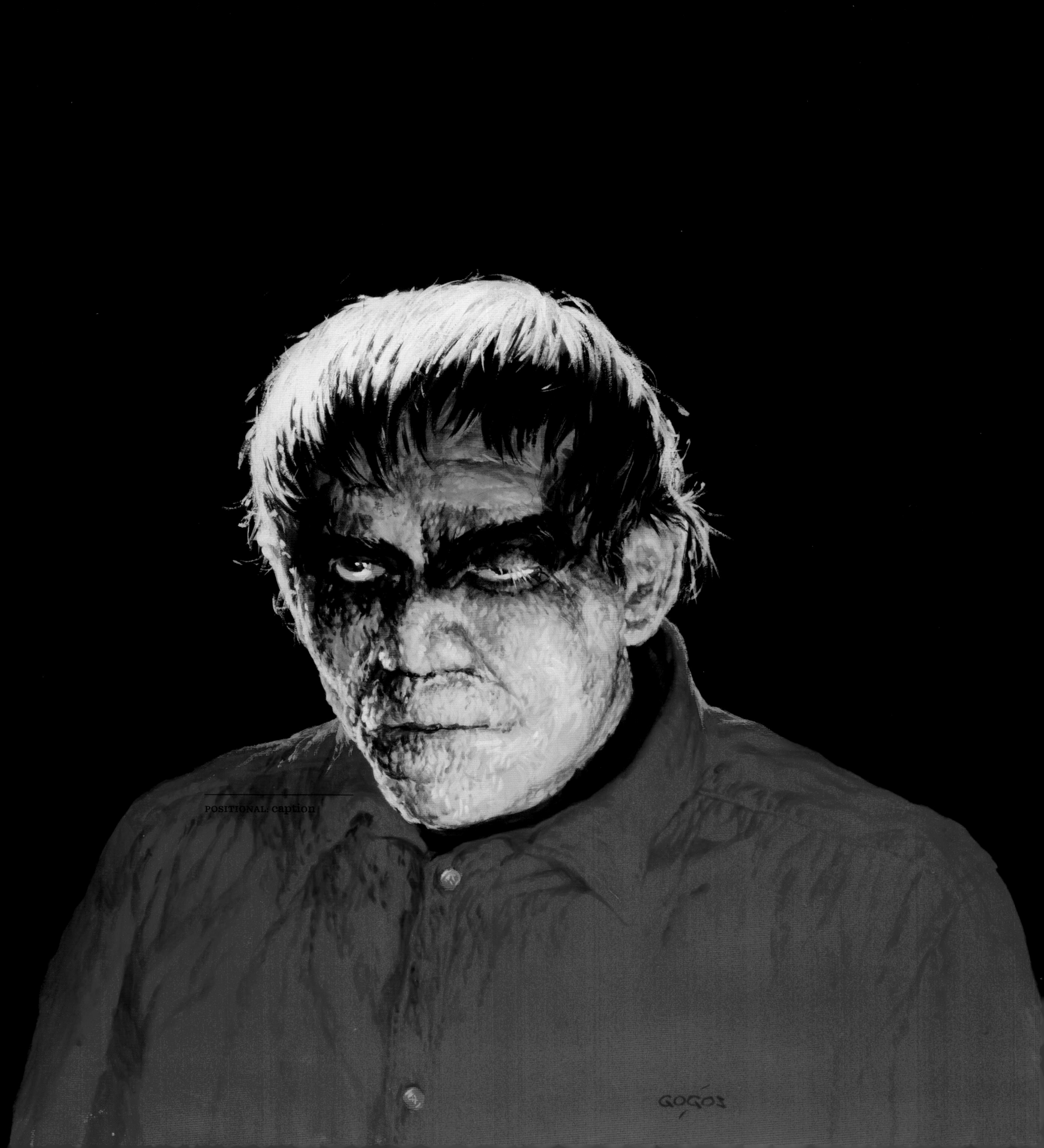

POSITIONAL caption

OPPOSITE: Portrait of Boris Karloff in the title role from *The Ghoul* (1933) by the artist Basil Gogos (1929–2017). This image served as the cover for issue #110 of *Famous Monsters of Filmland*. Karloff made *The Ghoul* in Britain for Gaumont shortly after shooting both *The Mummy* and *The Old Dark House* (both 1932) for Universal, and *The Ghoul* shows the influence of both those films.

ABOVE LEFT: Japanese poster for *The Ghoul*. Until a copy was discovered in Czechoslovakia in 1969, *The Ghoul* was thought to be a lost film; that copy was missing eight minutes of footage. In the 1980s, the original negative was discovered in a forgotten film vault at Shepperton Studios, London, and new prints were struck by the British Film Institute.

ABOVE RIGHT: Original one-sheet poster for *The Ghoul* (1933). The film not only starred Boris Karloff and his *Bride of Frankenstein* co-star Ernest Thesiger (as well as Cedric Hardwicke), it also marked the debut of Ralph Richardson. Director T. Hayes Hunter had worked in Hollywood as a silent film director before moving to Britain in 1927; *The Ghoul* remains his best-known film.

Murder, She Wrote: Ardel Wray

When producer Val Lewton decided the script for *I Walked with a Zombie* needed a rewrite (the first draft was by veteran screenwriter Curt Siodmak), he turned to a woman he'd recently hired to research Haitian culture and voodoo practices: Ardel Wray. Wray had worked for nearly every studio as a story analyst and reader, but *I Walked with a Zombie* was her first screenplay. Lewton was pleased with the sensibility she brought to her draft and hired her to write other features for him, including *The Leopard Man* (1943), *Isle of the Dead* (1945), and the unproduced Boris Karloff vehicle *Blackbeard the Pirate*.

Wray's career foundered when she refused to name suspected Communists during the McCarthy era; although she later wrote for television, she never wrote another produced feature film. She died in 1983.

ABOVE LEFT: Italian *foglio* poster for *Isle of the Dead* (1945), featuring art by Rinaldo Geleng, who also created posters for a number of Federico Fellini films. The painting that inspired this film—"Isle of the Dead" by Swiss artist Arnold Böcklin—first appeared in another Val Lewton production: it hangs on the zombified Jessica's bedroom wall in *I Walked with a Zombie*.

ABOVE RIGHT: One-sheet poster for *Isle of the Dead* (1945). The film is a fine example of how Lewton used his stable of talent: Ardel Wray, who also wrote *The Leopard Man* for Lewton and director Jacques Tourneur, supplied the script, while director Mark Robson had previously worked as editor on *I Walked with a Zombie*.

ABOVE LEFT: Alternative poster for *I Walked with a Zombie* by Canadian artist Sara Deck. Although the onscreen credits go to Curt Siodmak and Ardel Wray (with story by Inez Wallace), producer Val Lewton, a former novelist, had considerable input on the script, which was based in part on Charlotte Brontë's *Jane Eyre*.

TOP RIGHT: This lobby card for *I Walked with a Zombie* captures some of the film's atmospheric lighting and shot composition. It was the second of three films Tourneur directed for Lewton (the other two are 1942's *Cat People* and the following year's *The Leopard Man*), and his personal favorite of the three.

BOTTOM RIGHT: Another lobby card for *I Walked with a Zombie*, showing Betsy (Frances Dee, center) flanked by zombies. Lewton's horror unit at RKO was given audience-tested titles and told to produce films to match them; *I Walked with a Zombie* cleverly subverts that by having the heroine openly mock the title in her first line.

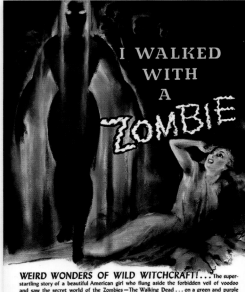

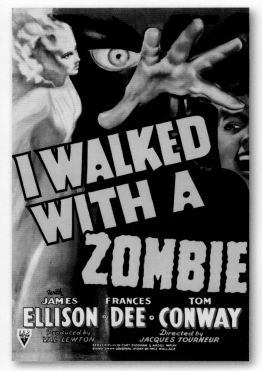

TOP LEFT: Black-and-white illustration based on *I Walked with a Zombie* by the American artist Doug Draper. An illustrator known for his contributions to numerous graphic novels, his work has been compared to the late Will Eisner's.

TOP RIGHT: Promotional ad for the *RKO Radio Pictures 1942–43* exhibitor book. Similar pieces were created for all of Lewton's films. The film's title was suggested by an article entitled "I Met a Zombie," as mentioned in this piece. The article's author, Inez Wallace, would receive credit for the film's story.

BOTTOM LEFT & RIGHT: One-sheet and lobby card for *I Walked with a Zombie*. An earlier draft of the screenplay included a scene in which Betsy, newly arrived on the island of San Sebastian, encounters a horribly scarred flower vendor; there was also a mention of the island displaying an American flag, suggesting it was a U.S. territory.

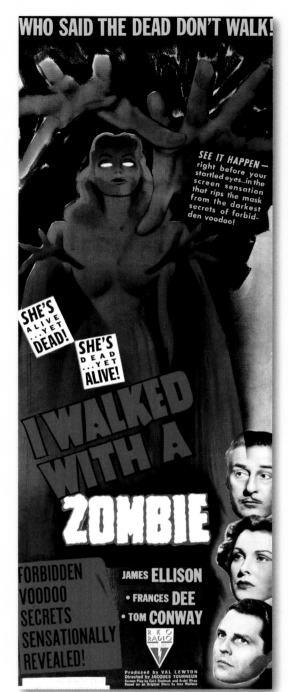

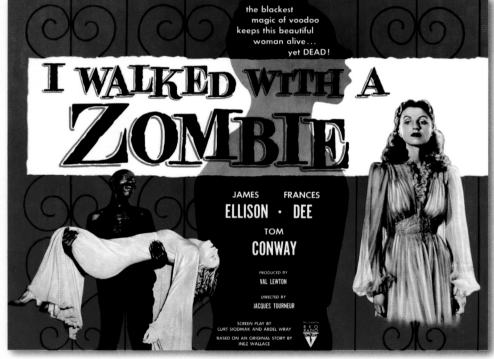

ABOVE LEFT: Insert poster for *I Walked With a Zombie*. Actor Tom Conway, who plays Paul Holland, starred in three films for producer Val Lewton (the others being *Cat People* and *The Seventh Victim*), and also frequently played detectives in serials, including Sherlock Holmes, the Saint, and the Falcon. He also appears in *Voodoo Woman* (1957) and was the brother of actor George Sanders.

TOP RIGHT: Is *I Walked with a Zombie*'s titular character Jessica (Christine Gordon), the catatonic wife of plantation owner Paul Holland (Tom Conway); or Carrefour, the blank-eyed native played by Darby Jones? There's an enigmatic shot beneath the opening credits that shows heroine Betsy (Frances Dee) walking with Carrefour, but she spends most of her time in the film beside Jessica.

BOTTOM RIGHT: Half-sheet poster for a 1956 re-release of *I Walked with a Zombie*. Co-screenwriter Ardel Wray noted in one interview that producer Val Lewton relied heavily on research and even included bibliographic references in his scripts.

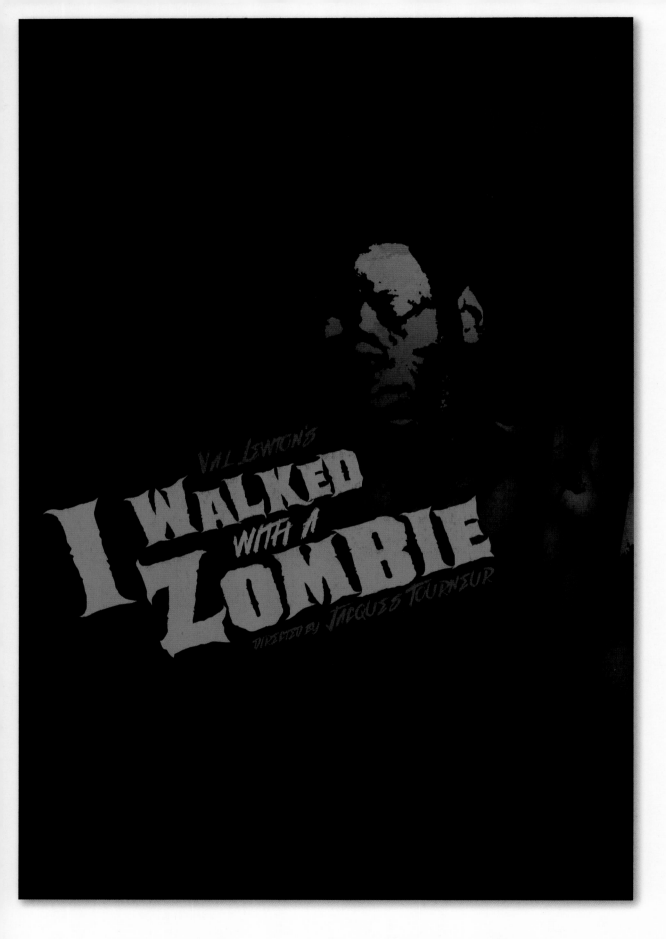

LEFT: Alternative poster for *I Walked with a Zombie* by Los Angeles–based artist Sister Hyde (Drusilla Adeline), who has provided art for numerous DVD releases by the Criterion Collection, A24, Arrow Video, Mondo, Paramount, and more.

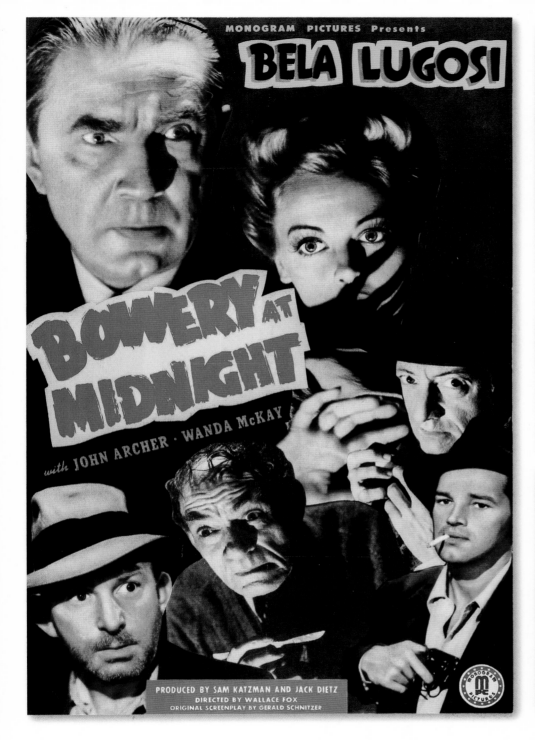

ABOVE LEFT: One-sheet for 1942's *Bowery at Midnight*, starring Bela Lugosi in a dual role (or is it?) as psychology expert Professor Brenner and criminal-posing-as-soup-kitchen-Samaritan Kurt Wagner. This was one of a number of films Lugosi made in the 1940s for schlock producer Sam Katzman at Monogram.

TOP RIGHT: French poster for *Bowery at Midnight*, the French title of which translates to *The Midnight Monster*. Lugosi received some good press for his performance in the film: the *Brooklyn Eagle* said, "Not since his portrayal of Dracula has Bela Lugosi appeared in finer fettle."

BOTTOM RIGHT: Mexican lobby card for *Bowery at Midnight*, the Spanish title here translating to *Grave Robbers*. The art is signed "Aguirre," so this may well be the work of prolific Mexican poster artist Aguirre Tinoco, whose whimsical imagery graced many Mexican posters and lobby cards.

Jungle Drums at Night: Voodoo on Film

The thirteen-year period from 1932 to 1945 could well be thought of as the golden age of voodoo-zombie movies; however, while zombie films at this time typically involved voodoo, not all voodoo film included zombies. There were dozens of voodoo films produced during this period (as well as some focused on related Caribbean beliefs, like Obeah), ranging from horror movies to melodramas to comedies.

In 1934, Columbia Studios brought out *Black Moon*, directed by Roy William Neill and starring *King Kong* lead Fay Wray (with two actors from *White Zombie*, Clarence Muse and Robert Frazer, in small parts). Its story focuses on a woman who returns to the island where her parents were murdered in a voodoo ritual when she was a child, and where she now finds herself at the center of a voodoo curse. Reviews and box office were poor, however, and the film quickly faded into obscurity.

Both *Obeah!* (1935) and *The Devil's Daughter* (1939) focus on someone who is controlled by an Obeah spell: the former, written and directed by F. Herrick Herrick, plays as an adventure tale about a search for a missing explorer; the latter, directed by Arthur Leonard, uses the plot of 1935's *Ouanga* to mix Obeah and romantic melodrama. Voodoo films came back in the 1950s, almost always featuring a white controller of a Black tribe; perhaps the most interesting of this crop—and the most laughable, because it sets its voodoo practitioners on a Pacific island—is Reginald Le Borg's *Voodoo Island* (1957), which stars Boris Karloff as a skeptic sent to an isolated island to investigate the disappearance of three hotel architects (and the zombie-like appearance of a fourth, who is still alive but blank-eyed and silent).

Voodoo films would continue to appear over the following decades, among them *The Dead One* (1961) and *Sugar Hill* (1974), although less frequently (and they were often critically derided), especially after the release in 1968 of *Night of the Living Dead*. Famed author and anthropologist Zora Neale Hurston, who studied and wrote about voodoo, once referred to all film and Broadway depictions as "laughable."

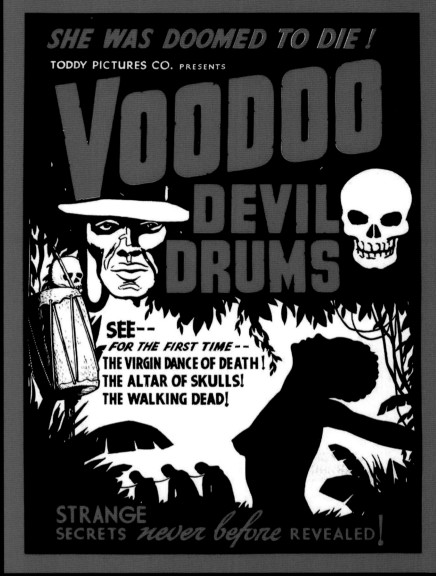

OPPOSITE, ABOVE LEFT: Title card from the original lobby-card set for *Black Moon* (1934). Inspired by the success of *White Zombie*, Columbia bought the rights to Clements Ripley's short story "Black Moon" and cast Kong Kong star Fay Wray and western star Jack Holt; *White Zombie* actors Clarence Muse and Robert Frazer also have small roles in the film.

OPPOSITE, ABOVE RIGHT: Poster for *She Devil*, the 1940 reissue of the 1934 film *Drums O' Voodoo*. Based on J. August Smith's Broadway play *Louisiana* (which closed after just eight performances), the film called on many of the play's cast, including Smith in the role of "Amos." *Drums O' Voodoo* received mixed reviews and did little at the box office.

ABOVE LEFT: One-sheet poster for *Voodoo Island* (1957). Both the art and the film emphasize the mysterious island's man-eating plants over its zombies, who are actually still alive but in a trance state.

ABOVE RIGHT: Released by Toddy Pictures, *Voodoo Devil Drums* (1944) was a forty-four-minute short also known as *Virgin Brides of Voodoo*. All that survives of the film now are lobby cards and this one-sheet poster, which lifted its art from a poster for 1934's *Chloe*.

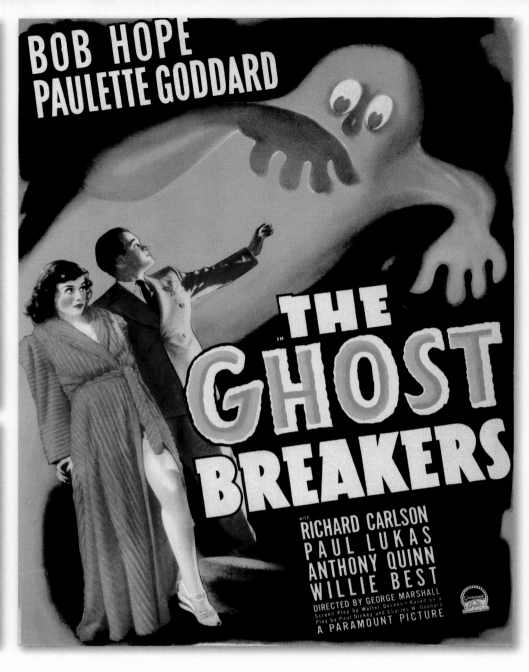

TOP LEFT: Belgian poster for
The Ghost Breakers (1940).
The film followed the 1939
pairing of Bob Hope and
Paulette Goddard in another
comedic thriller, *The Cat and
the Canary,* which was also
based on a play that had been
previously adapted for the
screen by Universal in 1930
as *The Cat Creeps* (now a
lost film).

BOTTOM LEFT: Lobby card for
The Ghost Breakers. The
film's zombie is played by
Noble Johnson, a Black actor
best known among horror
fans for playing the "Nubian"
in *The Mummy* (1932) and
the Native Chief in *King Kong*
(1933). Johnson was also a
producer whose company,
Lincoln Motion Picture
Company, was known for
producing films specifically
for Black audiences.

ABOVE RIGHT: Window card for
The Ghost Breakers. The
film's box-office success
inspired a third Bob Hope/
Paulette Goddard pairing
(1941's *Nothing but the
Truth*) and caused other
studies to rush horror
comedies into production,
including RKO's *You'll Find
Out* (1940) and Universal's
Hold That Ghost (1941), the
first comedic thriller starring
Abbott and Costello.

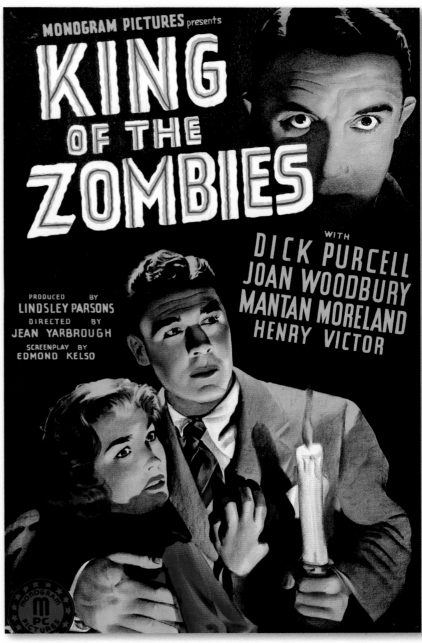

ABOVE LEFT: One-sheet poster for *The Ghost Breakers*, which was in fact the third filmed adaptation of the 1909 play *The Ghost Breaker* by Paul Dickey and Charles W. Goddard. In the play, the haunted estate is in Spain; in the 1940 film version, moving the location to a small Caribbean island allowed for the introduction of a zombie.

ABOVE RIGHT: One-sheet for *King of the Zombies* (1941). Inspired by the success of *The Ghost Breakers*, the film was originally intended as a vehicle for Bela Lugosi; when he proved unavailable, the part of the antagonist, Dr. Sangre, was offered first to Peter Lorre and finally to Henry Victor, a character actor who often played villains with German accents.

From Vaudeville to Horror: Mantan Moreland

Black comedian and actor Mantan Moreland was born in Louisiana in 1902; worked in Harlem, vaudeville, and Broadway theater; and went on to appear in over a hundred films. He's best known for portraying chauffeur Birmingham Brown in fifteen Charlie Chan films produced by Monogram; he also appeared in a number of comic horror films, including *King of the Zombies* (1941), *Mexican Spitfire Sees a Ghost* (1942), *Revenge of the Zombies* (1943), and *Spider Baby* (1967).

Although his pop-eyed expressions made him a popular comedic presence, Moreland eventually came to regret what he felt had been his participation in racial stereotyping. He hoped to score more serious dramatic roles in feature films, but he died in 1973 before realizing that goal.

ABOVE: Publicity still of Moreland and Robert Lowery in *Revenge of the Zombies* (1943). In a 1959 interview with the *Afro-American* newspaper, Moreland said, "Times have changed. The movies are growing up and I think my characterizations should keep pace with the times. Why shouldn't the role be written so that I solve the murder sometime?"

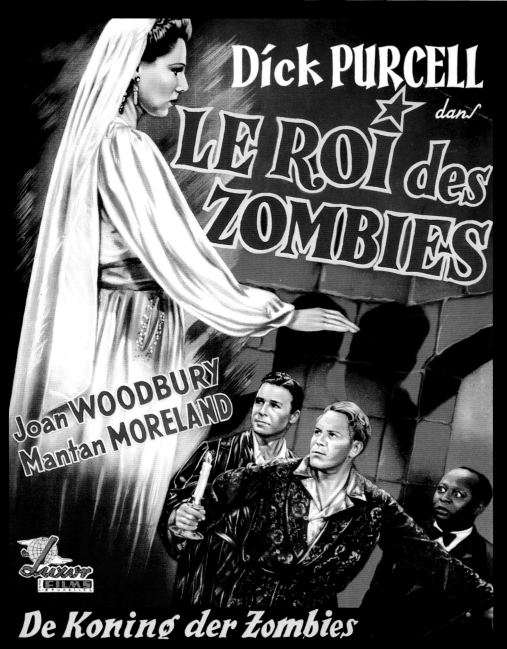

ABOVE LEFT: Belgian poster for *King of the Zombies.* Star Dick Purcell (shown at the bottom between John Archer and Mantan Moreland) is now best known for playing Captain America in a 1943 serial.

TOP RIGHT: *King of the Zombies* is now regarded by fans mainly for Moreland's performance. A frequently quoted gem is his ad-libbed line, after being zombified, "Move over, boys, I'm one of the gang now!"

BOTTOM RIGHT: One-sheet poster for *Lucky Ghost* (1941), starring Mantan Moreland and F. E. Miller. *Lucky Ghost* was distributed by Toddy Pictures Co., a company founded in 1941 that specialized in films with Black casts that were intended to be show in the roughly four hundred Black movie theaters and venues in operation around the U.S. at the time.

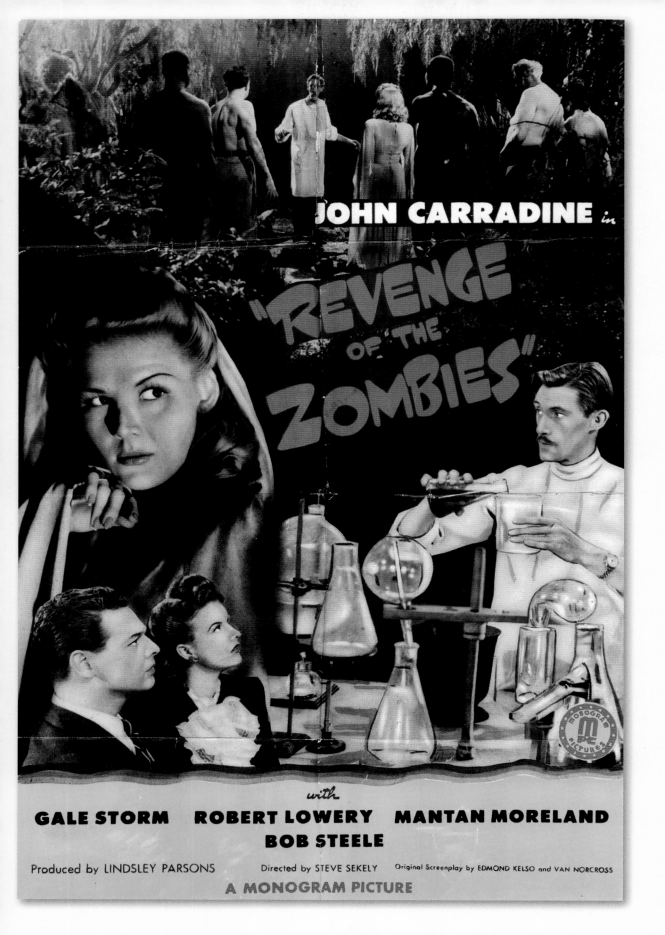

LEFT: One-sheet poster for *Revenge of the Zombies* (1943). Black actors Mantan Moreland and Madame Sul-Te-Wan had appeared two years earlier in *King of the Zombies*; the latter also appeared in the voodoo-themed *Black Moon* (1934) and *King Kong* (alongside *The Ghost Breakers'* Noble Johnson).

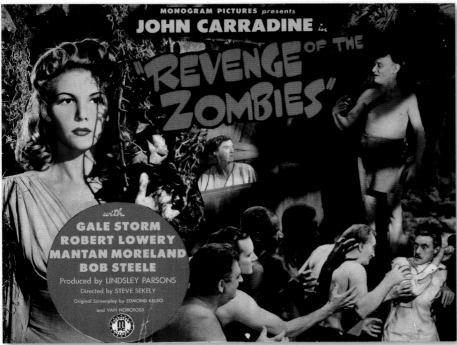

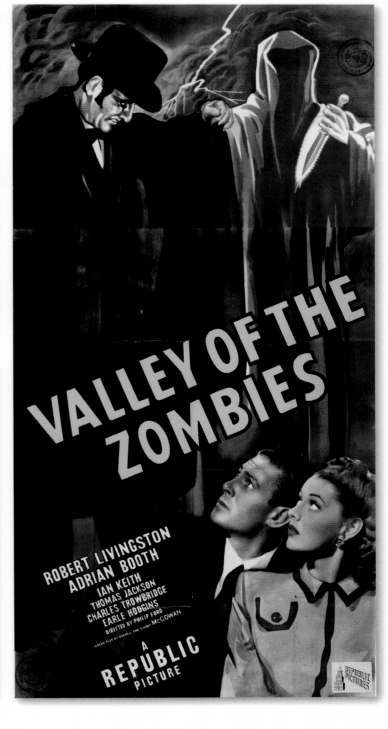

TOP LEFT: Half-sheet for
Valley of the Zombies (1946).
The film is set mainly in
urban locales; the title
derives from one line when
the villain, Ormand Murks
(Ian Keith), says that he
learned the secret of
immortality in "the valley
of the zombies."

BOTTOM LEFT: Half-sheet for
Revenge of the Zombies (1943),
which cast John Carradine as
the mad doctor intent on
creating a zombie army for
the Third Reich. A year later,
Carradine would appear in
Voodoo Man (playing a thug
who assists voodoo priests
Bela Lugosi and George
Zucco); he would also portray
Count Dracula in Universal's
House of Frankenstein.

ABOVE RIGHT: Three-sheet
for *Valley of the Zombies*.
Released by Republic
Pictures in 1946, it marked
the end of the cycle of 1930s
and '40s zombie films. In a
scathing review of the film,
Variety concluded that it
"features an unzombie-like
zombie and a fairly horrorless
story."

TOP LEFT: Mexican lobby card for the Bela Lugosi vehicle *Invisible Ghost* (1941), featuring typically colorful art by Aguirre Tinoco. *Invisible Ghost* was the first of the nine features Lugosi made for producer Sam Katzman and Monogram Pictures.

BOTTOM LEFT: Mexican lobby card for *Voodoo Man*, with art once again by the prolific Aguirre Tinoco. The Spanish title here falsely suggests that Lugosi had been cast once again as Dracula; in fact, he gives the best performance of his Monogram pictures here playing a doctor grieving the loss of his wife who has turned to voodoo to resurrect her.

ABOVE RIGHT: Three-sheet for *Voodoo Man* (originally titled *The Tiger Man*) from a 1950 re-release. The producers hoped to capitalize on the success of *White Zombie* by giving Lugosi's character, Dr. Marlowe, a similar beard and mustache. The voodoo god mentioned in the film, Ramboona, was a name concocted out of thin air.

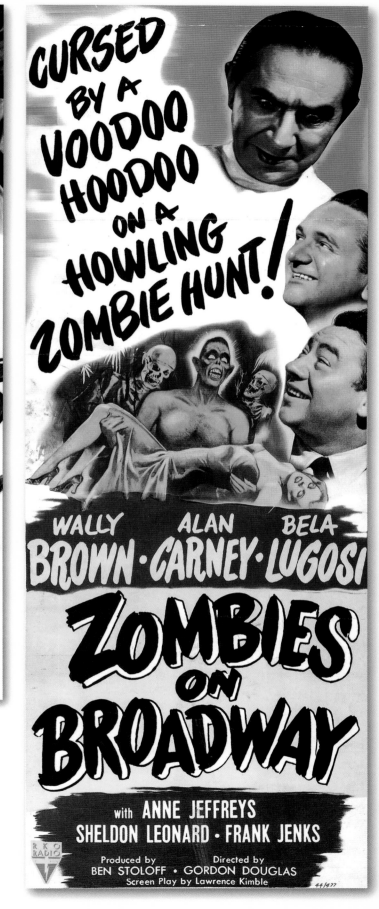

ABOVE LEFT: One-sheet poster for *Zombies on Broadway* (1945), in which Lugosi, as Dr. Paul Renault, supplies the foil to the comedic team of Wally Brown and Alan Carney—RKO's own version of Abbott and Costello. Unfortunately, the film is dismally unfunny.

ABOVE RIGHT: *Zombies on Broadway* not only took the name of the island San Sebastian from *I Walked with a Zombie* but also used two of the earlier film's Black actors: Darby Jones, so memorable as Carrefour, plays a zombie again here, while calypso singer Sir Lancelot also returns.

2

ZOMBIES IN THE 1950S AND '60S

"THAT CORPSE WANDERING ON THE MOORS IS AN UNDEAD. A ZOMBIE."

SIR JAMES FORBES IN *THE PLAGUE OF THE ZOMBIES* (1966)

> "They come from the bowels of hell—a transformed race of walking dead —zombies, guided by a master plan for complete domination of the earth!"
>
> Trailer for *Plan 9 from Outer Space* (1957)

A
s horror films of the 1950s turned away from supernatural to technological terrors—inspired by the atomic bomb—zombies went with them. Perhaps the most famous zombie flick of this decade is also beloved as one of the worst films of all time: Edward D. Wood, Jr.'s notorious *Plan 9 from Outer Space* (1957). The film's plot (such as it is) centers on an attempt by aliens to conquer Earth by raising the dead. Made on a micro-budget, *Plan 9* couldn't afford zombie hordes, but the sight of Swedish wrestler Tor Johnson staggering through a cardboard graveyard has become one of the great images of movie culture. The film also marked the final appearance of Bela Lugosi, whose footage was actually shot for another production but inserted into *Plan 9* instead; for additional shots, Lugosi was imitated by chiropractor Tom Mason.

However, the best zombie films of this decade all came from one director: Edward L. Cahn. By the 1950s, Cahn had been directing for more than two decades, making movies in virtually every genre; as markets shifted to science-fiction B-films intended for drive-ins, Cahn followed the money, making nearly a dozen science-fiction and horror films over the next ten years.

His first was 1955's *Creature with the Atom Brain*, about a police forensics expert (played by genre stalwart Richard Denning) investigating a series of mysterious murders by unstoppable killers. He discovers that the slayings are related to a case from ten years ago, involving a vengeful gangster named Frank Buchanan (Michael Granger) and renegade scientist Steigg (Gregory Gaye), who has discovered a way to remote-control dead bodies. The script, by veteran screenwriter Curt Siodmak (who also cowrote *I Walked with a Zombie*), keeps the stiff, stone-faced style of earlier zombies but adds a circular scar around the top of the head, due to the surgery Steigg performs to transform each corpse.

Cahn's 1957 entry, *Zombies of Mora Tau*, is a more conventional zombie picture, bringing back supernatural elements and a tropical setting in a story of a submerged treasure guarded by zombies. This slight but enjoyable thriller is notable mainly for being the first to show a horde of shambling corpses attacking humans trapped in a confined space (in this case, a boat).

The most interesting of Cahn's zombie trilogy is 1959's *Invisible Invaders*, whose script (by Samuel Newman) has the earth conquered by invisible aliens who are so weakened by the planet's atmosphere that they must inhabit dead human bodies to wage their war. While parts of the story are decidedly nonsensical (why do the aliens even want a planet that leaves them so debilitated?), *Invisible Invaders* is also the first movie to show a widespread zombie apocalypse, and to center, in part, on a clash between science and the military. Like George A. Romero's *Day of the Dead*, which would come nearly thirty years later, *Invisible Invaders* shows a team of scientists forced to shelter in an underground bunker, where they work desperately to find ways to stop the zombies—including experimenting on a captured specimen—while under the no-nonsense supervision of Major Bruce Jay (John Agar). Shots of zombies staggering over hillsides uncannily presage similar

No other film laid the zombie groundwork so effectively as 1964's *The Last Man on Earth,* an Italian American coproduction starring Vincent Price and based on Richard Matheson's 1954 novel *I Am Legend.*

visuals in *Night of the Living Dead* (despite the odd fact that all of *Invaders*' zombies seem to be middle-aged men dressed in business suits). Whether *Invisible Invaders* was actually ever seen by Romero is unknown, but—despite its obvious cheapness and illogic—it deserves a small spot in film history for getting there first.

In the '50s, horror cinema also tried to capture the youth market with such titles as *I Was a Teenage Frankenstein* and *Teenage Caveman*, so *Teenage Zombies* was perhaps inevitable. Although the film is close to unwatchable, it does at least boast a female mad scientist (played by Katherine Victor) who attempts to zombify some teens after they've been stranded on her isolated island.

During the societal chaos of the 1960s, as old norms were questioned and new countercultural movements like hippies and yippies arose, cinema transformed along with everything else. The atomic terrors of the last decade were out; television was bigger than ever, and movies changed to compete. Independent and exploitation movies found audiences on the drive-in circuit and second-run walk-in theaters; sex, violence, and blood appeared in greater (and more explicit) quantities than ever before.

PREVIOUS SPREAD: *Astro-Zombies* art by Tim Baron, an American artist who specializes in skateboard and monster art. Although the zombie is shown wielding a machete as it does in the movie, Baron—who created this for a personal project—admits the similarities end there.

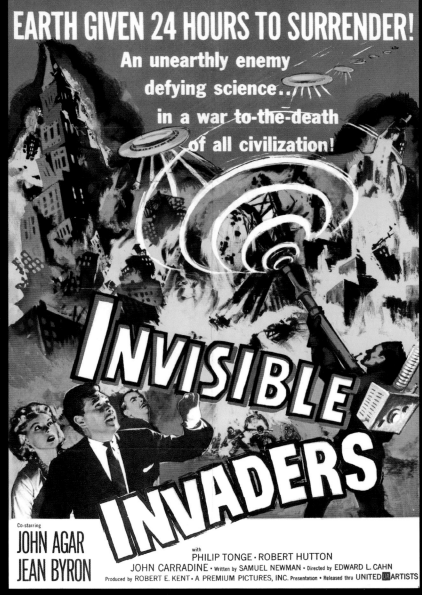

TOP LEFT: Mexican lobby card for *Creature with the Atom Brain* (1955), directed by Edward L. Cahn. The film's climax centers—for the first time in a zombie movie—on a group of undead creatures advancing through a rain of bullets.

BOTTOM LEFT: Cover art for a 2020 Japanese Blu-ray release of *Plan 9*. In 1992, gaming giant Konami released a point-and-click videogame based on *Plan 9*; the game's plot is centered on locating missing reels of the movie.

BOTTOM MIDDLE: One-sheet poster for Edward L. Cahn's *Zombies of Mora Tau* (1957). The eponymous walking dead are sailors who once tried to rob an African temple of its diamonds and now guard the gems as seaweed-bedecked zombies. They are vulnerable only to fire (one is imprisoned simply by a ring of candles) and attack their prey both on land and underwater.

ABOVE RIGHT: One-sheet poster for Cahn's *Invisible Invaders* (1959). In most theaters across the United States, *Invisible Invaders* was released as the second feature alongside headliner *The Four Skulls of Jonathan Drake* (also directed by Cahn). Later on, it was paired in some markets with another early zombie feature, *Doctor Blood's Coffin* (1961).

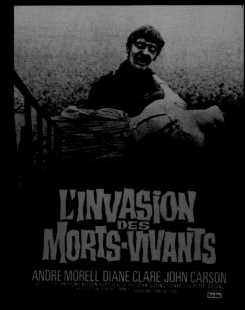

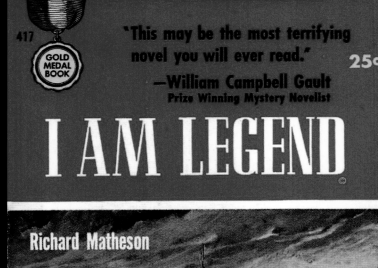

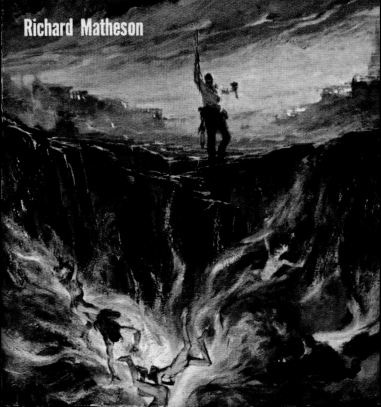

TOP LEFT: One-sheet poster for *Doctor Blood's Coffin* (1961), one of the first two color zombie films (alongside *The Dead One*, also released 1961). That makes the lack of color in this art surprising, even though it proclaims the film to be "in gori-est Eastman color."

TOP MIDDLE: French *affiche* poster from a 1970s re-release of *The Plague of the Zombies*, directed by John Gilling, who made *The Reptile* for Hammer Films in the same year, 1966. The two films also shared a shooting location, several cast members, and the idea of a mysterious plague in an isolated village.

BOTTOM LEFT: Mexican lobby card for *The Dead One* (1961), written, directed, and produced by Barry Mahon. The film adds vampire tradition to its zombie (Jonas) by making him vulnerable to sunlight.

ABOVE RIGHT: Cover for the true first edition of Richard Matheson's *I Am Legend*, featuring art by American artist Stanley Meltzoff. The publisher, Gold Medal Books, was known mainly for mystery and "sleaze" fiction.

In 1961, the first two zombie movies of the new decade appeared: Barry Mahon's *The Dead One* and the British *Doctor Blood's Coffin*. Although they take different approaches to their resurrected dead—*The Dead One* employs voodoo, while *Doctor Blood's Coffin* involves a Frankenstein-like mad doctor—both featured green-tinged, decaying zombies, pointing the direction for the future, and both were shot in color, a first for zombie films. *Doctor Blood's Coffin* is ambiguously a zombie film, since the creature (which only appears at the story's climax) may possess will and intelligence; however, the film is notable for its graphic shots of still-beating hearts as the eponymous scientist (played by Kieron Moore) engages in the transplant technique that allows him to restore life to a long-dead body. Directed by the Canadian Sidney J. Furie (who would go on to direct much more acclaimed films, including the poltergeist horror movie *The Entity*), *Doctor Blood's Coffin* thus takes the first shambling step on the trail of zombie gore.

Another early British entry in the zombie field was *The Earth Dies Screaming* (1964), directed by Terence Fisher—taking a break from his work for Hammer Studios, where he'd made such classics as *The Curse of Frankenstein* (1957), *Dracula* (1958), and *The Curse of the Werewolf* (1961)—a

---

"They're dead, I tell you! They have no morality, no free will."

Grandmother Peters in *Zombies of Mora Tau* (1957)

---

more staid production, shot in black-and-white, about a group of survivors of an alien attack who take refuge in a small British village, where they contend with both deadly robots and zombies.

Italy's *War of the Zombies* (*Roma contro Roma*), from 1964, provides the earliest historical zombie epic. After a Roman legion is decimated by barbarians, a witch arrives to claim the bodies of the dead centurions, who are turned into zombie warriors. *War of the Zombies* is unique in its sword-and-sorcery/zombie mash-up, providing a few moments of genuine atmosphere in both its scenes of pagan magic and its final confrontation between living and dead armies.

Mexico's wrestling hero Santo took on the undead in 1962's *Santo vs. the Zombies* (*Santo contra los zombies*). The film follows the standard formula of Santo movies, pitting the masked star against both mundane criminals and otherworldly creatures. The zombies here are costumed thugs who can withstand bullets and are controlled by an old professor who has studied Haitian voodoo and is now forced to put his knowledge to use in service to the villainous Genaro; the zombies can be bested by yanking off the silver belt that connects them to their controller. *Santo vs. the Zombies* was the first Santo film shot in Mexico, inaugurating

a long cycle. A year later, he would fight zombies again in *Santo vs. las mujeres vampiro* (released internationally as *Samson vs. the Vampire Women*), this time in the form of three zombified henchmen serving Queen Zorina (Lorena Velázquez, who had also starred in *Santo vs. the Zombies*).

In 1966, Great Britain's Hammer Film Productions, which had successfully brought Dracula and Frankenstein back to the silver screen with gore, style, and the considerable talents of stars Christopher Lee and Peter Cushing, turned its sights on zombies with *The Plague of the Zombies*. Directed by John Gilling, it lacks the major Hammer stars but features the studio's trademark high production values and whiff of social relevance (despite a depiction of voodoo that's even less authentic and more colonialist than the films of the '30s and '40s). The story begins in 1860, in a small Cornish village that has been ravaged by a mysterious plague. When famed physician Sir James Forbes (Andre Morell) arrives to investigate, he discovers that the local squire (John Carson) has been applying the voodoo techniques he learned during time spent in Haiti to turn the villagers into free labor for his tin mine. (Oddly enough, the earlier *Doctor Blood's Coffin* was also set in Cornish tin mines.) The zombies' gray-skinned white-eyed appearance (created by Roy Ashton) set a new standard for makeup.

However, no other film laid the zombie groundwork so effectively as 1964's *The Last Man on Earth*, an Italian-American coproduction starring Vincent Price and based on Richard Matheson's 1954 novel *I Am Legend*. Adapted by Matheson (under the pseudonym "Logan Swanson") and William J. Leicester, with direction by Sidney Salkow and Ubaldo B. Ragona, *The Last Man on Earth* is technically a vampire film, but its influence can be heavily felt in later zombie films, and it's also worth noting that the film's original trailer refers to its creatures by both names. Price plays Robert Morgan, a doctor who has survived a global plague that has killed the rest of mankind but resurrected them as hollow-eyed, slow-moving corpses that thirst for human blood. Morgan has survived for three years, living off a gasoline-run generator and hunting the creatures by day, but his willpower is crumbling in the face of the relentless attacks the creatures wage on his house night after night, led by his former colleague and friend, Ben Cortman. Although the film suffers from some obvious budget constraints—most notably in the simple makeup of the vampires—it nonetheless remains an effective thriller, and the most truthful adaptation of Matheson's classic novel. The film's depiction of life in a postapocalyptic world full of the undead would also influence later zombie movies.

The Last Man on Earth is notable for other reasons, too: its images of the staggering corpses barraging the boarded-up house at night had a serious impact on a young filmmaker named George A. Romero, who, four years later, would produce what is almost certainly the most important work in the history of zombie cinema: *Night of the Living Dead*.

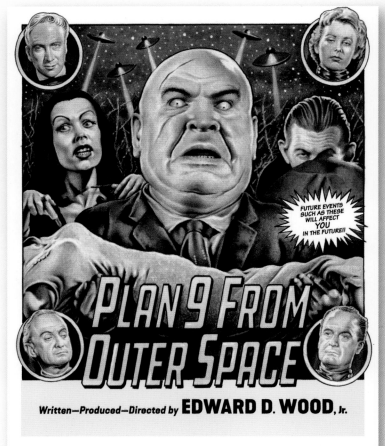

ABOVE LEFT: Original one-sheet poster for Edward D. Wood Jr.'s *Plan 9 from Outer Space* (1957). This is the rare two-color version; there's also a version that incorporates blue as well as red. The poster art is far more dramatic than the film itself.

TOP RIGHT: Over the years, the much-derided *Plan 9 from Outer Space* has become a popular live-performance piece. This promotional art by Drew Friedman, an American illustrator noted for his detailed caricatures, was created for an event held at Largo in Los Angeles on October 29, 2019.

BOTTOM RIGHT: Box art for Polar Lights' plastic model kit of the flying saucer from *Plan 9*. The kit is in 1/48 scale and was released in 2019; it comes complete with a "Conquered Planet Base."

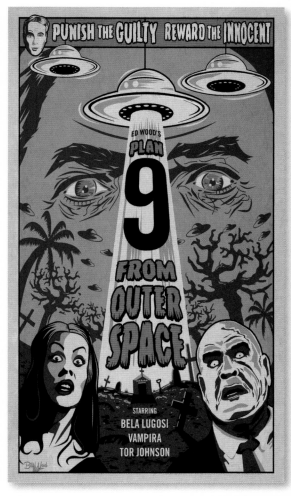

TOP LEFT: Digital art for *Plan 9* by the artist Bill Wood. A veteran of the Hollywood print-advertisement industry who studied under United Artists art director Donald Smolen, Wood says, "Despite its reputation as one of the worst films ever made, I absolutely love Ed Wood's *Plan 9*. It strikes a vital nerve every time I watch it."

BOTTOM LEFT: Mexican lobby card for *Plan 9 from Outer Space*. The Spanish-language title, *Espectros del Espacio*, translates to *Specters of Space*. The still image in the upper right corner of this card features Dudley Manlove and Joanna Lee as aliens Eros and Tanna, shown here confronting Lt. Harper (Duke Moore).

ABOVE RIGHT: This poster for *Plan 9 from Outer Space* was produced by artist Sara Deck in 2017, in a limited edition of twenty-five. Deck, a Canadian artist who has also created covers for books, home video releases, and soundtrack albums, has here chosen to emphasize the film's three undead: Vampira, Tor Johnson, and Bela Lugosi.

ABOVE LEFT: One-sheet poster for *Creature with the Atom Brain* (1955), Edward L. Cahn's first zombie film. The method used to create zombies in the film is actually an updating of "galvanism" (applying electricity), a theory first proposed by the eighteenth-century scientist Luigi Galvani. In Cahn's film, the electrical stimulation is applied to the amygdala.

ABOVE RIGHT: Australian day-bill poster for *Creature with the Atom Brain*, featuring the apt warning, "Not Suitable for Children." The film's zombies are dead bodies with receivers implanted in their brains so they can obey basic orders transmitted to them, but they're only good for a few days before they "disintegrate."

ABOVE LEFT: Belgian poster for *Creature with the Atom Brain*. Curt Siodmak, who wrote the film, was also one of the screenwriters on *I Walked with a Zombie*. His credits also include such horror classics as *The Wolf Man*, *The Invisible Man Returns*, *Son of Dracula*, and many more.

ABOVE RIGHT: Italian poster for *Creature with the Atom Brain*. The film's Italian title translates to *Atomic Bandits*, although in fact the antagonist, the ruthless Buchanan, intends on using the zombies mainly to wreak revenge against his enemies.

ABOVE LEFT: Italian *quattro-foglio* poster for Edward L. Cahn's *Zombies of Mora Tau* (1957), featuring artwork by Anselmo Ballester. Allison Hayes, the statuesque actress who plays the zombified Mona, also starred as a wild voodoo priestess in the same year's *The Disembodied*, but she's probably best known for playing the title role in *Attack of the 50 Foot Woman* (1958).

TOP MIDDLE: Insert poster for *Zombies of Mora Tau*. Co-starring in the film as the sensible Dr. Eggert is Morris Ankrum, a popular character actor who appeared in numerous movies and television shows, including *Rocketship X-M* (1950), *Invaders from Mars* (1953), *Earth vs. the Flying Saucers* (1956), and *Kronos* (1957).

TOP RIGHT: Italian *duo-foglio* poster for *Zombies of Mora Tau*, again featuring artwork by Anselmo Ballester. These are among the last works by Ballester (1897–1974), an Italian artist who painted film posters from the 1910s through the 1950s.

BOTTOM RIGHT: Title lobby card for *Zombies of Mora Tau*, complete with some badly drawn fish. This film may well mark the first time in cinematic history that a human killed by zombies (in this case Mona, played by Allison Hayes) herself becomes a zombie.

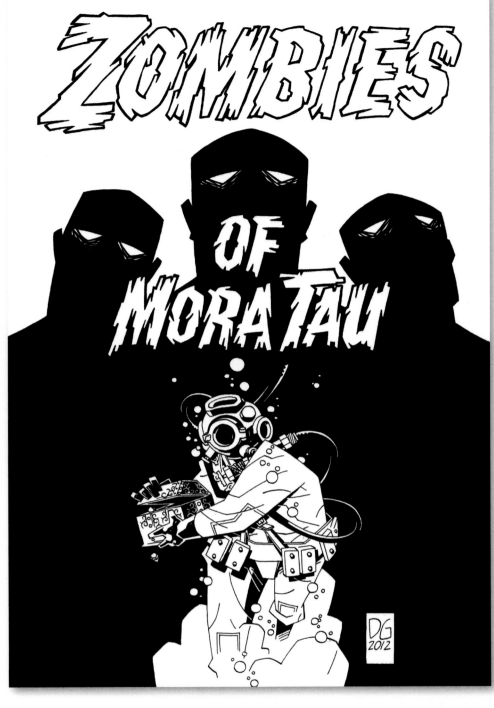

ABOVE LEFT: Newspaper ad for *Zombies of Mora Tau*. The film was initially released as half of a double feature with *The Man Who Turned to Stone*, another 1957 horror feature. Both films were produced by Sam Katzman.

ABOVE RIGHT: Alternativee poster for *Zombies of Mora Tau*, by the American artist Joe DellaGatta. The zombies in this film, created to guard a treasure of diamonds, are a throwback to the voodoo-generated movie zombies of the previous era.

THE LAST MAN ON EARTH AND OTHER VILLAINS: VINCENT PRICE

"I can't afford the luxury of anger. Anger can make me vulnerable. It can destroy my reason, and reason's the only advantage I have over them."

Dr. Robert Morgan in *The Last Man on Earth* (1964)

Unarguably one of the greatest horror icons of all time, Vincent Leonard Price, Jr. was born into an affluent American family (his grandfather made a fortune on his branded baking powder) and originally planned on pursuing a career in fine arts before discovering a love of theater in his early twenties. (He would later become a noted art collector.) Price realized he felt completely at home on the stage, and he quickly established himself as a lead without any formal training as an actor. In 1935, he began working with Orson Welles's Mercury Theatre in London; later the same year, he appeared on Broadway in the hit play *Victoria Regina*. Later in his career, Price returned to the stage to play Oscar Wilde in the one-man show *Diversions and Delights* (1978), a performance he personally considered to be his best.

By the 1940s, Price had made the transition to Hollywood and was appearing in such films as *The Song of Bernadette* (1943) and *Laura* (1944); his first horror film was 1939's *Tower of London*, but it wasn't until 1953's *House of Wax* that he was established as a true horror star. He followed that film with *The Fly* (1958), *Return of the Fly* (1959), and *The Tingler* (1959); his performance in *House on Haunted Hill* (1959) as a debonair but snide millionaire has been admired, imitated, and parodied for decades.

In 1960, Price began collaborating with Roger Corman on a series of films based on the works of Edgar Allan Poe: *House of Usher* was followed by *The Pit and the Pendulum* (1961), *Tales of Terror* (1962), *The Comedy of Terrors* (1963), *The Raven* (1963), *The Masque of the Red Death* (1964), and *The Tomb of Ligeia* (1964). All but the last two of those films boasted screenplays by Richard Matheson, and as noted elsewhere Price also starred in the 1964 adaptation of *The Last Man on Earth*, based on Matheson's *I Am Legend*. Despite the film's obvious low budget and pedestrian direction, Price's performance as Robert Morgan is considered to be one of his best, perfectly capturing the balance between melancholy and determination.

Among Price's other finest performances were 1968's *Witchfinder General* (released in the United States as *The Conqueror Worm*), in which he plays the cruel seventeenth-century inquisitor Matthew Hopkins; *The Abominable Dr. Phibes* (1971), a lush, Art Deco–styled black comedy directed by Robert Fuest and starring Price as the horribly scarred yet diabolically elegant title character (who would return for 1972's *Dr. Phibes Rises Again*); and 1973's *Theatre of Blood* (directed by Douglas Hickox), which pairs Price with Diana Rigg as Shakespearean actors seeking revenge against critics.

Price is also revered by music fans for his work on Alice Cooper's seminal horror rock album *Welcome to My*

Despite the obvious low budget and pedestrian direction, Price's performance as Robert Morgan in *The Last Man on Earth* is considered to be one of his best , perfectly capturing the balance between melancholy and determination.

Nightmare (1975) and Michael Jackson's "Thriller" (1982). His last major film appearance was in Tim Burton's *Edward Scissorhands* (1990), in which he appears as the lonely inventor of the wild-haired, blade-handed title character (played by Johnny Depp).

Price, who died in 1993, left behind a remarkable legacy beyond his body of acting work. He wrote several books, including a memoir, *I Like What I Know* (1959); the bestselling coffee table book *The Vincent Price Treasury of American Art* (1972); and a cookbook and restaurant guide co-written with Mary Price, *A Treasury of Great Recipes* (1965). As an art buyer for Sears-Roebuck in the 1950s, he exposed American consumers to fifty-five thousand works of art; his museum in East Los Angeles, the Vincent Price Art Museum, continues to present his love of fine art. He was also memorably kind to his fans, never turning down a request for an autograph. Ironically, he disliked referring to his best films as "horror," preferring the term "Gothic."

TOP LEFT: This poster by the artist Unlovely Frankenstein is for a movie that never was: *Herbert West: Reanimator*, with Vincent Price in the title role. The artist has explained that this imagined version would have been made in 1958, directed by Jacques Tourneur (*I Walked with a Zombie*), and shot in color.

BOTTOM LEFT: Lobby card for *The Last Man on Earth* (1964), showing Dr. Robert Morgan (Vincent Price) grappling with some of the film's undead creatures. The photo is in color; sadly, the film is not.

ABOVE RIGHT: This alternative poster for *The Last Man on Earth* by the Canadian artist "Ghoulish" Gary Pullin emphasizes the protagonist as vampire hunter. George A. Romero would later admit that Richard Matheson's novel *I Am Legend* was an influence on him, but added that he wanted to explore the events that come *before* the post-apocalyptic world of the novel.

ABOVE LEFT: This one-sheet poster for *The Last Man on Earth* seems to suggest that the film has a haunted house setting, perhaps playing on Vincent Price's 1959 hit *House on Haunted Hill*. This was the first of three movie adaptations of Richard Matheson's 1954 novel *I Am Legend*.

ABOVE RIGHT: One-sheet poster for *The Omega Man* (1971), the second film adaptation of Richard Matheson's classic vampire novel. This time, the plague survivors are turned into albino mutants who have formed a cult called "The Family."

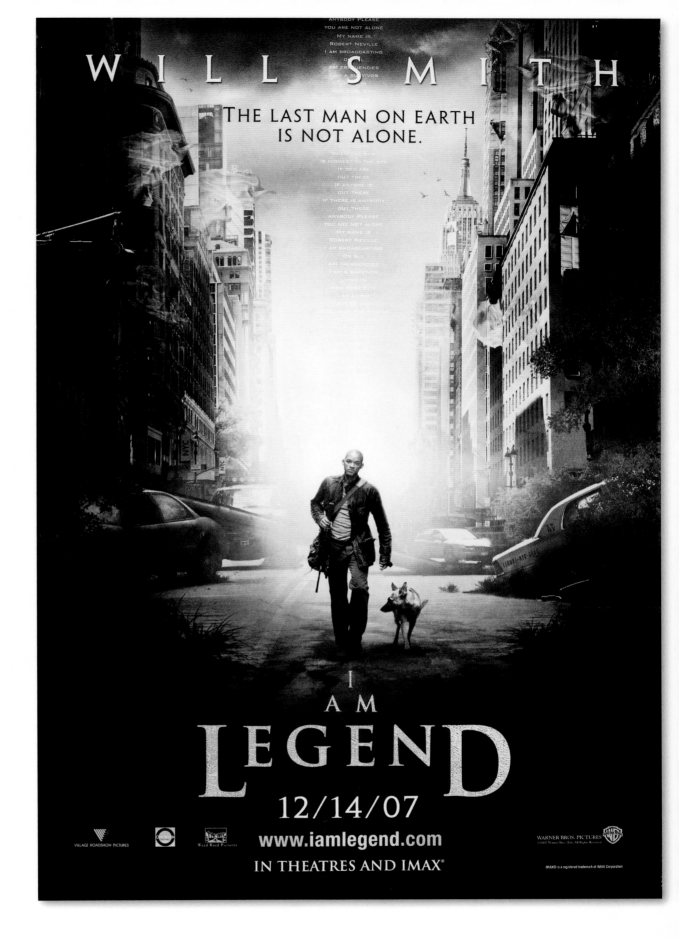

RIGHT: Bus-shelter poster for *I Am Legend* (2007), the third adaptation of Richard Matheson's novel. This version calls its plague survivors "Darkseekers" and depicts them as violent, rampaging mutants who must avoid sunlight.

ABOVE LEFT: One-sheet poster for *Voodoo Woman* (1957), another low-budget thriller by Edward L. Cahn. *Voodoo Woman* has a mad scientist (played by Tom Conway, a long way from his lead role in *I Walked with a Zombie*) working with a voodoo priest to turn a young woman into the monstrous embodiment of a voodoo god.

TOP RIGHT: One-sheet poster for *Teenage Zombies* (1959), which features, well . . . not zombies. The film's plot centers on a scientist working for a foreign power who has created a way to brainwash the American public via the water supply and turn them into mindless workers. Oh, and there's also a gorilla.

BOTTOM RIGHT: British quad poster for *Voodoo Woman* (1957). The "voodoo god" costume in *Voodoo Woman* is from another film by producer Alex Gordon, *The She-Creature*; for *Voodoo Woman*, the head was altered and a wig added. The creature was played by Paul Blaisdell, who built the suit.

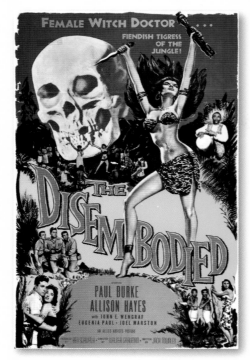

TOP LEFT: One-sheet poster for *The Disembodied* (1957). Like *Voodoo Woman,* this film centers on an unhappy couple living deep in the heart of a jungle; unlike that earlier work, however, *The Disembodied* makes the unsatisfied wife (Allison Hayes) the priestess of a multicultural voodoo cult.

BOTTOM LEFT: Italian *quattro-foglio* poster for *Voodoo Island* (1957). Screenwriter Richard Landau also wrote *The Lost Continent* (1951), and he mixes elements of a primeval world into this story as well, including primitive man-eating plants. Note that the Italian title, which translates to *The Haunted Island of Zombies,* focuses on the undead rather than voodoo.

ABOVE RIGHT: One-sheet for *The Dead One* (1961), which extends the previous cinematic trope of a white priest (or, in this case, priestess) presiding over Black voodoo rituals. It may also be the only zombie film which has a scene of children pretending to be zombies.

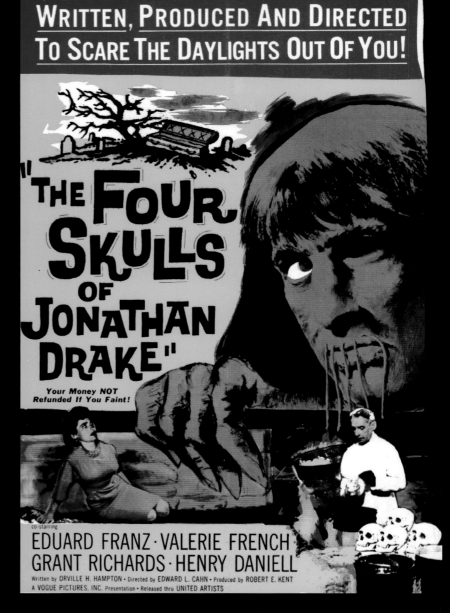

Romero's Zombie Granddaddy: Edward L. Cahn

Edward L. Cahn, nicknamed "Fast Eddie" because of how quickly he shot his films, was born in 1898 and started in Hollywood as an editor at Universal. By the 1930s, he'd moved to directing, becoming most well-known then for a string of *Our Gang* comedies. Cahn worked in all genres, but in the 1950s he made a trio of zombie films (*Creature with the Atom Brain*, *Zombies of Mora Tau*, and *Invisible Invaders*), as well as three films that would go on to attain cult status: *The She-Creature* (1956), a tale of reincarnation featuring one of the most famous monsters of the '50s, sporting a suit created by Paul Blaisdell; *Invasion of the Saucer Men* (1957), which

popularized the look of aliens as "bug-eyed monsters"; and *It!: The Terror From Beyond Space* (1958), featuring another Paul Blaisdell monster (this one would reappear in Cahn's *Invisible Invaders*), which would become notable for its influence on *Alien* (1979). He also directed the fantastically silly *Voodoo Woman* (1957), about a mad scientist (Tom Conway) working with a voodoo priest (Martin Wilkins) in an attempt to create an invincible female monster (for which the suit from *The She-Creature* was repurposed, with a wig and a different face mask). Cahn, whose last film was 1962's *Beauty and the Beast*, passed away in 1963.

OPPOSITE, TOP LEFT: Half-sheet poster for *It! The Terror from Beyond Space* (1958). This film would indirectly become Edward L. Cahn's most famous production after it inspired screenwriter Dan O'Bannon to create *Alien* (1979).

OPPOSITE, BOTTOM LEFT: Lobby card for *Creature with the Atom Brain* (1955). Seen here is the film's first zombie, who even appears under the opening credits. He's the resurrected thug Willard Pearce, played by professional wrestler turned actor "Killer" Karl Davis, who also appears in Edward L. Cahn's *Zombies of Mora Tau* (1957).

OPPOSITE, ABOVE RIGHT: One-sheet poster for *The Four Skulls of Jonathan Drake* (1959), also directed by Cahn. The film, which deals with a curse placed on a family by an Ecuadorian witch doctor, was released in a double bill with Cahn's *Invisible Invaders*.

ABOVE LEFT: Insert poster for Cahn's *Invisible Invaders* (1959). Producer Robert E. Kent started his career working as a screenwriter at Columbia for producer Sam Katzman; Katzman subsequently moved to Monogram, where he produced Bela Lugosi's 1940s zombie films.

ABOVE RIGHT: One-sheet poster for *The She-Creature* (1956). This is another of the better-known movies directed by Cahn, mainly due to the iconic creature suit created by Paul Blaisdell, as adapted for re-use in *Voodoo Woman*.

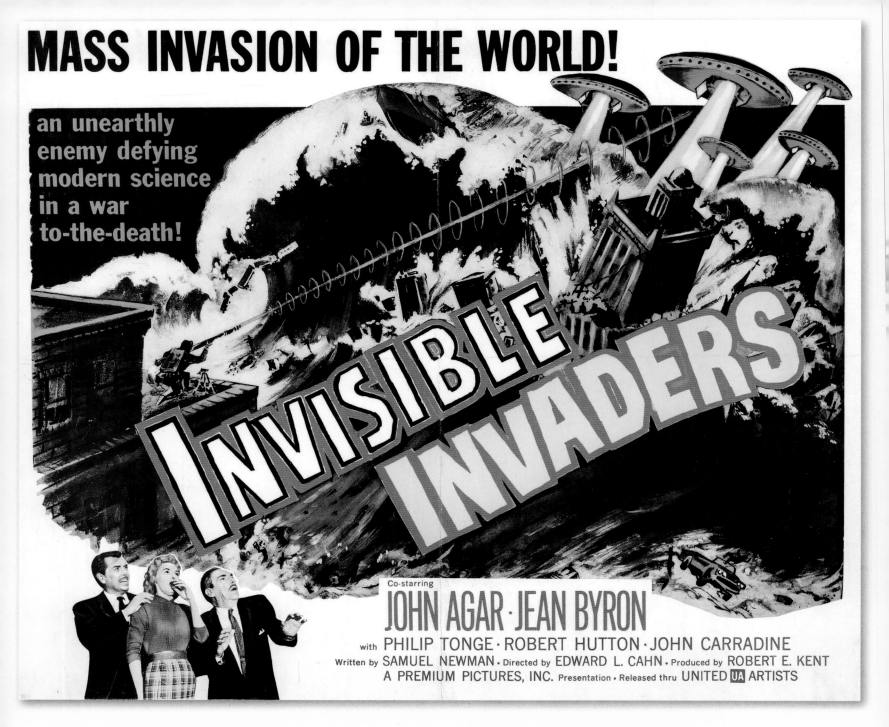

MASS INVASION OF THE WORLD!

an unearthly
enemy defying
modern science
in a war
to-the-death!

INVISIBLE INVADERS

Co-starring

JOHN AGAR · JEAN BYRON

with PHILIP TONGE · ROBERT HUTTON · JOHN CARRADINE

Written by SAMUEL NEWMAN · Directed by EDWARD L. CAHN · Produced by ROBERT E. KENT

A PREMIUM PICTURES, INC. Presentation · Released thru UNITED UA ARTISTS

ABOVE: Half-sheet poster for Edward L. Cahn's *Invisible Invaders* (1959). The low-budget film was shot in six days in December 1958, with horror star John Carradine working just one of them. The budget allowed for $4,000 of stock footage, which included shots from 1958's *Thunder Road* (a car crash) and 1938's *Born to Be Wild* (a truck crash).

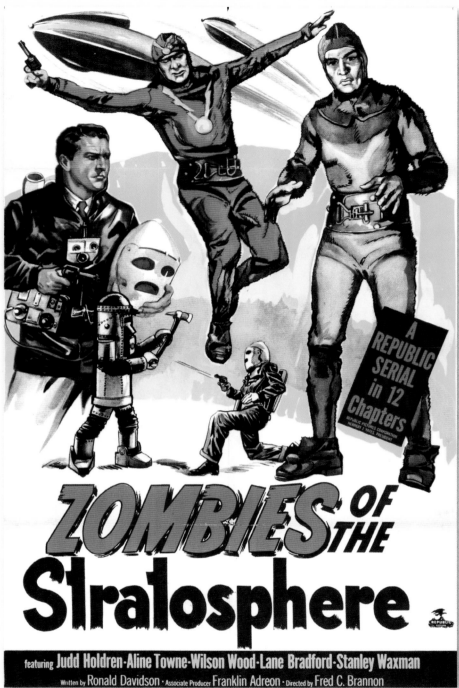

TOP LEFT: Lobby card for *Zombies of the Stratosphere* (1952), subtitled "Chapter 1: The Zombie Vanguard." The twelve-part serial, which was later recut into a feature film, *Satan's Satellites* (1958), is now known chiefly for the performance of a young Leonard Nimoy as the Martian "Narab."

BOTTOM LEFT: Lobby card for *Invisible Invaders* (1959). The uncredited producer of *Invisible Invaders* was the prolific but modest Edward Small, who started working in movies in 1926 but preferred to stay out of the limelight, so often chose to take no credit for his films.

ABOVE RIGHT: One sheet poster for *Zombies of the Stratosphere*. One of the great mysteries of modern cinema is why this serial is so called, since it involves no zombies, only an attempted Martian invasion of Earth.

ABOVE LEFT: One-sheet for the 1964 British horror/sci-fi mash-up *The Earth Dies Screaming*, directed by Terence Fisher, which followed in the footsteps of both *Plan 9 from Outer Space* and *Invisible Invaders* by focusing on aliens whose invasion of Earth involves creating and controlling human zombies.

TOP RIGHT: This portrait of the villain Quinn Taggart (Dennis Price) from *The Earth Dies Screaming* (1964) by the artist Roger Koch shows Taggart after he returns as a zombie and leads the robots to a group of survivors. Koch is an American artist specializing in portraits based on classic horror films.

BOTTOM RIGHT: Faux trading card created by Bruce Schneider for *The Earth Dies Screaming*. The film's zombies can be stopped by a shot to the chest—the Romero headshot was still a few years in the future. The invasion is thwarted by destroying a central transmitter that controls both the robots and the zombies.

TOP: This British quad poster for *Doctor Blood's Coffin* (1961) at least features color artwork, even if the tag line, "A Monster created from the depths!," is somewhat confusing.

BOTTOM LEFT: Lobby card for *Doctor Blood's Coffin* featuring the climactic zombie. The makeup on actor Paul Stockman was created by Freddie Williamson, who also worked with director Sidney J. Furie on another genre film in 1961, *The Snake Woman*.

BOTTOM RIGHT: Belgian poster for *Doctor Blood's Coffin*. Although the film's story could be considered a direct descendent of *Frankenstein*— it centers on a doctor trying to resurrect a dead body by replacing parts—its final creature seems driven by the mindless rage of the next generation of zombies.

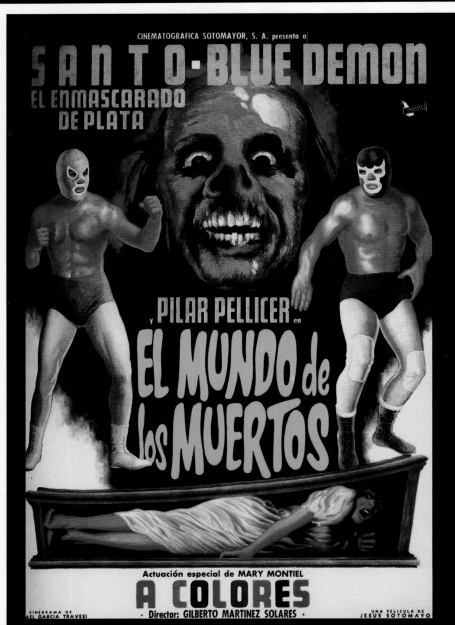

"The Greatest Luchador of Them All": El Santo

In the rowdy, raucous world of Mexican wrestling, no *luchador* was as famous or beloved as El Santo. Born Rodolfo Guzmán Huerta in 1917, El Santo ("The Saint") was easily identified by his silver mask (which he wore in every public appearance, removing it himself only once shortly before he died). In addition to his sports career, he starred in more than four-dozen movies, and also licensed himself out to a series of comic books that ran for thirty-five years. His first two films, *El Cerebro del Mal* (*The Evil Brain*) and *Hombres Infernales* (*The Infernal Men*), were both shot in 1958 in Cuba, with Santo playing a masked sidekick to the main hero (the producers later inserted his name into the titles).

It wasn't until his third film, 1962's *Santo vs. the Zombies*, that he took on the role of himself: a superstar wrestler who also fights crimes the police can't solve. *Santo vs. the Zombies* established the template of the Santo movie, with its star as muscled folk hero battling a fantastical evil, all while caped, masked, and driving a luxury convertible. Santo went on to make a total of fifty-two movies, often pairing up with other famed luchadores like Blue Demon to battle mobsters, mad scientists, vampires, witches, werewolves, mummies, headhunters, and other villains. Santo retired from both wrestling and acting in 1982, and passed away in 1984, at the age of sixty-six.

OPPOSITE, ABOVE LEFT: Mexican poster for *El mundo de los muertos* (a.k.a. *The World of the Dead*, 1970), which pairs Santo with fellow luchador Blue Demon to face off against a three-hundred-year-old witch. Oddly, the poster artist has chosen to place a portrait of Lon Chaney's Phantom of the Opera between the two wrestlers.

OPPOSITE, ABOVE RIGHT: Mexican poster for *Santo vs. las mujeres vampiro* (*Santo vs. the Vampire Women*, 1962), in which a coven of vampire women controls three zombified henchmen. When producer K. Gordon Murray acquired and released two dubbed Santo films in the U.S. (this film and 1963's *Santo in the Wax Museum*), both actor and character were renamed "Samson."

ABOVE LEFT: Mexican one-sheet for *Santo contra los zombies* (*Santo vs. the Zombies*, 1962). Fernando Osés, who co-created the film's story, also plays one of the zombie wrestlers who is vanquished by Santo.

ABOVE RIGHT: Portrait of Santo by the Mexican company Kimbal Estudio. This image is included in the company's "Mexican Curious" line, alongside the explanatory note, "Wrestling is an expression of Mexican popular culture, endowed with graphic and conceptual richness."

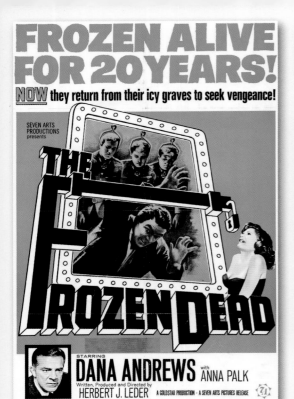

TOP LEFT: One-sheet for *The Frozen Dead* (1966). Written, produced, and directed by Herbert J. Leder, the film continues the "Nazi zombies" subgenre, first seen in 1941's *King of the Zombies*, by having a German scientist (Dana Andrews) trying to resuscitate frozen Nazis, only to end up with shambling, braindead failures.

BOTTOM LEFT: Original poster art created in watercolor for *The Frozen Dead* by artist Jack Thurston. While this striking image did not appear on the main one-sheet at the time of the film's release, it was used on other promotional materials.

ABOVE RIGHT: Italian *locandina* poster for *Il teschio di londra* (*The Zombie Walks*, 1969), based on the novel *The Hand of Power* by prolific suspense author Edgar Wallace. The titular zombie is actually an earthly killer dressed in a black cloak, hat, and skull mask.

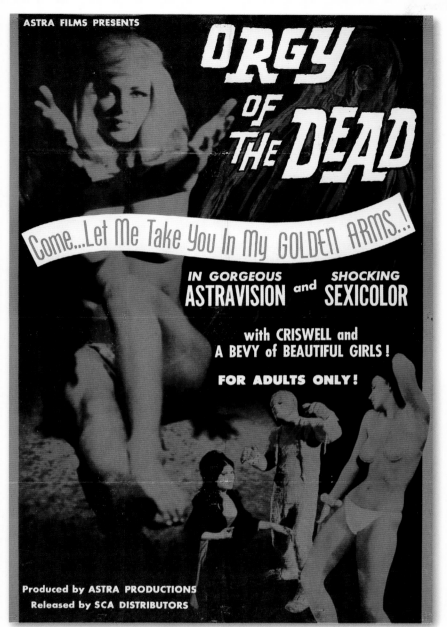

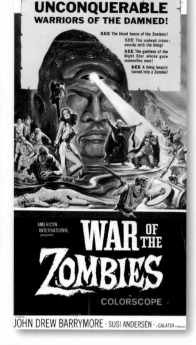

ABOVE LEFT: One-sheet for *Orgy of the Dead* (1965), directed by "A. C. Stephen" (Stephen C. Apostolof) and written by Edward D. Wood Jr. This is less a movie than a series of dance performances by topless young women, including a stiff-armed dancer who is introduced with the inexplicable line, "She lived as a zombie in life, so she will remain forever a zombie in death!"

TOP MIDDLE: Movie tie-in paperback for *Orgy of the Dead*, written by Edward D. Wood Jr. The screenplay credits for the film of the same name state that it's based on this novel. The cover artist, Robert Bonfils, worked as art director for publisher Greenleaf Classics and often produced fifty covers a month.

TOP RIGHT: Three-sheet for *War of the Zombies* (1964). The Italian title, *Roma contro Roma*, refers to the central plot point about a Roman centurion who is dispatched to a distant outpost, where he finds that the administrator has fallen under the thrall of an evil magician (played by John Drew Barrymore, the son of John Barrymore and father of Drew Barrymore).

BOTTOM RIGHT: Original artwork for the *War of the Zombies* by Reynold Brown (1917–1991), an American illustrator who created many iconic movie posters, including *The Creature from the Black Lagoon* and *Attack of the 50 Foot Woman*.

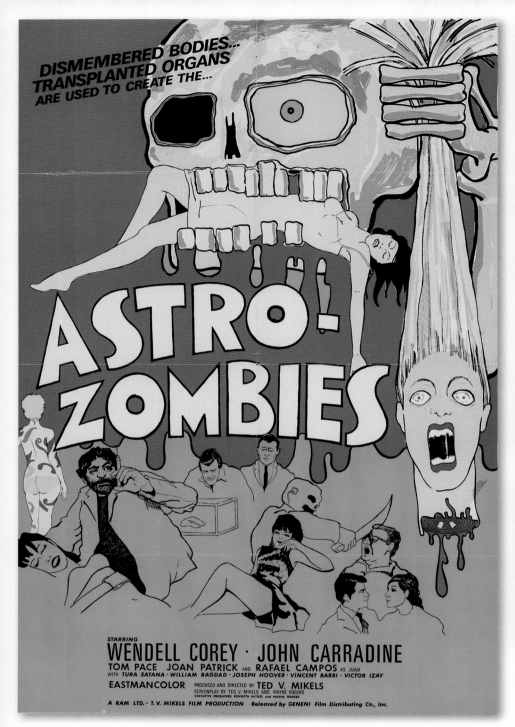

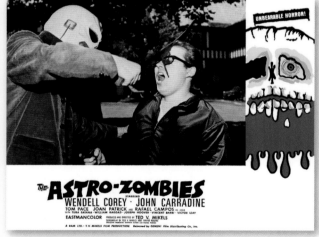

ABOVE LEFT: One-sheet for Ted Mikels's *Astro-Zombies* (1968), the title of which is derived from the idea that American scientists are creating cyborg-style astronauts for the space program. Things go very wrong, of course, and the prototypes run amok with machetes.

TOP RIGHT: One-sheet for the 1971 re-release of *Astro-Zombies*. Twelve years earlier, in *Invisible Invaders*, John Carradine played a scientist turned into a zombie by aliens; here, he is the scientist creating the zombies (after he's been canned by the feds).

BOTTOM RIGHT: Lobby card for *Astro-Zombies*. In keeping with the exploitation horror movies of the 1960s, *Astro-Zombies* offered more (obviously fake) blood and gore than any previous zombie film. The costumes for the title creatures involved rubber masks with a few metal bits glued on . . . and turtlenecks.

ABOVE LEFT: One-sheet for Ray Dennis Steckler's *The Incredibly Strange Creatures Who Stopped Living and Became Mixed-Up Zombies* (1964), which features musical numbers but is not a musical. "Cash Flagg," the film's star, was a pseudonym for Steckler; co-star Carolyn Brandt was his wife.

ABOVE RIGHT: Mexican and U.S. lobby cards for *The Incredibly Strange Creatures*. The film is most notable for its cinematographers: Joseph V. Mascelli, who wrote *The Five C's of Cinematography*; Vilmos Zsigmond, who later worked on *Close Encounters of the Third Kind*; and László Kovács, winner of multiple lifetime achievement awards.

The Sexiest Zombie: Vampira

Although she occupies less than three minutes of screen time in Edward D. Wood Jr.'s *Plan 9 from Outer Space* and never utters a single word, Vampira's stiff-armed graveyard stalking and striking appearance made an unforgettable impression in the notorious (anti)classic. Born Maila Nurmi in 1922, she set out to be an actress and model while still in her teens but found her first real success when Los Angeles TV station KABC hired her to host a horror-movie show called *The Vampira Show* in 1954. Although the show aired for only a year, it generated fans around the world and led to her appearances in *Plan 9* and Bert I. Gordon's 1962 fantasy film *The Magic Sword*, as well as non-genre films like *The Big Operator* and *The Beat Generation*. Her personal life was almost as extraordinary as her screen persona: she had a child (given up for adoption) with Orson Welles, was friends with James Dean, and worked from the 1960s onward laying linoleum. She later inspired the look of the immensely popular horror personality Elvira, while in Tim Burton's 1994 film *Ed Wood* she was played by actress Lisa Marie. Nurmi died in 2008 and was buried at Hollywood Forever Cemetery.

ABOVE LEFT: This artwork was created for a 1998 video release of *Plan 9 from Outer Space* (1957), emphasizing Maila Nurmi as Vampira. Nurmi claimed that she was paid $200 for her appearance in the film, and that she insisted her part be mute—in order to avoid having to speak any of Wood's dialogue.

ABOVE RIGHT: Vampira tattoo flash art by Russian artist Kate Markova (a.k.a. Red Selena). Nurmi said Vampira's costume was based on the cartoons of Charles Addams, who gave his own name to his best-known series, *The Addams Family*.

RIGHT: Maila Nurmi as Vampira in *Plan 9 from Outer Space*. The film credits call her character "Vampire Girl"; Nurmi noted in interviews that part of Vampira's appearance was based on the evil Queen from Disney's *Snow White and the Seven Dwarfs* (1937).

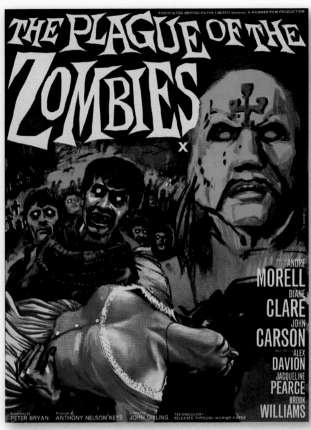

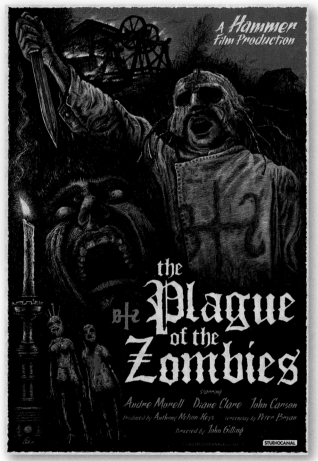

ABOVE LEFT: Italian *quattro-foglio* poster for *La lunga notte dell'orrore* (*Plague of the Zombies*, 1966). The Italian title translates to *The Long Night of Horror*; the poster emphasizes the film's occult aspect over its zombies.

TOP RIGHT: This image for *The Plague of the Zombies* (1966) was first used as the right half of a British quad poster, when the film was released in a double bill with Hammer's *Dracula, Prince of Darkness*. It was also used as the cover art for the film's 2019 Blu-ray release.

BOTTOM RIGHT: Alternative poster art for *The Plague of the Zombies*, by the British graphic designer Richard Wells, who has also created striking works based on other Hammer productions, as well as the literary works of M. R. James.

ABOVE LEFT: Insert poster for *The Plague of the Zombies* (1966). Hammer first began thinking about producing a zombie movie in 1962, when the writer John Bryan outlined an idea called *The Zombie*; a 1964 promotional ad showed the title *Horror of the Zombies*. Roy Ashton's makeup for the zombies is a high point of the film.

ABOVE RIGHT: French *petite* poster for *L'invasion des morts-vivants* (*The Plague of the Zombies*), featuring the work of Boris Grinsson (1907–1999), a Russian-born artist who, after moving to Paris in 1932, created over two thousand French film posters in virtually every genre. The French title translates to *The Undead Invasion*.

3

THE BIRTH OF THE MODERN ZOMBIE

"DO YOU BELIEVE THE DEAD ARE RETURNING TO LIFE AND ATTACKING THE LIVING?"

DR. JAMES FOSTER IN *DAWN OF THE DEAD* (1978)

> "Zombies to me were those boys in the Caribbean who do the wet work for Lugosi. I thought I was creating a completely new monster."
>
> George A. Romero, from a 2013 video interview for Vice Films/Grolsch Film Works

By now, the story of the twenty-eight-year-old Pittsburgh filmmaker who decided that his first feature film would be a horror movie about the dead returning to eat the living is the well-known stuff of much-repeated legend, and deservedly so, because that feature film not only changed the horror film forever but splattered all over pop culture in every direction.

Prior to *Night of the Living Dead*, George Romero had made his living shooting newsreels and commercials. After he formed Image Ten Productions, he began thinking about what he wanted to make for his debut feature film; his first attempt was a period drama called *Whine of the Fawn*, which failed to find financing. Examining profit-making pictures of years past, he decided that a horror movie might be a better bet. A partner in Image Ten, John Russo, cowrote the script with Romero, who would also direct, edit, and photograph the film (and have a cameo as a newsman, a role he'd also play in *Dawn of the Dead*).

Night of the Living Dead was originally called *Night of the Flesh Eaters*, although one early workprint of the film bears the title *Night of Anubis*. Shot in black-and-white on a budget of $114,000, it begins with a brother and sister, Johnny and Barbara, arriving at a rural cemetery to pay their respects to their late father. Within the first eight minutes, a tall, grimacing, ragged zombie has arrived and killed Johnny, leaving Barbara to flee. She winds up in a farmhouse with six other survivors; news reports indicate that this is happening on a wide scale, implying the beginning of an apocalypse. As tensions among the group escalate, Ben (Duane Jones) emerges as the cool-headed natural leader. During the long night, the farmhouse is besieged by dozens of "ghouls" who consume any living human they can drag down. One by one, the beleaguered survivors are taken down by their own terrible mistakes. Before the night is over, armed mobs have begun patrolling the countryside, suggesting a coming war. The film ends on footage of a fire.

Night of the Living Dead went on to become one of the most successful independent features ever made, opening to strong numbers both domestically and internationally. After its success, Romero made several other films, including the vampire movie *Martin*, but none generated either the profits or controversy of *Night of the Living Dead*, which outraged some critics who thought its gore went too far.

It wasn't until 1977, when Italian horror maestro Dario Argento (*Suspiria*, *Deep Red*) teamed up with Romero and producer Richard Rubinstein to put the financing into place, that Romero began production on what is now widely considered to be the finest zombie film ever made. Released in 1978, *Dawn of the Dead* took only the zombie outbreak from the first film and grafted in a new cast of characters and settings. It begins as a group of survivors are fleeing the massive meltdown of society in the face of the carnivorous walking dead (one expert in the film notes that these are not cannibals, since they don't prey on their own kind). Steven (David Emge), Fran (Gaylen Ross), Peter (Ken Foree), and Roger (Scott H. Reiniger) are the quartet who end up taking

With a running time of over two hours, *Dawn of the Dead* is an intense, ultraviolent, blackly funny masterpiece that forever united zombies with the end of the world.

refuge in a shopping mall, which they are able to effectively barricade against the zombies. Establishing residence in a palace of consumerism, they initially revel in their confinement and take the opportunity to live out fantasies, but they soon realize the mall is also a trap. When a biker gang successfully overcomes the barriers to break in, they allow the zombies to enter as well, forcing the heroes to fight dual battles. Only Fran and Black trooper Peter survive, suggesting that the only way forward is to abandon old stereotypes and begin anew.

For the first time, Romero had a reasonable budget to work with. He brought in a young makeup effects wizard named Tom Savini to provide more elaborate gore, which was displayed in full color this time; hired a gifted cinematographer, Michael Gornick, as part of a larger crew (as compared to eight on *Martin*); and had an extraordinary setting in the Monroeville Mall, where his crew shot for eight weeks each night from 11 p.m. to 7 a.m. before taking a hiatus during December because of Christmas decorations.

PREVIOUS SPREAD: Portrait of George A. Romero by the Australian artist Greg Chapman. Romero's father was a commercial artist, but although George too showed early promise as an artist—he even designed the logo for his first company, the Latent Image—his heart was always in filmmaking.

TOP LEFT: George A. Romero is surrounded by his zombie creations in this promotional still from his 1985 film *Day of the Dead*. The film was a happy production for Romero, who called it his personal favorite of all of his zombie films.

BOTTOM LEFT: Lobby card from *Night of the Living Dead* (1968). The zombies in the film were friends and family of the crew, and by way of payment they were provided with food and beer on location. (Romero later said that they were also paid after the film began to make money.)

ABOVE RIGHT: Alternative poster for *Night of the Living Dead* by the American artist Anthony Petrie, who says, "My goal was to recreate the zombies-breaking-into-the-house scene, so when it was framed on someone's wall, the image would be to scale and look like zombies were breaking through a window."

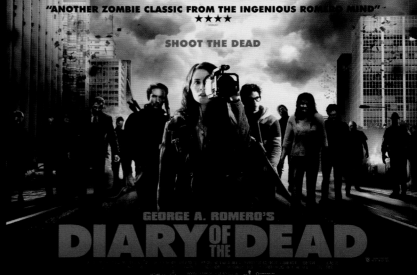

ABOVE LEFT: Alternative poster for *Night of the Living Dead* by the British artist Graham Humphreys. The half-eaten head shown at bottom right (discovered atop the staircase of the farmhouse in the film) was sculpted on a plastic skull model by Romero himself.

TOP MIDDLE: One-sheet for Romero's fourth zombie film, *Land of the Dead* (2005). Romero wrote his first draft just before 9/11; when he started shopping it after that catastrophic event, he found that softer films were in vogue, so he put his script on the shelf for a few years. Some critics and viewers still found echoes of 9/11 (and the Iraq War) in *Land of the Dead*.

TOP RIGHT: Italian DVD cover for Romero's sixth and final zombie film, *Survival of the Dead* (2009). It is the closest Romero came to making a direct sequel, since it follows several National Guardsmen who were first seen going AWOL in *Diary of the Dead*. Romero later said the film was inspired by William Wyler's 1958 western *The Big Country*.

BOTTOM RIGHT: British quad poster for *Diary of the Dead* (2007). Romero was happy to return to the independent style of filmmaking after 2005's *Land of the Dead*, in part because he was dismayed by the amount of money that the previous production spent on its stars.

With a running time of over two hours, *Dawn of the Dead* is an intense, ultraviolent, blackly funny masterpiece that forever united zombies with the end of the world. After *Dawn*, zombies would never again be stiff, wide-eyed slaves to a voodoo master; now, they were the shambling, gore-smeared harbingers of the end (with the heroes as heavily armed, resolute survivalists). *Dawn* was an instant critical and commercial success—Roger Ebert called it "one of the best horror films ever made"—and led to dozens of knockoffs, especially in Italy, where filmmakers like Lucio Fulci made careers out of low-budget zombie gorefests.

Romero went on to make two further features—1981's *Knightriders*, a drama about a group of motorcyclists who stage Renaissance fairs and jousting tournaments; and 1982's *Creepshow*, an anthology horror movie written by

---

"Zombies, man … they creep me out."

Paul Kaufman in *Land of the Dead* (2005)

Stephen King—before returning to the world of the undead in 1985 with *Day of the Dead*. Set some time after the zombie holocaust has destroyed most of the world, *Day* centers on the conflicts between a group of scientists and the military men assigned to guard them, all sequestered deep underground in a series of tunnels. The lead character, Sarah (Lori Cardille), is both a capable scientist searching for a cure to the zombie virus and possibly the last living woman, putting her in constant danger from her all-too-human, testosterone-driven cohorts. The film also introduces Bub (Howard Sherman), a semi-intelligent zombie who indicates that the walking dead can perhaps be trained. *Day* brought Tom Savini back for even better, more realistic gore effects that would have likely earned the film an X-rating had Romero not opted to simply release it without a rating (a strategy that had worked well with *Dawn*).

Day of the Dead was less successful than its predecessors, but it still earned well enough at the box office to merit another chapter in Romero's zombie saga . . . which didn't come for another twenty years. In the meantime, Hollywood beckoned, and Romero made several bigger-budget pictures (*The Dark Half*, *Monkey Shines*), but then something terrible happened: because *Night of the Living Dead* made the mistake of not including a copyright notice on the final print, Romero lost ownership of the film. Almost immediately, *Night* was colorized, remade by other filmmakers, and earning money for a lot of people who were *not* George A. Romero.

In 1990, in an attempt to regain control of his creation, Romero rewrote the film and turned the direction over to Savini. Unfortunately, outside producers severely curtailed Savini's ability to pursue his vision for the film, and it was a

disappointment to both fans and critics alike. However, its performances (mainly from Tony Todd and Patricia Tallman, in the roles of Ben and Barbara), effects, and style have weathered time well, and the film now has a following.

It wasn't until 2005 that Romero returned to the director's chair for a new zombie movie, *Land of the Dead*. This time he had not only a major studio (Universal) behind him but also a cast that included Dennis Hopper, John Leguizamo, Asia Argento (daughter of Dario), and Simon Baker. *Land* is set in a postapocalyptic world where the wealthy live in secure high-rises with euphemistic names like "Fiddler's Green" while the poor scrabble for scraps, sometimes forced to fight zombies in sporting events. The real star of the movie, though, might just be Dead Reckoning (also the film's original title), the armored and armed vehicle that the rich send out to scavenge outside of their safe complex. The plot revolves around insurrection attempts from both humans and zombies (led by the towering and sympathetic "Big Daddy," played by Eugene Clark), and a scheme on the part of Cholo (Leguizamo) to extort money from the wealthy by stealing Dead Reckoning.

Although the script's threads don't always tie together well, *Land of the Dead* was another victory for Romero. Zombie fans appreciated its creative gore (by KNB Effects Group) and action set pieces, and critics lauded its take on a society in which the rich exploit and abuse the poor.

Two years later, Romero was back with another independently produced zombie film, *Diary of the Dead*. Employing a found-footage style allowed him to explore new film technologies while revisiting his zombie apocalypse. *Diary* returns to the beginning of the meltdown, following a crew of student filmmakers who attempt to document what's happening. Although some reviewers praised the film's inventiveness, others felt that it was heavy-handed and slow, and it wasn't as profitable as the earlier films.

Romero returned one last time to zombie territory for 2007's *Survival of the Dead*, which would be his last feature film as director. *Survival* marks the first time that he carried characters over from one of the earlier films, since it follows a group of National Guard soldiers seen in *Diary of the Dead* as they abandon their posts and flee to an isolated island where they're embroiled in a longstanding feud between two families. *Survival of the Dead* had a limited release and was the first of Romero's zombie films to fail financially. It fared equally poorly with critics, who found it lacking in originality.

When George Romero died in 2017, he left behind dozens of unproduced projects, including two sequels to *Survival of the Dead*. He also left a legacy that has expanded to literature, merchandising, and academic study (his archives are now housed in a special collection at the library of the University of Pittsburgh), although he took no credit for what his legacy spawned. "I'm not a student of the genre," he told the *AV Club* in a 2008 interview. "My stuff is my stuff."

George A. Romero's
Horror Masterpiece...

NIGHT
OF THE
LIVING
DEAD
x

Produced by RUSSEL W. STREINER and KARL HARDMAN Directed by GEORGE A. ROMERO Screenplay by JOHN A. RUSSO and GEORGE A. ROMERO
Starring JUDITH O'DEA · DUANE JONES · MARILYN EASTMAN · KARL HARDMAN · JUDITH RIDLEY · KEITH WAYNE

ABOVE: British quad poster for
a 1978 re-release of *Night of
the Living Dead*, featuring
artwork by British poster
artist Tom Chantrell.
Romero scoffed at critics who
derided the film's grainy,
obviously low-budget
aesthetic, noting that his
company, the Latent Image,
had made successful
commercials for years.

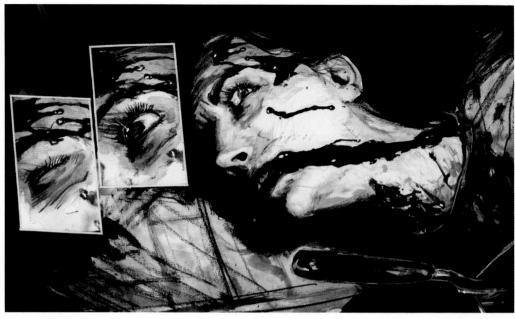

ABOVE LEFT: Australian day-bill poster for *Night of the Living Dead*. The first modern, flesh-eating zombie appears on page five of the shooting script with this simple description: "In the distance, a huddled figure is walking among the graves." Romero later noted that the script wasn't finished when shooting began.

TOP RIGHT: Original *Night of the Living Dead* art by American comics artist Stephen R. Bissette, who is best known for providing the art for Alan Moore's *Swamp Thing* comics.

BOTTOM RIGHT: British quad poster for the original 1968 release of *Night of the Living Dead*. Contrary to one oft-misquoted "fact," *Night of the Living Dead* was shot on 35mm film, not 16mm. It is true, however, that the film was shot in black-and-white for budgetary reasons.

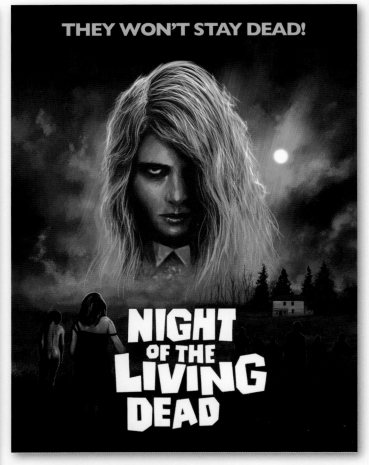

ABOVE LEFT: Promotional poster for Living Dead Media's fiftieth-anniversary screenings of *Night of the Living Dead* on October 24 and 25, 2018. The company also released a DVD box set with similar cover artwork.

TOP RIGHT: Alternative poster for *Night* by the British artist Daryl Joyce. The child zombie Karen Cooper (played by Kyra Schon) is one of the film's most iconic characters. Schon's father, Karl Hardman, portrays her onscreen father, Harry; Marilyn Eastman, who plays her mother, was Karl's business partner and later became his life partner.

BOTTOM RIGHT: Alternative movie poster for *Night of the Living Dead,* as produced for the seminal alternative movie poster company Mondo in 2010 by artist Florian Bertmer in a limited-edition run of two hundred screen prints.

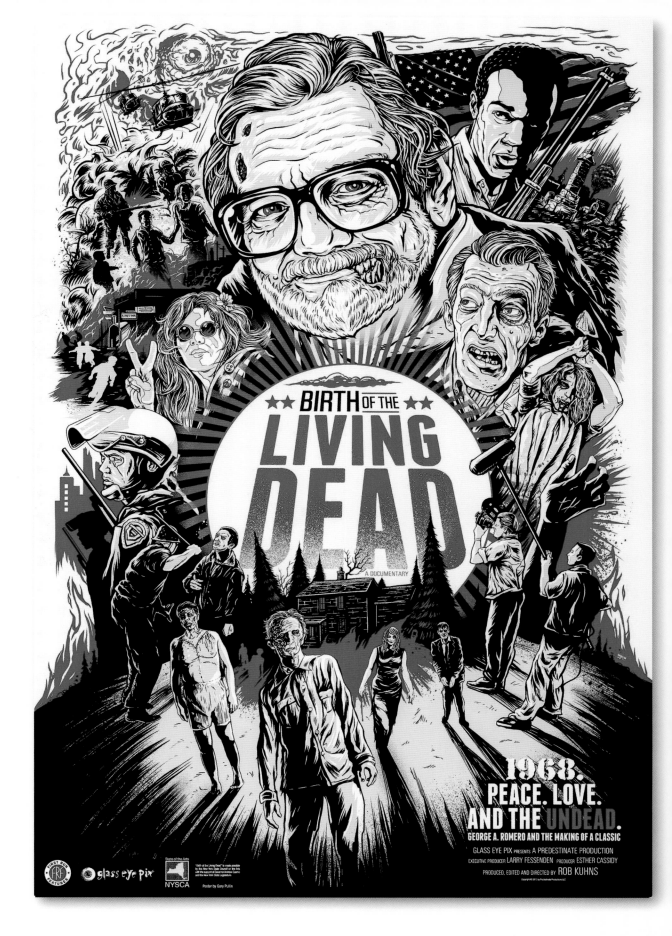

RIGHT: One-sheet poster for the 2013 documentary *Birth of the Living Dead*, directed by Rob Kuhns. The film details the making of *Night of the Living Dead* and emphasizes how it reflected the turbulence of the 1960s, especially the Vietnam War and the Civil Rights Movement.

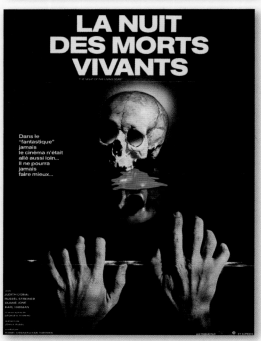

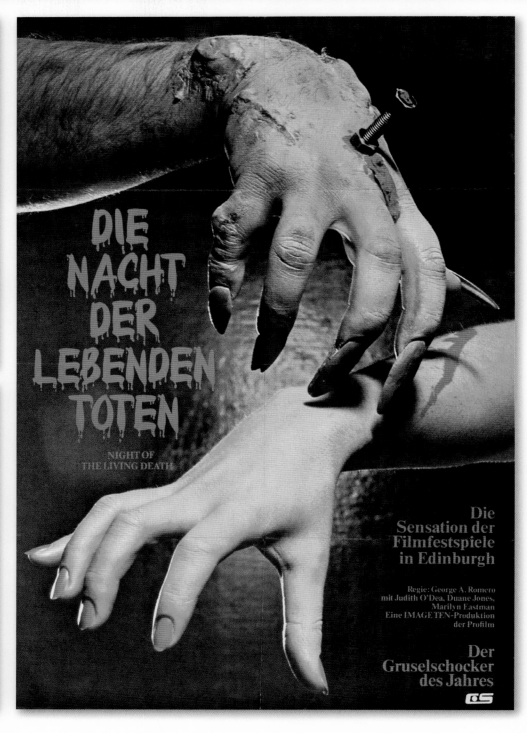

TOP LEFT: Poster for a 1981 Spanish re-release of *Night of the Living Dead*, featuring artwork by Macario Gómez Quibus (1926–2018), who signed his works "MAC." The Spanish artist worked in a variety of styles and reportedly produced over four thousand posters during his long career.

BOTTOM LEFT: French *grande* poster for a 1980s re-release of *Night of the Living Dead*. Romero ascribed part of the film's success to the rave reviews it received from French critics. The poster certainly reflects this: the ad copy near the center translates to, "In the fantastic never had the cinema gone so far . . . it can never do better."

ABOVE RIGHT: This German A1 poster notes *Night of the Living Dead*'s success at the Edinburgh International Film Festival (EIFF), which was established in 1947 and remains the world's longest continually running film festival. Romero's films were frequently screened at the festival over the years.

ABOVE LEFT: Alternative movie poster for *Night of the Living Dead*, featuring artwork by the American artist Jason Kauzlarich, who has also created similar posters for *Dawn of the Dead* and *Day of the Dead*.

ABOVE RIGHT: Italian *locandina* poster for *Night of the Living Dead*. This particular poster is part of the George A. Romero Archival Collection at the University of Pittsburgh, and it was signed by Romero with his typical inscription: "Stay scared!"

WORKING WITH ZOMBIES ON BOTH SIDES OF THE CAMERA: KEN FOREE

survived the carnage and flew off to further adventures with Fran (Gaylen Ross) in the helicopter. It was a huge deal for many African Americans but others as well; and I didn't realize for decades after the film how big a deal that was and how people were happy."

Ken Foree discussing *Dawn of the Dead* in a 2020 interview

Actor Ken Foree originally went to New York to pursue a career as a photographer, but he found himself considering other pathways after his equipment was stolen. After accompanying a friend to a theater audition, he began landing parts in Off-Broadway stage productions. He landed small parts onscreen in *Kojak* and the feature film *The Bingo Long Traveling All-Stars and Motor Kings* but was back to doing stage work in the East Village when a friend suggested that he audition for *Dawn of the Dead*.

Foree, who knew *Night of the Living Dead* lead Duane Jones from their mutual involvement with the civil rights movement in Harlem, auditioned several times—including with David Emge, Scott Reiniger, and Gaylen Ross, who would end up being cast in the film as Steven, Roger, and Fran, respectively. Although some reviewers were too stunned by the film's gore to appreciate the performances, audiences remembered Foree's resonant, somber reading of one of the most famous advertising lines in history: "When there's no more room in hell, the dead will walk the earth." In recent interviews, Foree has recalled loving the script and having a great time during the shooting, but little did he know that his performance as no-nonsense S.W.A.T. team member Peter Washington would establish him as a horror actor for the next few decades. In fact, he didn't even expect it to acquire a US distribution deal.

After *Dawn of the Dead*, Foree appeared in Romero's *Knightriders* (with Ed Harris, Tom Savini, and Patricia Tallman) as "Little John." For the next few decades, he would become a popular television performer, appearing in dozens of series including genre favorites *Beauty and the Beast*, *Quantum Leap*, *Babylon 5*, and *The X-Files*. (He also appeared in the television series *Knight Rider*, not to be confused with Romero's film.) He was a regular from 1996 to 2000 on the Nickelodeon sitcom *Kenan and Kel*, playing the father of mischievous Chicago high-school student Kenan Rockmore. During this time, he also appeared in Stuart Gordon's cult favorite *From Beyond*, portraying heroic but doomed detective Bubba Brownlee, who

eventually loses his fight against the Lovecraftian horrors unleashed by Dr. Edward Pretorius (Ed Sorel). He also appeared in *Leatherface: The Texas Chainsaw Massacre III* (1990), battling the ultraviolent Sawyer family; had a cameo in Zack Snyder's remake of *Dawn of the Dead* (2004); and faced zombies again in the Serbian horror film *Zone of the Dead* (2009).

Foree gained a fresh horror genre following in 2005, when he appeared in a different kind of Zombie movie, working for musician turned filmmaker Rob Zombie in *The Devil's Rejects* (2005) as brothel owner and antihero Charlie

---

Although some reviewers were too stunned by the film's gore to appreciate the performances, audiences remembered Foree's resonant, somber reading of one of the most famous advertising lines in history: "When there's no more room in hell, the dead will walk the earth."

Altamont. Next, he pleased fans around the world when he challenged masked killer Michael Myers in Zombie's 2007 reboot of *Halloween* with the words, "Let me introduce myself: I'm Joe Grizzly, bitch!"; unfortunately, Grizzly, a truck driver, loses his knife fight with the famed slasher in a truck-stop restroom. In 2012's *The Lords of Salem*, Zombie cast Foree as Herman "Munster" Jackson, a hip DJ partnered with Heidi (Sheri Moon Zombie), who is descended from a line of witches and finds herself drawn into an ancient cult. Foree also supplied the voice of Luke St. Luke, agent to the title character in Zombie's 2009 animated comedy *The Haunted World of El Superbeasto*.

Over the years, Foree has worked as a producer (most recently on 2017's *The Midnight Man*, in which he also starred) and as a writer (2010's *D.C. Sniper*). In 2007, he was inducted into the Phoenix International Horror and Sci-Fi Film Festival Hall of Fame.

omotional photo
of the Dead
ving Scott
Roger"), Gaylen
"), David Emge
, and Ken Foree
rmed and ready to
hordes of both
d human bikers
ng Pittsburgh's
e Mall. The mall
atively new when
Dead shot there.

BOTTOM LEFT: Promotional
photo of Foree as "Big Joe
Grizzly" in Rob Zombie's
2007 remake of John
Carpenter's *Halloween*.
Foree makes the most of his
brief appearance by loading
his lines with attitude.
Particularly notable is the
moment when he first
meets Michael Myers.

ABOVE RIGHT: Alternative
movie poster by the British
artist Andrew Swainson, also
available in a blue variant.
The idea for *Dawn of the Dead*
first came to Romero when he
visited Monroeville Mall—
Pennsylvania's first indoor
shopping mall—before it
opened and saw trucks
delivering products to the
various stores.

When there is no more room in hell...
the dead will walk the earth

George A. Romero's

DAWN OF THE DEAD

In 1968 George A. Romero began a three film trilogy tracing the growth of a "Zombie" Society. The first film was the now classic "Night Of The Living Dead."

"DAWN OF THE DEAD" (in 'Living' color) is his long awaited second film. The last film, "Day Of The Dead" should hit the screens about 1988.

Anyway, while you're waiting for "DAWN OF THE DEAD's" premiere you can enjoy a limited edition T-Shirt. To order send a check for $6.00 plus 60 cents (postage & handling) to The Laurel Group, Inc. 150 East 58th St., N.Y., N.Y. 10022. Let us know your name, address, zip code, and size (S,M,L,XL.) Please print or type and allow 4 weeks for delivery.

P.S. We didn't show you the whole shirt on purpose. Life, like the movies, should have some surprises! Also accept our apology for not providing an order form to clip out, this magazine is too nice to cut up.

PHOTO: K. KOLBERT   © 1978 DAWN ASSOCIATES

TOP: Art by James Warhola, taken from the *Dawn of the Dead Poster Book*. Warhola, the nephew of Andy Warhol, is an American artist who worked on the Garbage Pail Kids trading cards in the 1980s. The poster book, which was published in 1978, is now a highly sought-after collectible.

BOTTOM: Back cover for the *Dawn of the Dead Poster Book* (1978). Note the line in the text that declares, "The last film, *Day of the Dead*, should hit the screens about 1988." While the date is three years off (*Day* was released in 1985), it proves that by 1978, Romero was already thinking of the "Dead" films as a trilogy.

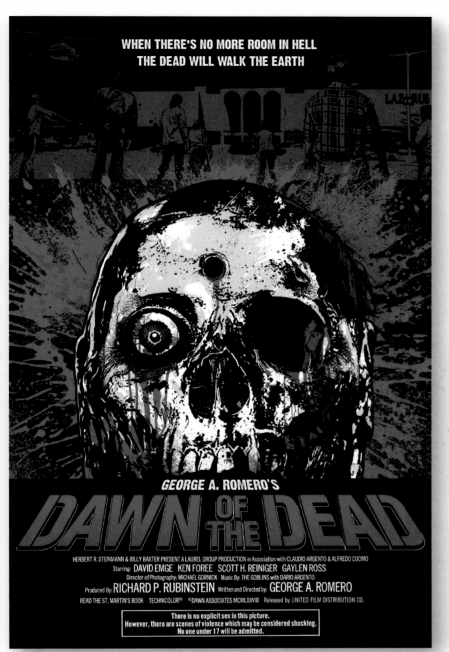

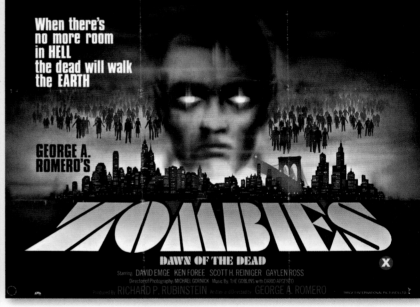

ABOVE LEFT: Alternative movie poster for *Dawn of the Dead* by the American artist James Rheem Davis, produced as a screen print limited to twenty-five copies. The famous ad slogan used here—"When there's no more room in hell the dead will walk the earth"—is uttered by actor Ken Foree, who would say the line again in Zack Snyder's 2004 remake of *Dawn of the Dead*, although this time as a television preacher rather than a trooper.

TOP RIGHT: Portrait by the American artist Frederick Cooper of *Dawn of the Dead* character Roger DeMarco (played by Scott H. Reiniger), showing the moment he returns from the dead.

BOTTOM RIGHT: British quad poster for *Dawn of the Dead* featuring artwork by Tom Chantrell. Although this poster depicts what looks like New York (which would figure as a location in Lucio Fulci's zombie films), *Dawn of the Dead* is set in and around Romero's then hometown of Pittsburgh.

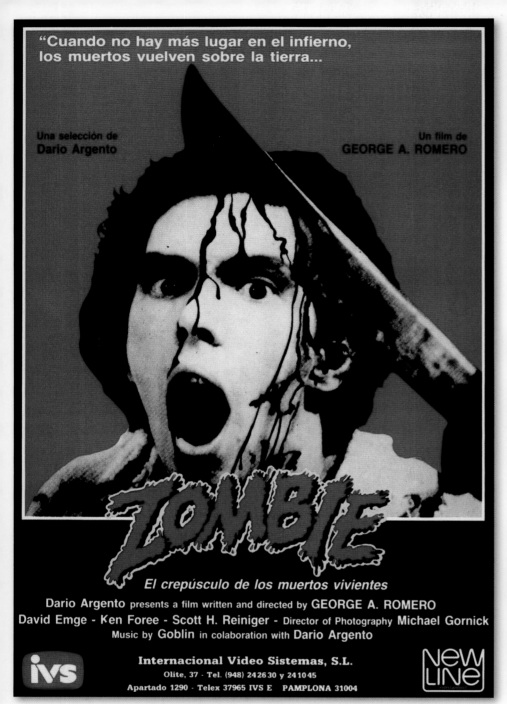

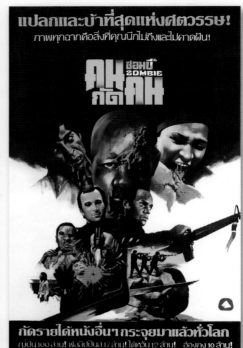

ABOVE LEFT: Promotional poster for the Spanish videocassette release of *Dawn of the Dead*. The film's producer, Richard Rubinstein, referred to the gore effects provided by makeup guru Tom Savini as "the moneymakers." In the film, that machete is wielded by Savini himself, playing the role of the biker "Blades."

TOP RIGHT: Thai poster for *Dawn of the Dead*. The film had a combined international box-office take of nearly $50 million, with a domestic gross of $16 million, against a total budget of $640,000, making it the most profitable of all of Romero's zombie films.

BOTTOM RIGHT: Japanese B2 poster for *Dawn of the Dead*. Romero first conceived of *Dawn* as an extremely dark piece about a couple living in the crawlspace above the mall, foraging naked among the stores. As script development progressed, he lightened the tone, even adding a pie fight between the bikers and the zombies.

ABOVE LEFT: Portuguese poster for *Dawn of the Dead,* here billed as *Zombie o despertar dos mortos* but more commonly known in Europe as *Zombi.* Italian producer Fabrizio de Angelis took advantage of a loophole in Italian copyright law that allowed anyone to market a film as a sequel and rushed *Zombi 2* (1979) into production under the direction of Lucio Fulci.

ABOVE RIGHT: Italian *quattro-foglio* poster for *Dawn of the Dead.* In exchange for providing financing for *Dawn,* Italian filmmaker Dario Argento took the foreign rights (except for South America, which Laurel Entertainment retained), and even did his own cut of the film, making more prominent use of the score by Goblin. Romero preferred to use cues from a stock music library.

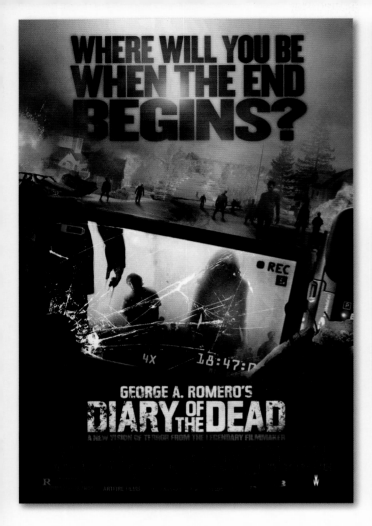

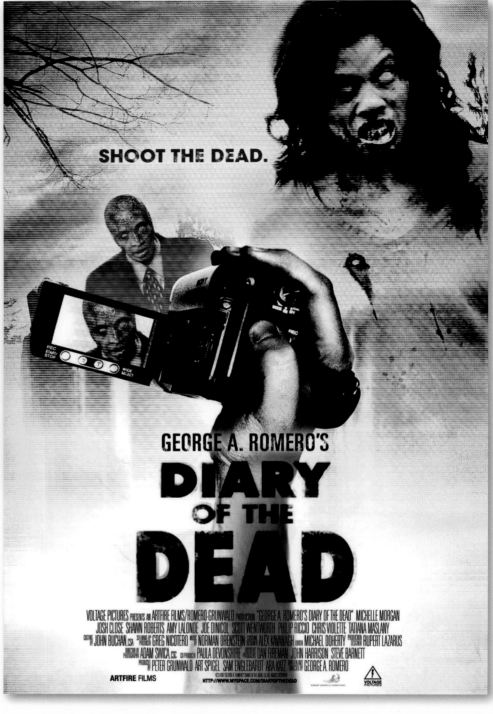

ABOVE: A pair of one-sheets for *Diary of the Dead* (2007). Romero's original vision for the film was to make it in one single take, but that proved unfeasible (although the 2017 Japanese film *One Cut of the Dead* pulled it off, at least for its first half). In press interviews for *Diary*, Romero claimed that he was not a political filmmaker and that his films were overanalyzed.

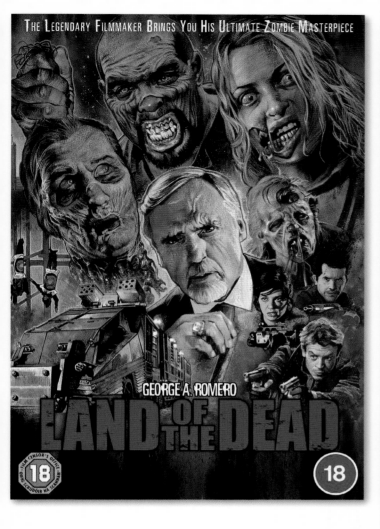

ABOVE LEFT: Poster for the U.K. home video release of *Land of the Dead*, featuring artwork by the British illustrator Graham Humphreys. The massive success of *Shaun of the Dead* (2004) helped *Land* finally go into production, twenty years after *Day of the Dead*; Romero paid homage by casting Edgar Wright and Simon Pegg as zombies in *Land*.

ABOVE RIGHT: One-sheet for *Land of the Dead* (2005), signed by Romero. Although *Land of the Dead* is the only Romero zombie film to receive distribution by a major studio, Universal came on board relatively late, after producer Mark Canton sold the company the rights, and as such had input on the cast but not the script or the location (Toronto).

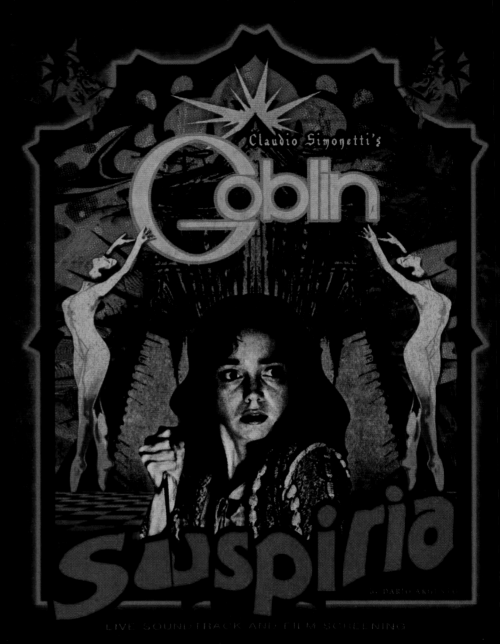

Scoring the Undead: Goblin

When Italian horror maestro Dario Argento stepped in to assist with financing *Dawn of the Dead*, he brought with him the prog-rock group that had scored several of his films: Goblin. In 1975, Argento hired the group for his thriller *Deep Red*, and the resulting soundtrack led to a successful album. Their greatest success came two years later, when they provided the thunderous score for Argento's witch epic *Suspiria*. Although Goblin's roster of members changed frequently over the years, they continued to score such films as the Australian horror entry *Patrick*, Luigi Cozzi's *Contamination*, and Argento's *Tenebrae, Phenomena,* and *Sleepless*. They have also performed their soundtracks live.

ABOVE LEFT: A production still from *Dawn of the Dead* showing Dario Argento and George Romero at the Monroeville Mall. Argento was crucial in making *Dawn of the Dead* happen: he provided early financing and even put up Romero in a hotel room in Rome while he completed work on the screenplay.

ABOVE RIGHT: A concert poster for a 2019 screening of Dario Argento's 1977 film *Suspiria* accompanied by a live performance of the film's score. Although the score was composed and performed by Goblin (or "The Goblins," as the onscreen credit read), the group's current incarnation includes only one original member, hence their billing as "Claudio Simonetti's Goblin."

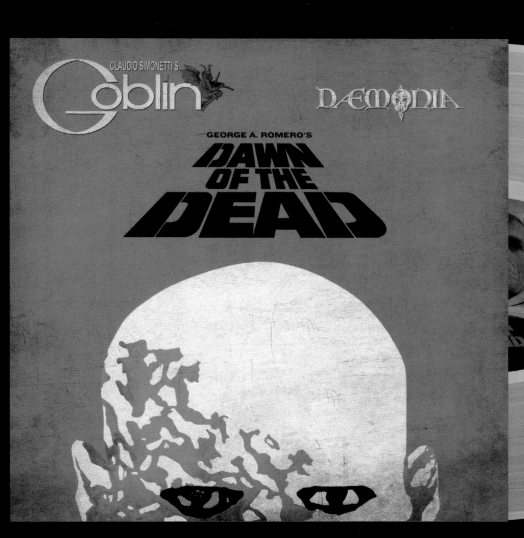

ABOVE: A limited-edition "lime vinyl" edition of the soundtrack for *Dawn of the Dead* was released in 2018, with "Claudio Simonetti's Goblin" and the band Daemonia playing new interpretations of the film's musical cues. There was also a deluxe edition, limited to 199 copies, that included a T-shirt, tote bag, posters, and more.

RIGHT: Goblin's official logo. Although some of the band's members played together earlier under other names, they officially became Goblin in 1975, when Dario Argento invited them to compose the score for his film *Deep Red*. The resulting album was immensely successful, but the band split up in 1978, just after recording the score for *Dawn of the Dead*.

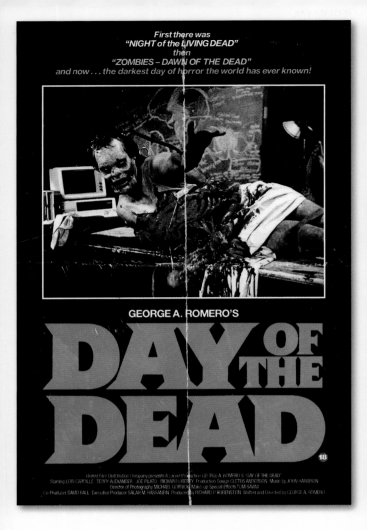

ABOVE LEFT: Faux one-sheet poster for *Day of the Dead*, as created by Lev Brahas (a.k.a. Levtones), heralding "the darkest day of horror the world has ever known." In 2013, a list of the "Top 100 Goriest Horror Movies of All Time" at the Internet Movie Database (IMDb) ranked *Day* at #5.

ABOVE RIGHT: Advance one-sheet poster for *Day of the Dead*. Romero called it his personal favorite of all of his zombie films, although he was disappointed at having to trim down his first draft, a sprawling, gory epic in which the military (assisted by scientists studying zombie behavior) has been training the undead into an army by feeding them human meat.

ABOVE LEFT: Turkish poster for *Day of the Dead*. The film was shot in seven weeks at a former limestone mine turned storage facility located near Wampum, Pennsylvania. The location was so cold that machinery (including Savini's cable-operated puppets) sometimes failed, and members of the cast and crew often fell ill.

ABOVE RIGHT: Thai poster for *Day of the Dead*. The "wall of arms" shot that appears near the beginning of the film was difficult to achieve: on the first attempt, the zombies positioned behind the wall knocked it over rather than punching through it.

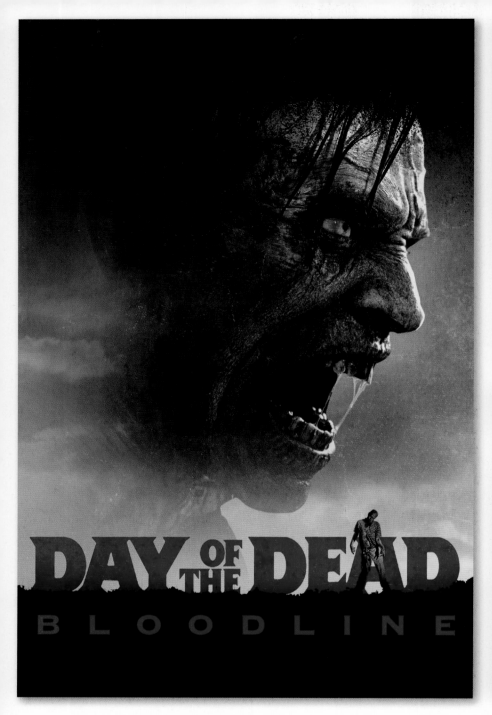

ABOVE LEFT: One-sheet for *Day of the Dead: Bloodline* (2018), which followed 2008's remake of *Day of the Dead* and used the ad slogan, "A bold new reimagining of the George A. Romero classic." *Bloodline*, which is mainly set five years into a zombie holocaust, actually bears almost no resemblance to Romero's 1985 film and was poorly received by critics.

TOP RIGHT: *Day of the Dead* poster design by the American artist Terry Callen of Screaming Brain Studios. The disemboweling of Captain Rhodes—who famously growls, "Choke on it!" at the zombies—provides the film's bloody climax.

BOTTOM RIGHT: Cover art for the special-edition Blu-ray release of *Day of the Dead*, by the American artist Thomas "The Dude Designs" Hodge. Noting that much of the art for the film focuses on the zombies, Hodge concentrated instead on the protagonist, Sarah (Lori Cardille). The green palette was inspired by the fluorescent lighting of the underground rooms.

ABOVE LEFT: Alternative poster for *Day of the Dead* by Jairo Guerrero. Twenty years would elapse between *Day of the Dead* and *Land of the Dead*. In fact, between 1993, when Romero made *The Dark Half*, and 2005, when he finally made *Land*, he directed only one feature: the little seen, French-financed thriller *Bruiser* (2000).

ABOVE RIGHT: One-sheet for the 2008 remake of *Day of the Dead*. In this version, Sarah Bowman (Mena Suvari) is a corporal under the command of Captain Rhodes (Ving Rhames); Bub's creator, Dr. Logan (Matt Rippy) is here, now working for the CDC, but Bub is not. Poorly reviewed, the film failed to receive a theatrical release and went straight to DVD.

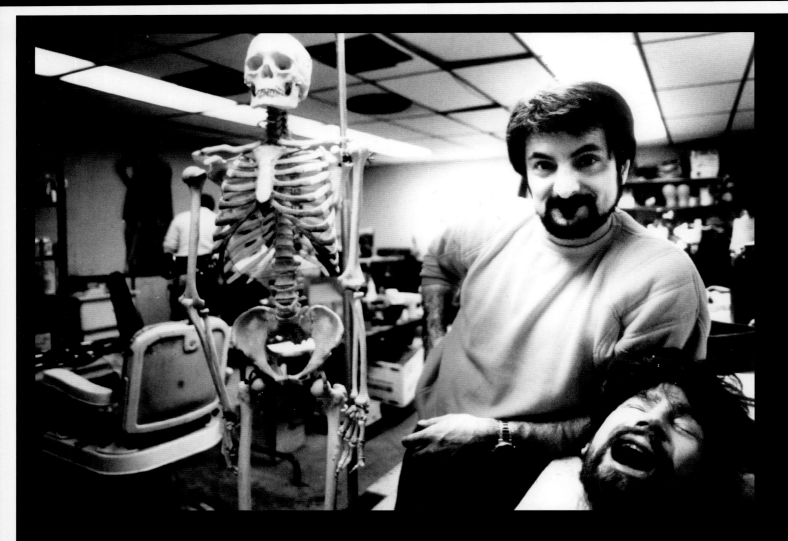

The King of Splatter: Tom Savini

Born in Pittsburgh in 1946, young Tom Savini became fascinated with movie monsters, in particular the startling creations of Lon Chaney. He had originally wanted to offer his makeup services to Romero for *Night of the Living Dead*, but he was instead sent to Vietnam, where he served as a combat photographer—a job that would later inspire his makeup effects. He came to prominence with his work on *Dawn of the Dead*, which included heads lopped in half by spinning helicopter blades and machetes driven into skulls. Savini also had a supporting role in *Dawn* as the adrenaline-fueled biker Blades (a role he would briefly reprise in *Land of the Dead*); he took on a bigger part in Romero's *Knightriders* as Morgan, the Black Knight. Throughout the '80s Savini provided gore effects for such films as *Friday the 13th*, *Maniac*, *The Texas Chainsaw Massacre 2*, and *H. P. Lovecraft's Necronomicon*, in addition to also working on Romero's *Day of the Dead*, *Creepshow*, and *Two Evil Eyes*. When Romero put together the 1990 remake of *Night of the Living Dead*, he asked Savini to direct. As an actor, Savini has appeared in *From Dusk Till Dawn*, the 2004 remake of *Dawn of the Dead*, *Grindhouse*, *Django Unchained*, and more. A champion fencer, he has also performed stunts in a number of films.

ABOVE: A production still from *Day of the Dead*, showing Tom Savini in his makeup lab. *Day* was a frustrating experience for Savini. He didn't enjoy the new chain of command on the film, which made access to George Romero difficult, and was keen to focus more on directing, having recently helmed an episode of the television series *Tales From the Darkside* ("In the Closet").

OPPOSITE: One-sheet for the documentary *Smoke and Mirrors: The Story of Tom Savini* (2021), with artwork by the American artist Terry Wolfinger. Savini, who delivered a charismatic performance as Morgan in Romero's *Knightriders* (1981), wanted to play the part of the villainous Captain Rhodes in *Day of the Dead*, but Romero worried that playing a lead role in addition to handling all of the film's makeup effects would be too much. He cast Joe Pilato as Rhodes instead.

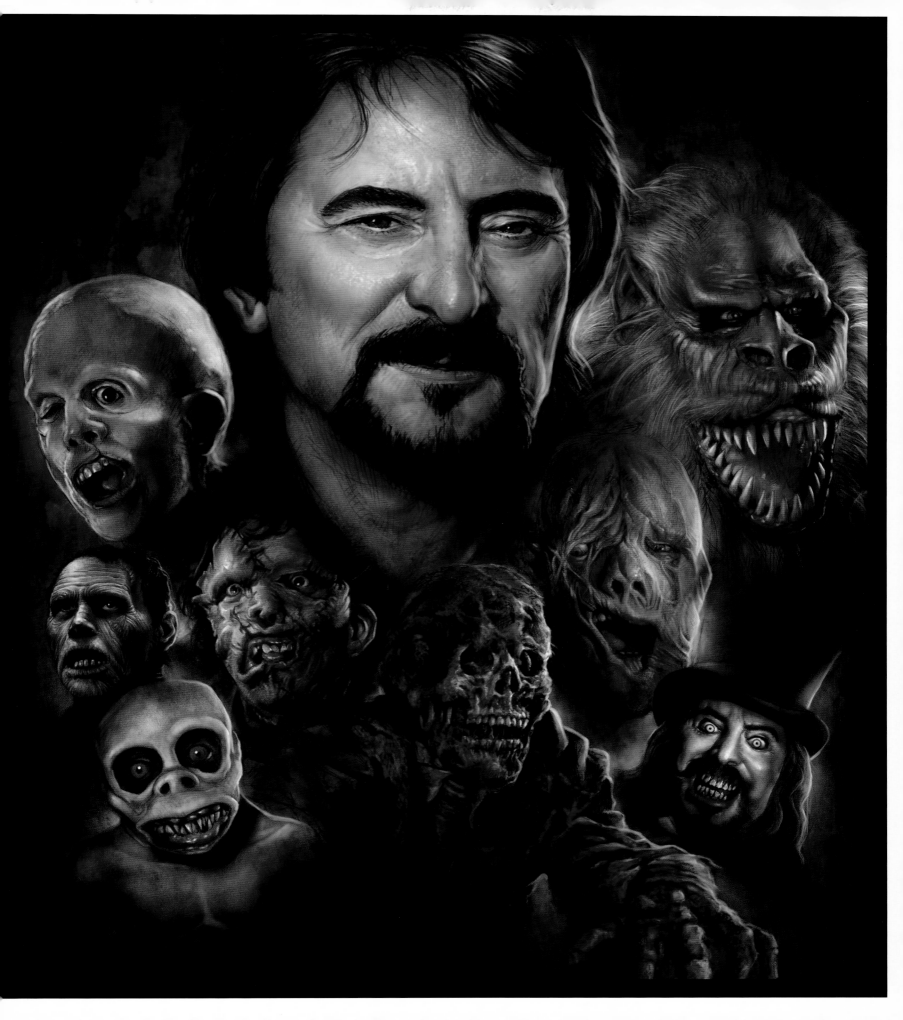

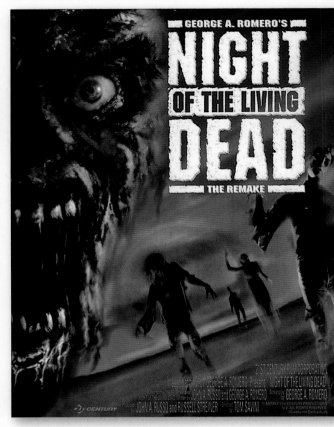

ABOVE LEFT: Poster for the home-video release of the 1990 remake of *Night of the Living Dead*, written by George A. Romero and directed by Tom Savini, who also supervised the makeup effects. It was made, in part, in an attempt to reestablish Romero's ownership of the copyright in the film series.

TOP RIGHT: Cover art from the DVD release of the *Night of the Living Dead* remake. Although directing the film was an unpleasant experience for Savini (who has yet to direct another feature film) and initial reviews were mostly negative, the film has found more favor with critics and fans in the years since.

BOTTOM RIGHT: German poster for the 1990 version of *Night of the Living Dead*. The film cast Tony Todd as Ben and Patricia Tallman as Barbara; in this version, Barbara is a more proactive character who becomes the only survivor, echoing a draft of the original *Night* that also had Barbara as the lone (albeit insane) survivor.

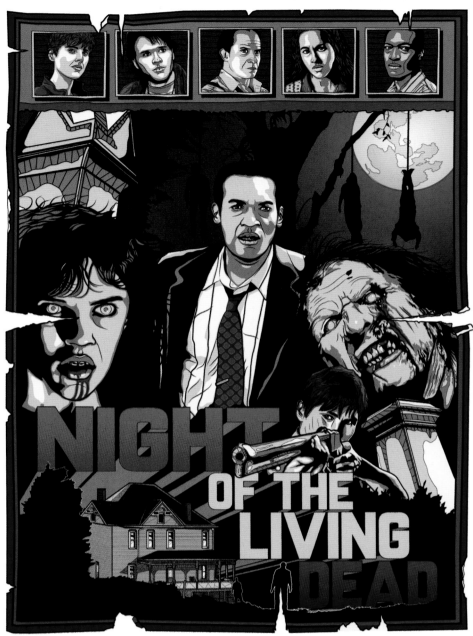

21ST CENTURY FILM CORPORATION AND GEORGE A. ROMERO PRESENTS A MENAHEM GOLAN PRODUCTION A FILM BY TOM SAVINI "NIGHT OF THE LIVING DEAD" TONY TODD PATRICIA TALLMAN
SCORE COMPOSED BY PAUL McCOLLOUGH DIRECTOR OF PHOTOGRAPHY FRANK PRINZI CO-EXECUTIVE PRODUCERS AMI ARTZI EXECUTIVE PRODUCER MENAHEM GOLAN AND GEORGE A. ROMERO BASED ON THE ORIGINAL SCREENPLAY NIGHT OF THE LIVING DEAD WRITTEN BY JOHN A. RUSSO AND GEORGE A. ROMERO
SCREENPLAY BY GEORGE A. ROMERO PRODUCED BY JOHN A. RUSSO AND RUSS STREINER DIRECTED BY TOM SAVINI
THERE IS A FATE WORSE THAN DEATH..

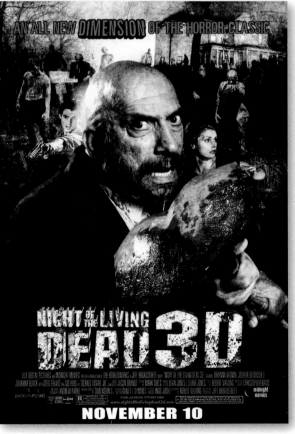

ABOVE LEFT: Alternative poster for the 1990 *Night of the Living Dead* by the British vector artist Mathew Lowe (a.k.a. NeonOddityUK). Tom Savini published a book in 2019 entitled *Night of the Living Dead 1990: The Version You've Never Seen*, in which he shared many of his original ideas and storyboards for the film.

TOP RIGHT: Poster art for *Night of the Animated Dead* (2021), an animated remake of *Night of the Living Dead*, directed by Jason Axinn and released by Warner Bros. Home Entertainment. Romero had no involvement with the film, which went direct to video and was maligned by critics for its lack of originality.

BOTTOM RIGHT: One-sheet for *Night of the Living Dead 3D* (2006), directed by Jeff Broadstreet, who also made a 2012 prequel, *Night of the Living Dead 3D: Re-animation*, which co-stars Jeffrey Combs as the younger brother of the mortician (Andrew Divoff) who creates zombies when he exposes corpses to hazardous medical waste.

監督/脚本 ジョージ・A・ロメロ
特殊効果 トム・サビーニ

DAY OF THE DEAD

今、死者は甦った……。
人は獲物となり餌となる。

近未来の人類滅亡 人喰いゾンビ対人間の凄絶な死闘／そこに彼女が見たものは……!?

死霊のえじき

Keeping it in the Family: Bill and Lori Cardille

George Romero has always preferred packing his crews with friends and family members (for example, his second wife, Christine Forrest Romero, worked as an actress, associate producer, casting director, and assistant director across various films), but Bill and Lori Cardille are unique in being the only father and daughter he cast as actors in different films. Bill Cardille was the beloved host of the Pittsburgh-area *Chiller Theatre* from 1964 to 1983; he appeared in *Night of the Living Dead* as a news reporter interviewing the zombie hunters, and also played a zombie in *Day of the Dead*. His daughter Lori studied acting at Carnegie Mellon and worked in several soap operas before Romero cast her as Sarah in *Day of the Dead*; she also stars in *Night of the Living Dead 2* (2023) alongside *Day of the Dead* costars Terry Alexander and Jarlath Conroy.

ABOVE LEFT: Japanese poster for *Day of the Dead*, featuring Ralph Marrero as Rickles and Lori Cardille as Sarah. Sarah is a combination of two characters from Romero's first draft of the film: Sarah Bowman, a rebel fighter, and Mary Henried, a scientist who once had an affair with Captain Rhodes and now must work with him.

ABOVE RIGHT: Portrait of Lori Cardille as Dr. Sarah Bowman in *Day of the Dead* by the British artist Peter Johnson. When she was cast in *Day*, Cardille had never starred in a feature film before, and she found shooting out of order difficult. Nonetheless, her performance was praised by critics.

TOP: Promotional still from *Day of the Dead* showing Lori Cardille as Dr. Sarah Bowman, standing between Terry Alexander as John (left) and Jarlath Conroy as McDermott (right). The three actors are set to reunite in director Marcus Slabine's upcoming *Night of the Living Dead 2*.

BOTTOM LEFT: Bill Cardille appeared in *Night of the Living Dead* as a television news reporter. He showed up for the part with his own crew of news cameramen—a luxury Romero said the film production couldn't have afforded otherwise.

BOTTOM RIGHT: "Chilly Billy" Cardille in a photograph promoting his show *Chiller Theatre*, which aired on Pittsburgh's WIIC-TV. Romero praised Cardille's support, noting, "He would talk about us on the air a lot, and I think he had a lot to do with our ability to ultimately raise money and finish the movie."

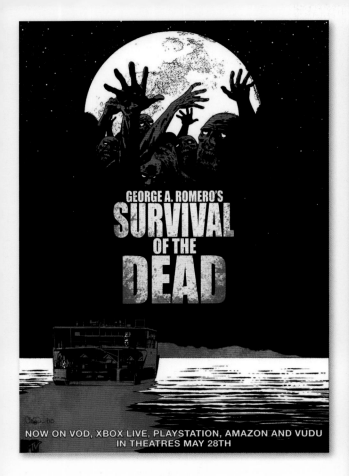

ABOVE LEFT: Poster for *Survival of the Dead* by Charlie Adlard, an artist known for his work on the *Walking Dead* comics. Released in 2009, *Survival* was made for a budget of about $4 million but earned back less than ten percent of that, making it the one flop of Romero's zombie hexalogy.

ABOVE RIGHT: DVD cover art for *Survival of the Dead*. In 2017, Romero announced a final zombie film, *Twilight of the Dead*, which he said would bring the series to a conclusion, but he died before he could make it. His widow, Suzanne, worked with screenwriters to finalize the script and, as of 2022, was looking for a director.

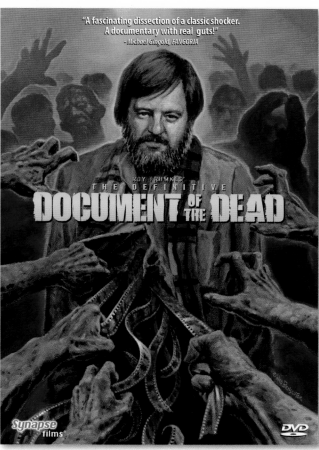

ABOVE LEFT: Japanese poster for *Survival of the Dead*, showing the patriarchs of the feuding O'Flynn and Muldoon families confronting each other above an image of the zombified Jane O'Flynn (Kathleen Munroe).

ABOVE RIGHT: Cover art from the DVD release of *The Definitive Document of the Dead*, Roy Frumkes's behind-the-scenes look at the making of *Dawn of the Dead*. Originally released in 1985, the 2013 DVD/Blu-ray includes additional material on *Two Evil Eyes* (1991), *Land of the Dead* (2005), and *Diary of the Dead* (2007).

4

THE NEXT WAVE

"WOE BE UNTO HIM WHO OPENS ONE OF THE SEVEN GATEWAYS TO HELL, BECAUSE THROUGH THAT GATEWAY, EVIL WILL INVADE THE WORLD."

THE BOOK OF EIBON FROM *THE BEYOND* (1981)

> "There was nothing Hollywood about it—it was just unrelenting and complete madness and very upsetting for me. It left a tremendous impression on me as a filmmaker and I think that's why *The Evil Dead* was so influenced by *Night of the Living Dead*, because that's really what a horror film was for me."
>
> Sam Raimi on *Night of the Living Dead*, from a 2019 interview with *Den of Geek*

The influence of the flesh-eating Romero zombie was felt within a few years of the release of *Night of the Living Dead*. Just as *White Zombie*'s specter loomed over the movies of the 1930s and '40s, so would Romero's hungry walking dead stand behind nearly every zombie movie released after 1968.

The first film to employ Romero's sensibilities was 1972's *Tombs of the Blind Dead*, a Spanish-Portuguese coproduction directed by Amando de Ossorio. The film is set in a ruined (and fictitious) medieval village called Berzano, situated in a wilderness near the border of Spain and Portugal and once home to medieval Templar knights who returned from the Crusades with the secret of immortality. Although the knights were hung for their heresy (the second film revealed that their eyes were burned out by angry villagers), they still rise from their graves to seek the blood of the living. The film is an interesting combination of Romero's zombies and older folkloric tales: the knights are not truly zombies (for one thing, their immortality is achieved through blood-drinking), but their victims, who return to shambling, mindless, hungry life after being murdered by the knights, certainly are. Although the film is generally considered to be slow-moving (and suffers from some serious gaps in logic—are the horses ridden by the reanimated knights also immortal vampires?), it benefits from spectacular locations and an eerie score by Antón García Abril. It was successful enough to start its own franchise, with *Return of the Blind Dead* (1973), *The Ghost Galleon* (1974), and *Night of the Seagulls* (1975) following.

Also released in 1972 was the low-budget American production *Children Shouldn't Play With Dead Things*, co-written by Alan Ormsby (who also stars and provided the zombie makeup) and Bob Clark (who directs). After a theatrical troupe led by the flamboyant Ormsby arrives on a small island to party, they hold a magic ritual to resurrect the dead in a graveyard but are far less successful in controlling them; flesh-eating mayhem ensues. The film is perhaps most notable for being the first obvious riff on *Night of the Living Dead*—except for the introduction of the occult and the color cinematography, these zombies could have been lifted directly from Romero's classic.

Zombies were given possibly their first art-house spin in the 1973 *Messiah of Evil*, written, produced, and directed by Willard Huyck and Gloria Katz, who would go on to write the screenplays for *American Graffiti* and *Indiana Jones and the Temple of Doom. Messiah of Evil* follows a young woman, Arletty (Marianna Hill), who has come to the isolated seaside town of Point Dume in search of her father, a renowned artist. What she finds instead are legends of a "dark stranger" who will return to the town during a "blood moon" to wreak havoc; soon after, she discovers the townspeople in the local supermarket, feasting on raw meat. Although the film was largely ignored upon its initial release, it was re-released in 1983 as *Dead People* and has since garnered critical acclaim.

Although Paul Maslansky's *Sugar Hill* (1974) likely wouldn't have existed without the success of *Night of the Living Dead*, the film returned to traditional voodoo

American zombie films from the early 1980s plainly followed Romero's basic aesthetic—featuring shambling, ragged corpses who, if not directly consuming human flesh, were still driven to violent impulses—but looked to put fresh spins on the mythology.

zombies. Set in the American South, not the Caribbean, *Sugar Hill* mixes the living dead with a traditional blaxploitation plot involving revenge by focusing on an eponymous heroine (played by Marki Bey) seeking revenge against the local gang that murdered her boyfriend. *Sugar Hill* upends previous voodoo-zombie films by featuring a Black voodoo priestess, Mama Maitresse (Zara Cully), who helps the eponymous heroine enact her payback; it also features the Vodou *loa* Baron Samedi (the wonderfully gleeful Don Pedro Colley) as a lead character throughout, directing the zombies in high style.

Shock Waves (1977) followed in the footsteps of 1941's *King of the Zombies* and 1966's *The Frozen Dead* to explore a trope that would show up again in 2009's *Dead Snow*: Nazi zombies. Here, the Nazis show up as the "Death Corps," zombies created to be super-soldiers who have been stuck on a deserted island for decades before being encountered by shipwrecked tourists. The film benefits from the presence of the venerable Peter Cushing as the human SS Commander in charge of the undead Germans.

PREVIOUS SPREAD: Promotional art by Graham Humphreys for the 2013 concert event "Frizzi 2 Fulci," in which composer Fabio Frizzi performed tracks from a number of Fulci films. For these performances, Frizzi rearranged the original music in order to include a larger ensemble.

ABOVE LEFT: One-sheet poster for *Children Shouldn't Play with Dead Things* (1972). Not only did Alan Ormsby co-write, star in, and provide makeup effects for the film, he also created the art for the poster, which might explain why it accurately captures the film's snarky, grimly funny tone.

TOP MIDDLE: Poster created for a 2021 screening of *Messiah of Evil* (1972) at Toronto's Revue Cinema. The film's zombies—who devour one victim in the meat section of a supermarket and another in a movie theater—are the result of a "Dark Stranger" who first visited the town of Point Dume one hundred years ago and will return during the "Blood Moon."

TOP RIGHT: Front cover of the pressbook for *Sugar Hill* (1974), from the collection of the Library of Congress. The book includes this lively description of Baron Samedi calling up zombies: "The Baron waves his cane. Thunder roars! Lightning flashes! The mounds of earth covering the surrounding graves begin to part asunder and from the moldy earth rises an army of Zombies, ready to do Sugar's bidding."

BOTTOM RIGHT: Mexican lobby card for *Tombs of the Blind Dead* (1972), the first of director Amando de Ossorio's "Blind Dead" quartet. Its success helped launch the Spanish horror film cycle of the 1970s. De Ossorio (1918–2001) had hoped to make a fifth "Blind Dead" film called *The Necronomicon of the Templars*, but he was unable to secure financing.

WE ARE GOING TO EAT YOU!

ZOMBIE

...THE DEAD ARE AMONG US!

Jerry Gross presents "ZOMBIE" starring Tisa Farrow • Ian McCulloch • Richard Johnson • Al Cliver
Story and Screenplay by Elisa Briganti • Produced by Ugo Tucci and Fabrizio De Angelis for Variety Film
Color by Metro Color • Directed by Lucio Fulci • Distributed by The Jerry Gross Organization

There is no explicit sex in this picture.
However, there are scenes of violence which may be considered shocking.
No one under 17 will be admitted.

THROUGH THE GATES OF HELL THEY CAME ...FROM

THE BEYOND

Starring **KATHERINE MacCOLL   DAVID WARBECK   SARAH KELLER**
ANTOINE SAINT JOHN   VERONICA LAZAR
Directed by **LUCIO FULCI**

EAGLE FILMS

ABOVE LEFT: One-sheet for *Zombie*, one of several titles given to Lucio Fulci's *Zombi 2* (1979) in the United States. The film was also released at various times as *Zombie Flesh Eaters*, *The Island of the Living Dead*, *Zombie: The Dead Walk Among Us*, and *Nightmare Island*.

TOP RIGHT: Cover art by Graham Humphreys for the 2014 vinyl release of Fabio Frizzi's score for Fulci's *City of the Living Dead*. This release by Death Waltz Recording Company came in a limited pressing of 350 copies on orange and yellow vinyl; a regular edition on red vinyl was also available.

BOTTOM RIGHT: British quad poster for Fulci's *The Beyond* (1981). A push during the early 1980s for the British Board of Film Censors to take more control when it came to excessively violent or bloody films led to the official creation of the "video nasties," a list of seventy-two films that were prosecuted under the Obscene

Publications Act and/or required to be edited. Fulci's *Zombi 2* and *The House By the Cemetery* were prosecuted; *The Beyond* was not, but Fulci was required to trim about two minutes of the film. *City of the Living Dead* was not officially classified as a video nasty, but Fulci was nonetheless required to cut about two minutes of gore.

One filmmaker seized on the idea of Romero's cannibalistic shamblers after *Dawn of the Dead* and made himself into a cult director in the process: Lucio Fulci. Fulci had been a minor figure in the Italian film industry for several decades, mainly producing *giallo* (or thriller) movies like *Don't Torture a Duckling* (1972). *Dawn of the Dead* was released in Italy under the title *Zombi*, and following its success there screenwriter Dardano Sacchetti wrote a sequel, which Fulci adapted. Confusingly titled *Zombi 2*, the film has no ties to Romero's film except the idea of zombies, which here are presented as the residents of Matul, a Caribbean island cursed by unseen voodoo masters (although, like Romero's creatures, these zombies consume human flesh upon resurrection). *Zombi 2* (also known as *Zombie* or *Zombie Flesh Eaters*, among other titles) is excessively gory even in a genre known for excessive gore, with scenes that graphically depict eyes gouged out (a recurring theme throughout Fulci's oeuvre), throat-rippings, and entrails consumed; it also follows in the exploitation tradition of presenting frequent, lingering shots of unclad women (one of whom even engages in scuba diving clad in nothing but a skimpy bikini bottom). The film is renowned among fans for its fight between a zombie and a shark—a scene that Fulci didn't shoot (producer Ugo Tocci brought

---

"Remember: whatever happens, death is not the end."

Lucien Celine in *The Serpent and the Rainbow* (1988)

---

in a second unit to take over when Fulci, who thought the scene sounded silly, refused).

Fulci went on to make a zombie-themed series known as the "Gates of Hell" trilogy: *City of the Living Dead* (1980, with zombies that operate more as ghosts, given their ability to instantly appear and vanish), *The Beyond* (1981), and *The House by the Cemetery* (1981). *The Beyond* (released in the United States in 1983 as *7 Doors of Death*) is the best of the series, following a young New Yorker (played by Catriona MacColl) who inherits a decaying Southern hotel that happens to be situated atop a gateway to hell; as workers die around the structure, they return as zombies. The film was shot on location around New Orleans, and the interior sets of the hotel—especially the perpetually flooded basement—are evocative, lending the film a rich Southern Gothic sensibility. Of course, Fulci's trademark gore is still present: the film's scenes include a woman's head destroyed by acid (as her young daughter watches), a man crucified to a wall and covered in hot wax, a spider attack, and assorted eye-poppings. Fulci was scheduled to direct *Zombi 3* but walked out after disputes with the producers, leaving it to be finished by codirector Bruno Mattei instead. The series continued on through *Zombi 5—Killing Birds*; confusingly,

in some countries, unrelated horror films were also titled *Zombi* to extend the franchise.

American zombie films from the early 1980s plainly followed Romero's basic aesthetic—featuring shambling, ragged corpses who, if not directly consuming human flesh, were still driven to violent impulses—but looked to put fresh spins on the mythology. Gary Sherman's *Dead and Buried* (1981)—co-written by Dan O'Bannon, who would go on to write and direct *Return of the Living Dead* four years later—turned its zombie creator into an aging mortician, played in a bravura performance by Jack Albertson, who uses ancient spells to create a town of resurrected dead who require periodic repairs to counteract their decay. Tom McLoughlin's *One Dark Night* (1982) has a dead psychic return to life inside a mausoleum, where he reanimates corpses to serve as his soldiers. Thom Eberhardt's playful *Night of the Comet* (1984) puts two valley girls (Catherine Mary Stewart and Kelli Maroney) into the middle of a zombie apocalypse engendered by a passing comet. Fred Dekker's *Night of the Creeps* (1986) offers up alien slugs that zombify their victims, interrupting a big party at the local college. And, in 1987, genre stalwart John Carpenter made *Prince of Darkness*, about a team of physicists investigating a secret chamber in a forgotten Catholic church where a canister of swirling green liquid might be the Devil, who kills various team members before resurrecting them to do his bidding.

Meanwhile, an independent American filmmaker was also embarking on a horror series that would veer more into zombie territory as it went and develop a large fan following in the process. Sam Raimi's *The Evil Dead* (1981) was a high-octane thriller that introduced the world to Ash (Bruce Campbell), a hapless hero who runs afoul of demonic forces in a backwoods cabin. Although the first film was heavily influenced by *Night of the Living Dead*—a fact commented on by Raimi himself, who noted, "You know, zombies and his cabin setting. It was so scary and intense. That really had a giant impact on me"—it kept strictly to possession. The 1987 sequel *Evil Dead II* turned more toward deliberate black comedy as Ash fights ballet-dancing zombies (his former girlfriend, who he watches in an elaborate scene that employs stop-motion animation) and his own severed hand.

One movie released in the '80s that offered a decidedly non-comedic take on zombies was Wes Craven's *The Serpent and the Rainbow* (1988). Based on the 1985 book by ethnobotanist Wade Davis, *The Serpent* mixes Haitian Vodou with science, as an American anthropologist played by Bill Pullman investigates the drug used to create zombies.

By the end of the 1980s, the zombie film had—like the hungry masses often shown in these movies—overrun the horror genre, to the point where terror became parody. Movies like *Dead Heat* (1988)—a buddy action movie with one undead partner—tried and failed to thrust zombies into other genres, while titles like *Redneck Zombies* (1987) and *Chopper Chicks in Zombietown* (1989) plainly pointed to a different way forward: the zom-com.

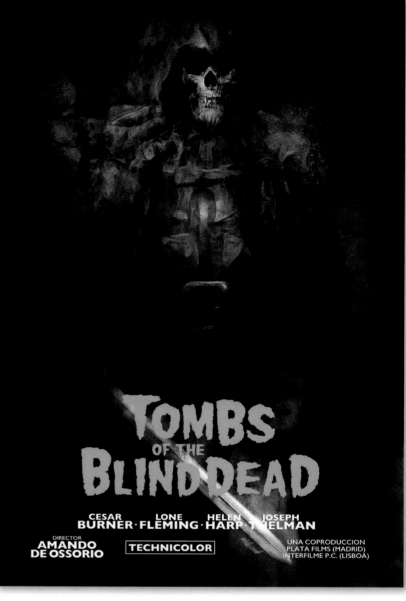

OPPOSITE, LEFT: Italian *duo-foglio* poster for *Tombs of the Blind Dead* featuring art by Renato Casaro, a famed Italian artist whose hundreds of posters have been gathered into five published collections, most recently 2017's *The Art of Movie Painting*.

OPPOSITE, TOP RIGHT: Australian day-bill poster for *Tombs of the Blind Dead*. The film's writer and director, Amando de Ossorio, objected to the use of the term "zombie" to describe his living dead, since they possessed will and purpose—an assertion that seems arguable, given that his undead monks do little beyond pursuing victims.

OPPOSITE, BOTTOM RIGHT: Cover art by Spanish comic-book illustrator Marc Gras Cots for a proposed print adaptation of *Tombs of the Blind Dead*. The limited-edition release would include a faux-travel poster encouraging readers to "Visit Berzano."

ABOVE LEFT: Spanish one-sheet for *Tombs of the Blind Dead*, featuring art by famed Spanish artist Francisco Fernandez Zarza-Pérez (1922–1992), who—working under the pseudonym "Jano" —is often referred to as "master of the Spanish film poster."

ABOVE RIGHT: Alternative movie poster for *Tombs of the Blind Dead* by the American artist Richard Hilliard. In 2020, Italian director Raffaele Picchio made *Curse of the Blind Dead*, which follows the cursed Templar knights as they resurrect in a postapocalyptic future.

ABOVE LEFT: Spanish poster for Amando de Ossorio's second "Blind Dead" film, *Return of the Blind Dead*, featuring art by the prolific Spanish artist Jose Montalban (1925–2020). This time, most of the action takes place in the village of Berzano during celebrations for the five-hundredth anniversary of the defeat of the evil Templar Knights—who of course wreak havoc on the festivities.

TOP MIDDLE: German A1 poster for the last of de Ossorio's Templar Knights films, *Night of the Seagulls* (1975). The German title shown here translates to *Blood Feast of the Blind Dead*. This film is set in an isolated coastal town where, every seven years, the undead Templars rise from the sea and demand a maiden to sacrifice.

TOP RIGHT: Spanish poster for *The Ghost Galleon* (1974), which is about a group of models and businessmen who stumble on a mysterious ship that holds a crew of the undead Templars. This is often considered the weakest of the "Blind Dead" series, with critics noting the poor special effects. The fiery destruction of the ship at the climax, for example, is obviously a small, cheap model.

BOTTOM RIGHT: Half-sheet poster for *Children Shouldn't Play with Dead Things*. "Orville," who is mentioned on the poster, is the corpse that the director of the theater troupe (played by Alan Ormsby) digs up, uses in an occult ritual, and then mocks.

ABOVE LEFT: One-sheet poster for *Messiah of Evil* (1973). The film's husband-and-wife director/writer/producer team of Willard Huyck and Gloria Katz would go on to a long association with George Lucas, writing *American Graffiti* (1973), *Indiana Jones and the Temple of Doom* (1984), and *Howard the Duck* (1986), the latter of which Willard also directed.

ABOVE RIGHT: American artist Francine Spiegel, who specializes in examining women's roles in horror movies, produced a limited-edition run of fifty prints of this image from *Messiah of Evil*. It focuses on Marianna Hill as Arletty, the young woman in search of her missing artist father.

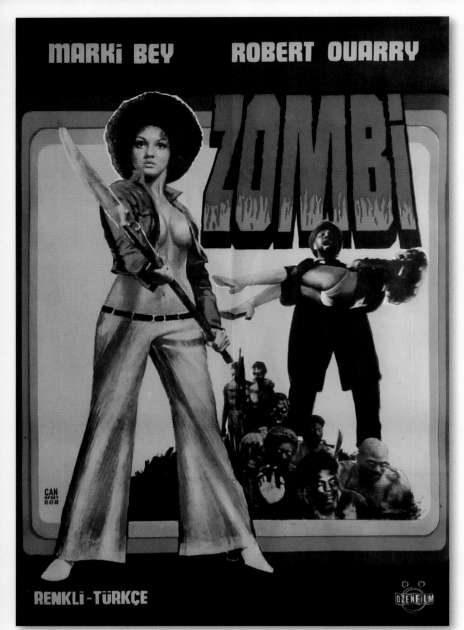

ABOVE LEFT: This Turkish poster for *Sugar Hill* (1974) has confusingly retitled the film *Zombi*, but it is not to be confused with either *Dawn of the Dead*, released in Europe as *Zombi*; or Lucio Fulci's *Zombi 2*, released in the U.S. as *Zombie*; or the plethora of other films from around the world simply called *Zombie*.

ABOVE RIGHT: U.S. one-sheet poster for *Sugar Hill* (1974). The film's zombies are fairly typical—grayish skin, draped in cobwebs—except for one interesting twist: their eyes are gleaming metal balls.

RIGHT: Probably the most memorable zombie from *Zombi 2* (1979), as rendered here by digital artist Grimbro. This iconic member of the undead is presented as an ancient conquistador who lurches up from his grave on the (fictitious) Caribbean island of Matul, where most of the action takes place.

ABOVE LEFT: Australian day-bill poster for *Zombi 2*, presented here under the alternate title *Zombie Flesh Eaters*. Shown here is the first zombie seen in the film, when the boat of a man who has gone missing in the Caribbean mysteriously shows up in New York Harbor; after two policemen board the vessel, they're attacked by this large, rotting zombie.

TOP MIDDLE: Alternative poster for *Zombie Flesh Eaters* by the British artist Pete Knight. After the success of this film, producer Fabrizio de Angelis rushed another zombie movie into production, *Zombie Holocaust* (1980). The latter film, directed by Marino Girolami, borrowed plot points, locations, sets, and stars from Fulci's hit. It was released in the U.S. in 1982 as *Doctor Butcher M.D.*

TOP RIGHT: Italian *duo-foglio* poster for *Zombi 2*. The film's screenwriter, Dardano Sacchetti, got his start on Dario Argento's *The Cat o' Nine Tails* (1971); that same year, he also provided the story for Mario Bava's seminal slasher *A Bay of Blood*. He would go on to write all three of Fulci's "Gates of Hell" films, as well as *Demons* (1985) and *Demons 2* (1986) for director Lamberto Bava (Mario's son).

BOTTOM RIGHT: Alternative movie poster for *Zombie Flesh Eaters* (*Zombi 2*), as issued by Alamo Drafthouse and Mondo in 2011 in an edition of 110, featuring art by the American artist Jock. Mondo specializes in working with artists to produce limited-edition posters, soundtrack LPs, toys, and even tiki mugs.

RIGHT: Alternative movie poster for *Zombie* by American artist Tom Whalen, designed for a special screening of Fulci's film at the Colonial Theatre in Phoenixville, Pennsylvania, on March 5, 2010. Whalen's unique style was influenced by comics artists Steve Ditko and Jack Kirby and graphic designers Saul Bass and Milton Glaser.

WELL, HELLO MR. FANCY-PANTS: BRUCE CAMPBELL

"Groovy."

Ash in *Evil Dead II* (1987)

In 1978, a nineteen-year-old filmmaker named Sam Raimi got together $1,600 and made a short horror film called *Within the Woods*. He cast his friend Bruce Campbell in the lead role of Bruce, one of four teenagers who encounter evil forces at an isolated cabin in the woods. Raimi was able to use the short to finance a feature film version called *The Evil Dead*; released in 1981, it became one of the most successful independent horror movies of all time, launching the careers of Raimi, Campbell, and producer Rob Tapert, and setting up Campbell's character of Ashley "Ash" Williams as an iconic horror hero.

Although the terrors of the first *Evil Dead* were engendered by demonic possession, the sequels featured demons and zombies and provided Campbell with plenty of opportunities to showcase his talents at both horror and comedy. *Evil Dead II* (1987) essentially remade the first film but swiftly set Ash up as the resourceful survivor who straps a chainsaw to his arm after severing his demon-possessed hand. Critics praised both Raimi's crazed, kinetic direction, and Campbell's slapstick-endowed performance.

After *Evil Dead II*, Campbell continued to appear in horror films like *Maniac Cop*, *The Dead Next Door*, *Waxwork II: Lost in Time*, and *Darkman* (also directed by Raimi), but it took the 1992 release of the third *Evil Dead* movie, *Army of Darkness*, to secure his status as a beloved cult actor. Originally titled *Medieval Dead*, *Army of Darkness* takes the unlucky Ash through an occult time-warp into the Middle Ages, where he finds himself caught up in a war between rival kingdoms and "deadites," or dead bodies possessed by demons. Campbell's performance is more comedic than ever, with his over-the-top delivery of lines like, "Gimme some sugar, baby," and "Groovy," endearing him to fans all over the world. In the *New York Times*, critic Janet Maslin praised Campbell's "manly, mock-heroic posturing," while in the *Bangor Daily News* Christopher Smith remarked on how camp drove the film's appeal, "with Bruce Campbell clearly happy behind the wheel." He received the Fangoria Chainsaw Award for his performance.

After *Army of Darkness*, Campbell appeared in a number of bigger film productions, including Joel and Ethan Coen's *The Hudsucker Proxy*, Frank Marshall's *Congo*, and John Carpenter's *Escape from L.A.* He returned to cult film territory in 2002 in Don Coscarelli's *Bubba-Ho-Tep*, playing an elderly Elvis Presley (or is he just another impersonator?) battling an ancient evil in a nursing home; he earned the best reviews of his career and received the Comedy Festival's Film Discovery Jury Award for Best Actor, the Fantasporto Film Festival International Fantasy Film Award for Best Actor, and the Fangoria Chainsaw Award for Best Actor.

In 2013, it was rumored that Campbell would be playing Ash Williams again in *Army of Darkness 2*, but instead in 2015 he reprised the role in the television series *Ash vs. Evil Dead*. The series ran for three seasons on the Starz network

> Although the terrors of the first *Evil Dead* were engendered by demonic possession, the sequels featured demons and zombies and provided Campbell with plenty of opportunities to showcase his talents at both horror and comedy.

and earned Campbell more Fangoria Chainsaw Awards and a Saturn Award for his performance.

Campbell also played the title role in the television series *The Adventures of Briscoe County, Jr.* (1993–1994) and lead character Sam Axe in 111 episodes of the television series *Burn Notice*. He has also guest-starred or had recurring roles in *Lois and Clark: The New Adventures of Superman*, *Hercules: The Legendary Journeys*, *The X-Files*, *Ellen*, *Xena: Warrior Princess*, and *Fargo*. A popular voice actor, he can be heard in cartoons like *Duck Dodgers*, *Robot Chicken*, and *Archer*, and videogames including *Spider-Man*, *Cars 2*, *Dead by Daylight*, and—of course—the *Evil Dead* games.

In 2001, Campbell hit the *New York Times* bestseller list with his autobiography, *If Chins Could Kill: Confessions of a B Movie Actor*. He followed that up in 2005 with *Make Love! The Bruce Campbell Way*, and in 2017 with *Hail to the Chin: Further Confessions of a B Movie Actor* (co-written with Craig Sanborn).

Campbell's eccentric charisma may have been best summed up when he described himself as a "mid-grade, kind of hammy actor."

RIGHT: "Ash vs. Evil Dead" by French artist Anthony Geoffroy. After playing Ash in three "Evil Dead" films for director Sam Raimi, Bruce Campbell took on the character again for the STARZ television series *Ash vs. Evil Dead* (2015–2018). An animated Ash series is now in development.

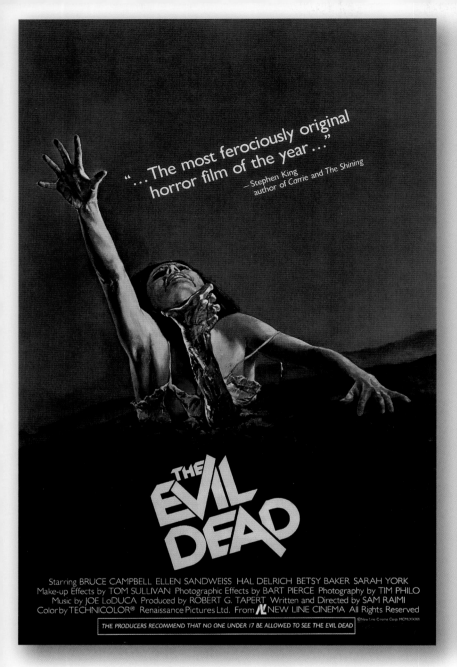

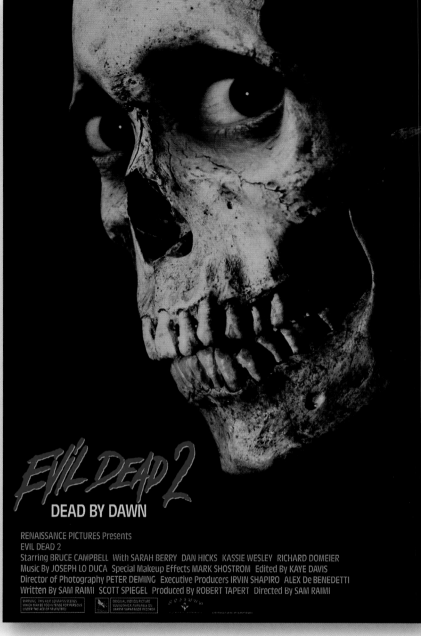

ABOVE LEFT: One-sheet for Sam Raimi's *The Evil Dead* (1981), with an endorsement quote by Stephen King. King saw the film at Cannes before it was acquired for distribution and wrote a rave review for *Twilight Zone* magazine subtitled, "Why you haven't seen it yet and why you ought to." Raimi has credited King with helping the film obtain release.

ABOVE RIGHT: One-sheet poster for *Evil Dead 2: Dead by Dawn* (1987). The second of Sam Raimi's "Evil Dead" entries is less of a sequel and more of a remake (sometimes referred to as a "requel"), since it begins as the first film did: with Ash arriving at an isolated cabin, where he discovers the work of a professor who was translating an ancient occult tome.

ABOVE: Poster advertising the home-video release of *The Evil Dead*, with art by the British illustrator Graham Humphreys. The film was classified as a "video nasty" in the UK and the videotape—which had already trimmed forty-nine seconds before the British censors granted it an "X" for theatrical release—was removed from distribution.

ABOVE LEFT: One-sheet for a 1998 re-release of Lucio Fulci's *The Beyond*, featuring artwork by Gerald Martinez. The blind woman depicted on many posters for *The Beyond* is not the female lead Liza, played by Catriona MacColl, but rather the enigmatic Emily (Sarah Keller), who tries to warn her before she herself falls victim to the supernatural evil at Liza's inherited New Orleans hotel.

TOP RIGHT: Thai poster for *The Beyond.* Actress Catriona MacColl, who starred in all three of Fulci's "Gates of Hell" films, noted that he didn't like "having to explain parts and psychological motivations to actors—he just likes one to get on with the job." She went on to suggest that the pressure of getting the effects right may have kept him from working more with his actors.

BOTTOM RIGHT: Alternative poster design for *The Beyond* by Silver Ferox Design, a.k.a. Jeremy Mincer, a graphic designer specializing in arthouse, horror, and exploitation movie genres. All three of the films that comprise Fulci's "Gates of Hell" trilogy contain exteriors shot in North America, while the interiors were filmed in Rome, at De Paolis Studios.

RIGHT: Italian *quattro-foglio* poster for *The House by the Cemetery*, featuring artwork by Enzo Sciotti (1944–2021). The monster in the film is an undead mad doctor who bears the somewhat silly collage name of "Dr. Freudstein," which Fulci claimed had been thought up by producer Fabrizio de Angelis.

Creating the Gore Score: Fabio Frizzi

Part of the success of Lucio Fulci's work is due to the throbbing, synth scores of Fabio Frizzi. Born in Bologna in 1951, Frizzi's first film score (for *Amore libero*, or *Free Love*) appeared in 1974, but it wasn't until he scored Fulci's *Zombi 2* in 1979 that he found his niche. He worked regularly from that point on, scoring more than forty films (including ten for Fulci). His last score to date was for 2018's *Puppet Master: The Littlest Reich*. Frizzi now releases music through his own company, Smuzzle Records, and continues to perform live.

ABOVE LEFT: Portrait of Lucio Fulci. When asked about being a horror-movie director, Fulci responded, "Horror is not a goal in itself to me. I am basically interested in the fantastic." He preferred writing, sound mixing, and editing to directing actors.

ABOVE RIGHT: Italian *foglio* poster for *Zombi 3*, with art by Enzo Sciotti, who has borrowed elements from a number of other movie posters here, including *A Nightmare on Elm Street 3: Dream Warriors*, *Force Five*, *Absurd*, and *Tales from the Crypt*.

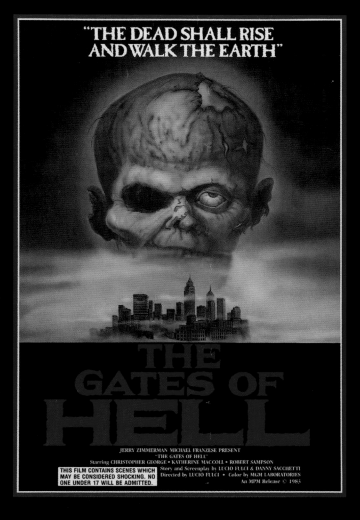

"THE DEAD SHALL RISE AND WALK THE EARTH"

THE GATES OF HELL

JERRY ZIMMERMAN MICHAEL FRANZESE PRESENT
"THE GATES OF HELL"
Starring CHRISTOPHER GEORGE • KATHERINE MACCOLL • ROBERT SAMPSON
Story and Screenplay by LUCIO FULCI & DANNY SACCHETTI
Directed by LUCIO FULCI • Color by MGM LABORATORIES
An MPM Release © 1983

THIS FILM CONTAINS SCENES WHICH MAY BE CONSIDERED SHOCKING. NO ONE UNDER 17 WILL BE ADMITTED.

PAURA
NELLA CITTÀ' DEI
MORTI VIVENTI

CHRISTOPHER GEORGE · KATHERINE MAC COLL · CARLO DE MEJO
ANTONELLA INTERLENGHI · GIOVANNI LOMBARDO RADICE
DANIELA DORIA · FABRIZIO JOVINE · e con JANET AGREN nel ruolo di SANDRA
Regia di LUCIO FULCI
Fotografia SERGIO SALVATI • Musiche FABIO FRIZZI · Colore LV LUCIANO VITTORI
Produzione DANIA FILM-MEDUSA DISTRIBUZIONE - NATIONAL CINEMATOGRAFICA

ABOVE LEFT: U.S. one-sheet for Fulci's *City of the Living Dead* (1980). The original American title for the film was *Twilight of the Dead,* but it was dropped when United Film Distributors, which had handled release of *Dawn of the Dead,* sent a cease-and-desist letter because of the similarity in the two titles. It was eventually released as *The Gates of Hell* instead.

RIGHT: Italian *quattro-foglio* poster for *City of the Living Dead (Paura nella citta' dei morti viventi),* featuring art by Renato Casaro. Fulci rode a wave of late 1970s and early '80s Italian horror that also included Dario Argento's films (*Deep Red, Suspiria, Tenebrae, Inferno*). By the late '80s, the trend faded, with horror largely replaced by comedy in Italian cinema.

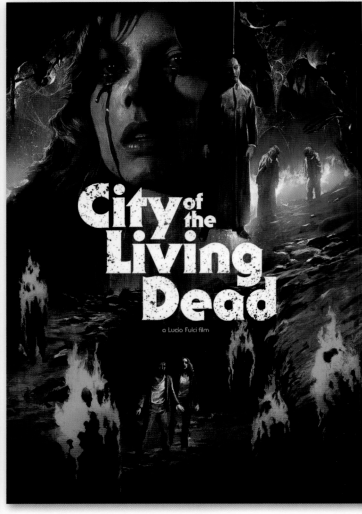

ABOVE LEFT: Thai poster for *City of the Living Dead*, which incorporates elements from Spiritualism (it opens with a séance), Biblical apocrypha (the medium warns the protagonists that terrifying events predicted in the Book of Enoch will soon come true), Halloween (the living dead will begin their invasion on All Saints' Day), and H. P. Lovecraft (the events all take place in the town of Dunwich).

ABOVE RIGHT: This tribute to *City of the Living Dead* was produced by the American artist Robert Sammelin. As the author Stephen Thrower notes in his book *Beyond Terror: The Films of Lucio Fulci*, the director's fascination with damage to eyes led to scenes that include "orbital rupture by glass shards, by giant splinter, by probing undead finger, by rusty nail, by beaks of stuffed birds."

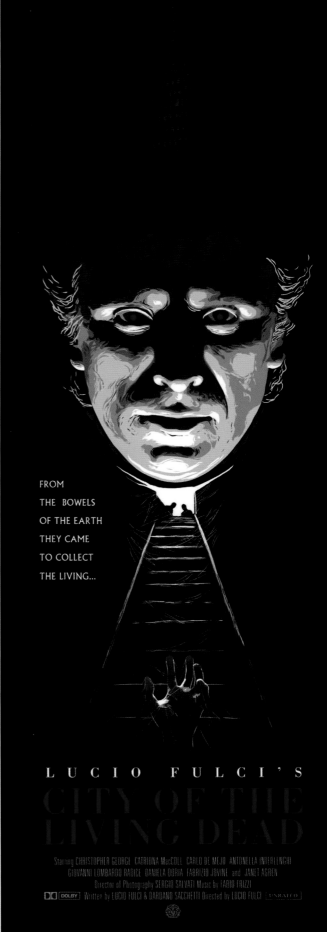

ABOVE LEFT: Argentine poster for *City of the Living Dead*. Probably the most famous gore effect in the film involves a woman vomiting up her own intestines. Fulci claimed the effect was achieved by making the actress swallow the tripe of a freshly slaughtered lamb, which she then vomited up on camera, although he did also admit that a puppet was used for closer shots.

RIGHT: Screen print of *City of the Living Dead* by the artist Randy Ortiz, created in a run of 125 prints for Mondo. The main antagonist in *City of the Living Dead* is the evil priest Father Thomas, played by Fabrizio Jovine, an idea that captures Fulci's own difficult relationship with Catholicism: "I have realized that God is a God of suffering. I envy atheists; they don't have all these difficulties."

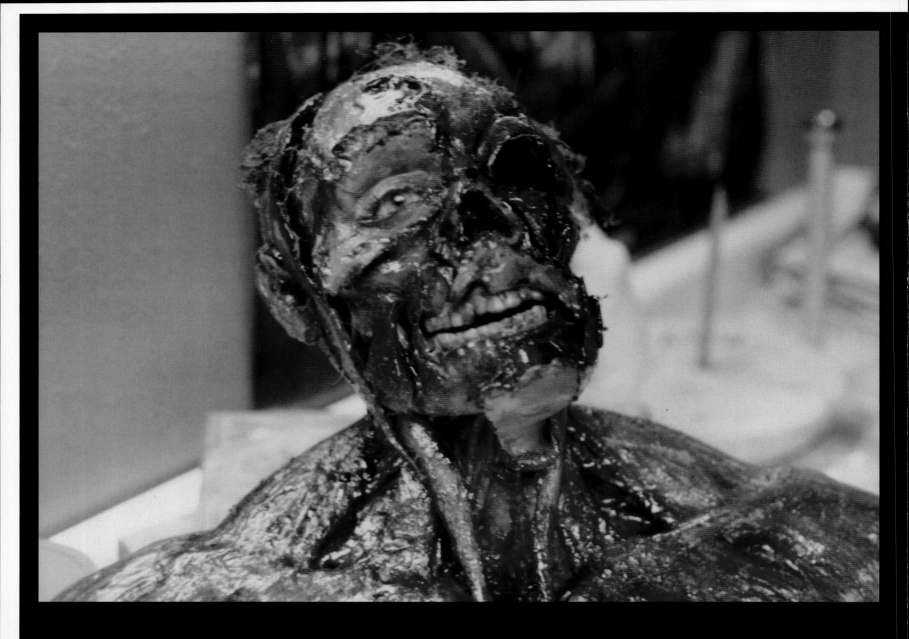

Corpse Kings: Tom Burman and Stan Winston

In the 1970s, new techniques in special makeup effects made stars of some of cinema's top artisans, among them Tom Burman and Stan Winston. Burman came from a family of film technicians; after working on *Planet of the Apes* in 1968, he set up the Burman Studios, and in the 1970s he provided monsters and creatures for such films as *The Island of Dr. Moreau, Invasion of the Body Snatchers, The Manitou,* and *Prophecy.* Winston, meanwhile, had originally come to Hollywood in search of work as an actor, but instead he turned to makeup, and in 1973 he won an Emmy (shared with Tom's brother, Ellis Burman, Jr.) for the television movie *Gargoyles.*

In 1981, Winston worked on Gary Sherman's *Dead and Buried,* creating the detailed corpses resurrected by the film's antagonist. A year later, Burman similarly provided the ultrarealistic dead bodies animated by psychic powers in Tom McLoughlin's *One Dark Night.* Winston went on to receive Academy Awards for his work on *Aliens, Terminator 2: Judgment Day,* and *Jurassic Park,* and another Emmy for *The Autobiography of Miss Jane Pittman;* Burman received an Academy Award nomination for *Scrooged* and Emmy Awards for *Grey's Anatomy, Nip/Tuck, Tracey Takes On . . . , The Tracey Ullman Show,* and *Young Indiana Jones* and the *Curse of the Jackal.* Stan Winston died in 2008, at the age of sixty-two; Tom Burman retired from makeup in 2017, but in 2019 he wrote and produced the documentary *Making Apes: The Artists Who Changed Film.*

ABOVE: The burned head of Freddie (Christopher Allport) created by Stan Winston's team for *Dead and Buried* (1981). Winston also directed the features *Pumpkinhead* (1988) and *A Gnome Named Gnorm* (1990), as well as the music video for Michael Jackson's "Ghosts." He went on to produce a series of five low-budget cable movies for HBO and Cinemax.

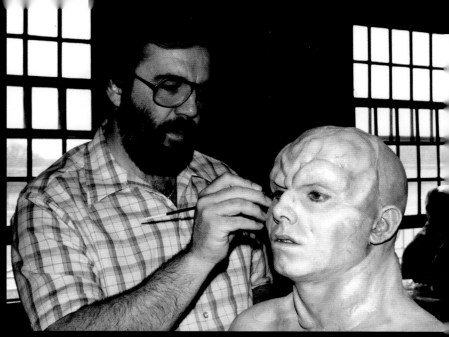

ABOVE LEFT: A child's corpse, as created by Tom Burman's crew for *One Dark Night* (1982). The effects artists created a number of bodies for the film by studying illustrated books on forensic pathology.

TOP RIGHT: Tom Burman makes up actor Paul Clemens for his transformation into a cicada-like monster in *The Beast Within* (1982). Burman also co-wrote and directed *Meet the Hollowheads* (1989) and wrote and produced *Making Apes: The Artists Who Changed Film* (2019), about John Chambers and the effects created for *Planet of the Apes* (1968).

BOTTOM RIGHT: Stan Winston at work on a head created for *Dead and Buried* (1981). This head is featured in one of the film's most spectacular effects sequences, as the mortician Dobbs (Jack Albertson) reconstructs the badly damaged corpse of a hitchhiker (Lisa Marie). Winston's own hands stood in for Jack Albertson's in the shots.

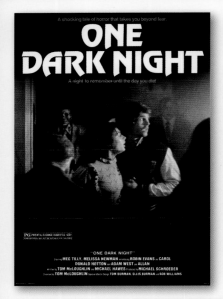

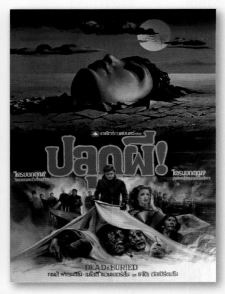

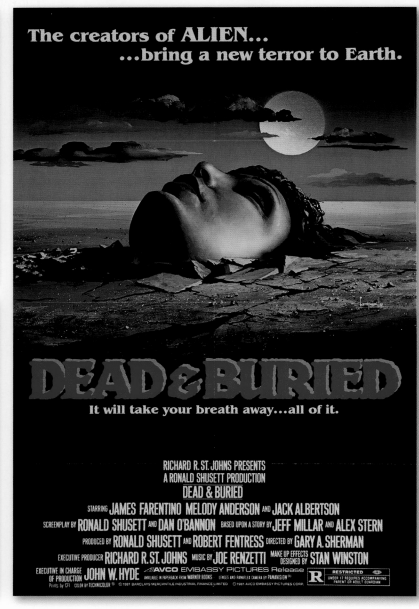

TOP LEFT: One-sheet for *One Dark Night* (1982), which marked the first major performance by Meg Tilly, who would receive an Academy Award nomination in 1985 for *Agnes of God*. Here she plays Julie, the unlucky heroine whose initiation into a club called the Sisters involves spending the night in a mausoleum, where the undead psychic Raymar has recently been entombed.

TOP MIDDLE: Thai poster for *Dead and Buried* (1981). In later interviews, credited co-screenwriter Dan O'Bannon would claim that he actually had very little to do with the film, which was mainly written by producer Ronald Shusett; he claimed that Shusett had asked him to put his name on the screenplay after he became bankable from writing *Alien* (1979).

BOTTOM LEFT: British quad poster for *One Dark Night*. The film was the debut of writer/director Tom McLoughlin, who would go on to write and direct *Friday the 13th Part VI: Jason Lives* (1986) and *Date with an Angel* (1987). Before that, McLoughlin worked as a mime; his credits include playing the mutated bear created by Tom Burman in *Prophecy* (1979).

ABOVE RIGHT: One-sheet for *Dead and Buried*, featuring art by Dario Campanile, an Italian-born artist now living in America. Campanile created a number of book and magazine covers in the 1980s, but he is now known chiefly as a fine artist. This striking poster is one of the most memorable movie images of the period.

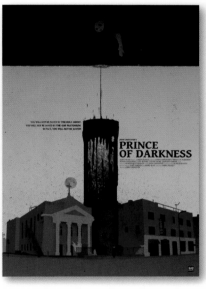

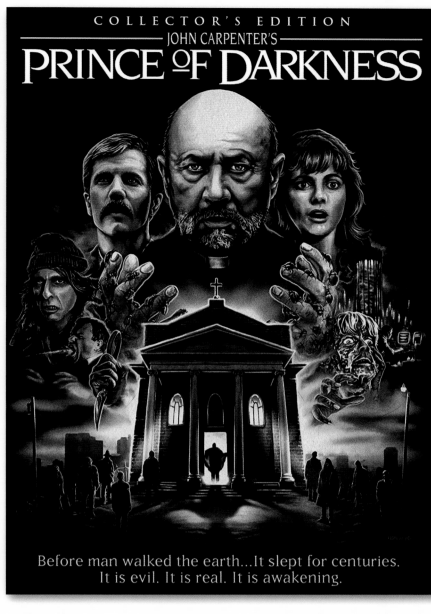

Before man walked the earth...It slept for centuries.
It is evil. It is real. It is awakening.

TOP LEFT: British quad poster for John Carpenter's *Prince of Darkness*. Carpenter wrote the screenplay under the pseudonym "Martin Quatermass," a direct homage to the renowned British author Nigel Kneale, who himself created the character of "Bernard Quatermass," the central figure in the films *The Quatermass Xperiment* (1955) and *Quatermass and the Pit* (1967).

BOTTOM LEFT: Artwork for the remastered 4K release of *Prince of Darkness* by the artist Matt Ferguson. Vice Press issued the work in a limited run of 184 editions in quad-style format, signed by the artist and available for purchase for only seven days. Ferguson also created artwork for 4K video releases of Carpenter's *The Fog* (1980), *Escape from New York* (1981), and *They Live* (1988).

BOTTOM MIDDLE: Alternative poster for *Prince of Darkness* by the French artist Grégory Sacré (a.k.a. Gokaiju). John Carpenter refers to this film as the second part of his "Apocalypse Trilogy," which begins with *The Thing* (1982) and concludes with the Lovecraftian *In the Mouth of Madness* (1994).

ABOVE RIGHT: Cover artwork for Scream! Factory's Collector's Edition release of *Prince of Darkness*, created by Justin Osbourn, a.k.a. Slasher Design Co. The film's church located in downtown Los Angeles's Little Tokyo district; built in 1923, it is now the Union Center for the Arts and houses East West Players, the nation's premier Asian American theater.

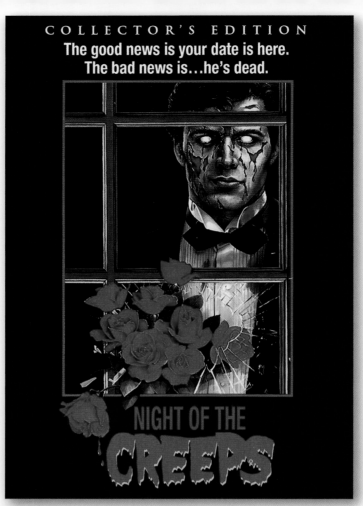

TOP LEFT: One-sheet for *Night of the Creeps* (1986). Writer/director Fred Dekker named virtually every character in the script after a horror film director: they include Chris Romero, Cynthia Cronenberg, Ray Cameron, Sgt. Raimi, and Officer Bava. Both this film and Dekker's *The Monster Squad* (1987) achieved cult status.

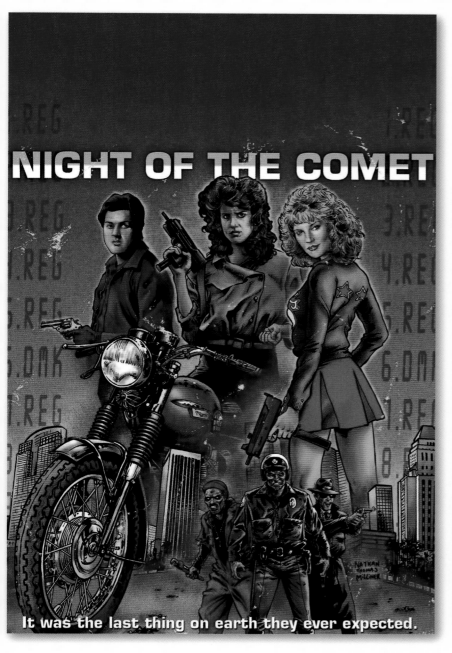

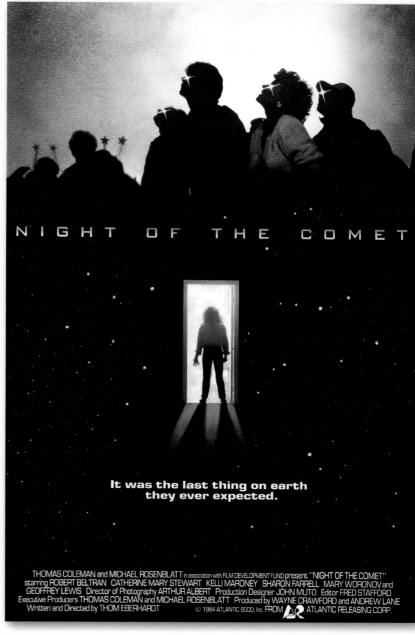

OPPOSITE, TOP RIGHT: Cover art for Shout! Factory's Blu-ray release of *Night of the Creeps*. This limited-edition release also included an eight-inch figure of Detective Ray Cameron, as played in the film by Tom Atkins.

OPPOSITE, BOTTOM: Alternative poster for *Night of the Creeps*, as created by the British artist Graham Humphreys. The film combines the 1950s idea of zombies created by aliens (in this case, slugs that enter through the victim's mouth) with the 1980s craze for teen movies.

ABOVE LEFT: Poster for *Night of the Comet* featuring art by American illustrator and filmmaker Nathan Thomas Milliner. The poster was included with the two-hundred-copy limited-edition Blu-ray release by Scream! Factory; the artwork also served as the cover for the company's Collector's Edition Blu-ray and DVD release of the film.

ABOVE RIGHT: One-sheet for *Night of the Comet*, in which zombies are created after the earth passes through the tail of a comet. The protagonists, played by Catherine Mary Stewart and Kelli Maroney, survive because they are inside lead-lined rooms at the time. Maroney's character, sixteen-year-old Sam, is said to have been an influence on Joss Whedon in creating *Buffy the Vampire Slayer*.

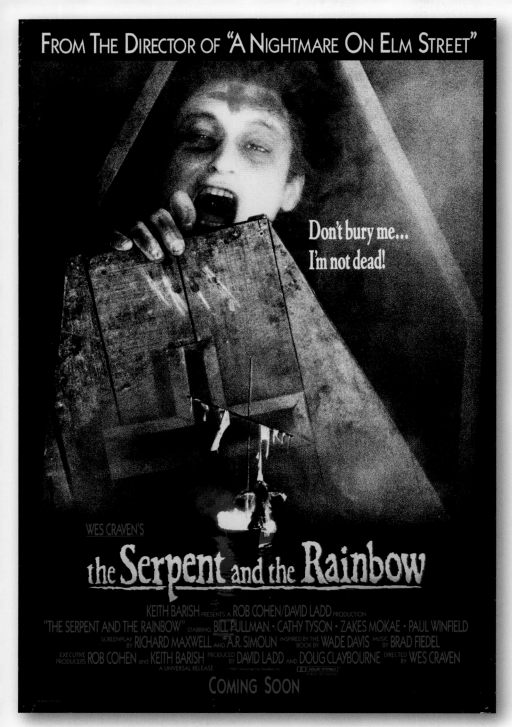

Don't bury me...
I'm not dead!

WES CRAVEN'S
the Serpent and the Rainbow

KEITH BARISH PRESENTS A ROB COHEN/DAVID LADD PRODUCTION
"THE SERPENT AND THE RAINBOW" STARRING BILL PULLMAN · CATHY TYSON · ZAKES MOKAE · PAUL WINFIELD
SCREENPLAY RICHARD MAXWELL AND A.R. SIMOUN INSPIRED BY THE BOOK BY WADE DAVIS MUSIC BY BRAD FIEDEL
EXECUTIVE PRODUCERS ROB COHEN AND KEITH BARISH PRODUCED BY DAVID LADD AND DOUG CLAYBOURNE DIRECTED BY WES CRAVEN
A UNIVERSAL RELEASE

COMING SOON

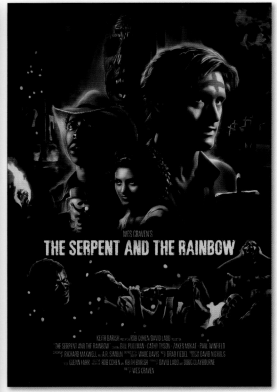

WES CRAVEN'S
THE SERPENT AND THE RAINBOW

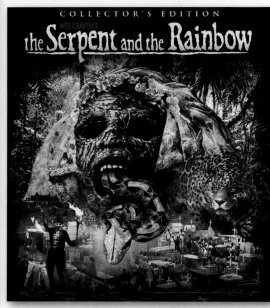

COLLECTOR'S EDITION
WES CRAVEN'S
the Serpent and the Rainbow

ABOVE LEFT: One-sheet for *The Serpent and the Rainbow* (1988), directed by Wes Craven and adapted by screenwriters Richard Maxwell and Alan Rodman from the 1985 nonfiction book of the same name by Wade Davis. The character of Christophe Durand (Conrad Roberts), who was once declared dead but is found alive, is based on the book's "real" zombie, Clairvius Narcisse, who claimed he'd been subjected to a potent combination of pufferfish venom and psychoactive substances that had turned him into a zombie slave.

TOP RIGHT: Alternative poster for *The Serpent and the Rainbow* by the German artist Ralf Krause. The film began location shooting in Haiti, where cast and crew members attended real Vodou ceremonies, but political upheaval forced the production to relocate to Santo Domingo.

BOTTOM RIGHT: Cover artwork for Scream! Factory's Collector's Edition Blu-ray release of *The Serpent and the Rainbow* by Joel Robinson. The image was also produced as a poster and issued in a limited-edition of two hundred copies.

RIGHT: British artist Chris Lambon created this image of *The Serpent and the Rainbow* for the German DVD release by Koch Films. A card at the start of the film explains the title: in Vodou, the Serpent represents the Earth, the Rainbow is Heaven, and Man lives between the two.

The creators of ALIEN... ...bring a new terror to Earth.

It will take your breath away...all of it.

RICHARD R. ST. JOHNS PRESENTS
A RONALD SHUSETT PRODUCTION
DEAD & BURIED
STARRING JAMES FARENTINO MELODY ANDERSON AND JACK ALBERTSON
SCREENPLAY BY RONALD SHUSETT AND DAN O'BANNON BASED UPON A STORY BY JEFF MILLAR AND ALEX STERN PRODUCED BY RONALD SHUSETT AND ROBERT FENTRESS DIRECTED BY GARY A. SHERMAN
EXECUTIVE PRODUCER RICHARD R. ST. JOHNS MUSIC BY JOE RENZETTI MAKE UP EFFECTS DESIGNED BY STAN WINSTON EXECUTIVE IN CHARGE OF PRODUCTION JOHN W. HYDE
JAVCO EMBASSY PICTURES Release

IT'S THE ONE STORY
YOU WON'T SEE
ON THE 6 O'CLOCK NEWS.

CUT AND RUN

ALESSANDRO FRACASSI presents A film by RUGGERO DEODATO
LISA BLOUNT LEONARD MANN · WILLIE AAMES in "CUT AND RUN"
RICHARD LYNCH RICHARD BRIGHT MICHAEL BERRYMAN VALENTINA FORTE
With the participation of JOHN STEINER Special Appearance by KAREN BLACK
Story and Screenplay CESARE FRUGONI and DARDANO SACCHETTI Edited by MARIO MORRA
Director of Photography ALBERTO SPAGNOLI Production Manager MAURIZIO ANTICOLI
Directed by RUGGERO DEODATO
Produced by ALESSANDRO FRACASSI for Racing Pictures
NEW WORLD PICTURES

Plucky Heroine: Lisa Blount

Although she received a Golden Globe nomination for her performance in the 1982 hit *An Officer and a Gentleman*, actress Lisa Blount had already made an impression on horror fans for her role as a flirtatious model who ends up becoming a deadly zombie nurse in 1981's *Dead and Buried*. In 1987, she scored the female lead in John Carpenter's *Prince of Darkness*, playing the heroine who eventually sacrifices herself to save the world from an incursion of evil (and zombies). She also appeared in *Radioactive Dreams* (1985), *Nightflyers* (1987), *Blind Fury* (1989), and *Needful Things* (1993). Although Blount never found tremendous success as an actress, she went on to win an Academy Award for a live-action short film she coproduced (with her husband Ray McKinnon and Walton Goggins) in 2001 called *The Accountant*. She died in 2010, at the age of fifty-three; no cause of death was listed, but she had suffered from a condition similar to multiple sclerosis for the

ABOVE LEFT: An 11×14 lobby card from *Dead and Buried*, showing Lisa Blount as the zombie nurse, about to kill photographer George LeMoyne (Christopher Allport). The "needle in the eye" effect was achieved by building a puppet head of the victim and then filming the needle being pulled from the

ABOVE RIGHT: One-sheet for Ruggero Deodato's *Cut and Run* (1985), starring Lisa Blount as a reporter who stumbles into a cult of cannibals in the South American jungle. The screenplay was co-written by frequent Lucio Fulci collaborator Dardano Sacchetti.

OPPOSITE: Five-color screen print of *Prince of Darkness* by the British artist Godmachine, as commissioned by Studio Canal/Frightfest. The film's executive producer, Shep Gordon, also managed rock superstar Alice Cooper, whom Carpenter cast as the silent leader of the entranced street people surrounding the church

PRINCE of DARKNESS

LOOK WHAT'S BURIED
INSIDE YOUR TELEVISION.

THE
VIDEO
DEAD

INTERSTATE 5 PRODUCTIONS IN ASSOCIATION WITH HIGHLIGHT PRODUCTIONS
PRESENT A ROBERT SCOTT FILM • THE VIDEO DEAD • ROXANNA AUGESEN • ROCKY DUVALL • MICHAEL ST. MICHAELS
AND JENIFFER MIRO AS THE WOMAN SPECIAL VISUAL EFFECTS BY DALE HALL JR. DIRECTOR OF PHOTOGRAPHY GREG BECKER
PRODUCTION DESIGNER LINDA HORWITZ ASSOCIATE PRODUCER WILLIAM S. WEINER
WRITTEN, PRODUCED AND DIRECTED BY ROBERT SCOTT
A MANSON INTERNATIONAL RELEASE © 1986 VIDEO DEAD, A CALIFORNIA LIMITED PARTNERSHIP

The Unbelievable.
The Unthinkable.

There is no escape from the nightmare
that has waited 100 years to return!

The SUPERNATURALS

"TERRIFYING...UNIQUE...SURREAL one of the most frightening films I have ever seen."
"TEXAS CHAINSAW MASSACRE"
"UNRELENTING EXCITEMENT a truly original haunted house thriller"
"POLTERGEIST"

7
DOORS OF
DEATH

DOLBY STEREO   R

ABOVE LEFT: One-sheet for the 1987 low-budget effort *The Video Dead*, written and directed by Robert Scott, in which a cursed television set that shows only one movie—titled *Zombie Blood Nightmare*—releases zombies into the real world.

TOP RIGHT: One-sheet for *The Supernaturals* (1986), about a modern army troop who encounter a horde of Confederate zombies while practicing maneuvers in the Deep South. The film is chiefly notable for its cast, which includes *Star Trek*'s Nichelle Nichols as Sgt. Leona Hawkins.

BOTTOM RIGHT: One-sheet for the 1983 U.S. release of *The Beyond* under the title *7 Doors of Death*, featuring artwork by Tom Tierney. When distributor Aquarius acquired the North American rights to the film, they re-titled it, re-scored it, re-cut it, and changed Fulci's name to "Louis Fuller."

TOP LEFT: One-sheet for *Pet Sematary* (1989), as adapted by Stephen King from his own novel about revenants who return from a cursed burial ground in the Maine woods. The book was first optioned by George Romero, who was set to direct but had to pull out due to scheduling conflicts with *Monkey Shines* (1988). Mary Lambert ended up directing instead.

BOTTOM LEFT: One-sheet for *The Vineyard* (1989), co-directed and co-written by James Hong, who also starred in the film. Hong is probably best known for his performances in *Blade Runner* (1982) and *Big Trouble in Little China* (1986); here he plays an elderly winemaker who uses Asian magic in his search for immortality, creating castoff zombies along the way.

ABOVE RIGHT: One-sheet for *Waxwork* (1989), written and directed by Anthony Hickox. The plot concerns a group of teens who visit a wax museum and find themselves trapped in some of the exhibits, one of which is a horde of zombies; the museum's owner, David Lincoln (David Warner), is trying to bring about the end of the world by resurrecting hungry zombies.

5

RISE OF THE ZOM-COMS

"BRAAAAAAAAINNNNNSSSS!"

ZOMBIES IN *RETURN OF THE LIVING DEAD* (1985)

> "The bloodier it gets, the funnier it is. It's like pop Buñuel; the jokes hit you in a subterranean comic zone that the surrealists' pranks sometimes reached, but without the surrealists' self-consciousness (and art-consciousness). This is indigenous American junkiness."
>
> From Pauline Kael's review of *Re-Animator* in the *New Yorker* (1986)

Maybe it was because George Romero had so artfully turned *Dawn of the Dead* into a satire, or maybe it was due to oversaturation, or perhaps the subject matter was just inherently ripe for poking fun at; whatever the reason, the 1980s saw humorous zombie films overtaking the more serious works.

Although it's probably fair to say the trend really did start with *Dawn* (1940s yuck-fests like *Zombies on Broadway* notwithstanding), it gained considerable momentum in 1985 with the release of two films: Dan O'Bannon's *Return of the Living Dead* and Stuart Gordon's *Re-Animator*. *Return of the Living Dead* sits slightly higher in the pantheon of zombie cinema for a new quirk it introduced: these zombies are most interested in eating brains. It also has a direct lineage to the Romero films via John Russo, who co-wrote (with Romero) the original *Night of the Living Dead*; when Romero and Russo split, Russo left with certain elements of *Night*, including the right to use "Living Dead" in a title.

In the 1970s, as George Romero was writing *Dawn of the Dead*, Russo was writing his own sequel novel, *Return of the Living Dead*. Originally intended as a vehicle for director Tobe Hooper (*The Texas Chainsaw Massacre*), *Return* was forced to find a new director when production on Hooper's film *Lifeforce* ran over. Dan O'Bannon was already a cult figure thanks to his involvement with *Alien* and *Dead and Buried* (almost a satirical zombie movie in itself), and he was eager to finally direct a feature. He rewrote Russo's story considerably, imbuing his tale of teenagers trapped in a cemetery during an outbreak with a punk sensibility and a liberal dose of humor; he also made the original *Night of the Living Dead* part of *Return*'s story by suggesting that it was created by the government as part of a cover-up. The film deftly sets a range of young actors—notably Linnea Quigley as Trash, whose striptease resurrection is one of the film's more memorable scenes—against veterans James Karen, Don Calfa, and Clu Gulager, and also has its secret government toxins returning long-dead animals to life.

Return of the Living Dead was successful enough both financially and critically to spawn a franchise, eventually leading to a total of five films (sadly, O'Bannon was not involved with any of the sequels). The same is true of Stuart Gordon's *Re-Animator*. Based on a story by H. P. Lovecraft, *Re-Animator* is centered on Herbert West (played to spiky perfection by Jeffrey Combs), a young medical student whose glowing green serum returns the dead to life . . . albeit mindlessly violent life. West achieves one victory, though, when he brings back to life the severed head of his one-time

Return of the Living Dead sits slightly higher in the pantheon of zombie cinema for a new quirk it introduced: these zombies are most interested in eating brains.

foe Dr. Hill (David Gale), who retains his intelligence—and his lust for the film's heroine (played by Barbara Crampton). The film's extraordinary amount of blood initially earned it an X rating, although it was later re-cut to an R. Gordon's direction is stylish, exciting, and very funny ("Who's going to believe a talking head? Get a job in a sideshow" is one of a number of lines much beloved by fans), so it's no surprise that *Re-Animator* gave rise to two sequels, *Bride of Re-Animator* (1990) and *Beyond Re-Animator* (2003). Oddly enough, series producer and *Bride* director Brian Yuzna was also involved with the *Return of the Living Dead* franchise, as director of *Return of the Living Dead 3* (1993). *Re-Animator*'s director, Stuart Gordon, had no more involvement with the films after the first installment, but he did go on to direct an Off-Broadway theatrical musical that liberally splattered audience members with blood.

For the next seven years, the zombie genre seemed bloodless (no pun intended); those films that emerged were largely low-budget exploitation movies and mostly sequels. Then, in 1992, two zom-coms arrived that reinvigorated the genre: Peter Jackson's *Braindead* (a.k.a. *Dead Alive*) and Sam Raimi's *Army of Darkness*. Before he was making *The Lord of the Rings* or adding "Sir" to his name, Peter Jackson was making low-budget gorefests in his native New Zealand.

PREVIOUS SPREAD: Alternative poster design for *Shaun of the Dead* (2004) by the artist Matt Ryan Tobin. The landmark comedy appeared just two weeks after the film's distributor Universal Pictures also released Zack Snyder's remake of *Dawn of the Dead*, and together they were responsible for reigniting interest in zombie movies.

HERBERT WEST HAS A VERY GOOD HEAD ON HIS SHOULDERS –

AND ANOTHER ONE IN A DISH ON HIS DESK

H. P. LOVECRAFT'S CLASSIC TALE OF HORROR

RE-ANIMATOR

DEATH IS JUST THE BEGINNING...

BRIAN YUZNA PRESENTS "H.P. LOVECRAFT'S RE-ANIMATOR" DAVID GALE ROBERT SAMPSON AND JEFFREY COMBS AS HERBERT WEST ASSOCIATE PRODUCERS BOB GREENBERG AND CHARLES DONALD STOREY SCREENPLAY BY DENNIS PAOLI WILLIAM J. NORRIS AND STUART GORDON SPECIAL EFFECTS MAKE-UP ANTHONY DOUBLIN AND JOHN NAULIN PRODUCED BY BRIAN YUZNA STARRING BRUCE ABBOTT BARBARA CRAMPTON EXECUTIVE PRODUCERS MICHAEL AVERY AND BRUCE CURTIS DIRECTOR OF PHOTOGRAPHY MAC AHLBERG MUSIC COMPOSED BY RICHARD BAND BASED ON THE LOVECRAFT'S "HERBERT WEST – THE RE-ANIMATOR" ADDITIONAL MAKE-UP EFFECTS JOHN BUECHLER DIRECTED BY STUART GORDON

RETURN OF THE LIVING DEAD 3

ABOVE LEFT: One-sheet for Stuart Gordon's *Re-Animator* (1985), with photography by Nels Israelson. Although this adaptation of H. P. Lovecraft's short story "Herbert West— Reanimator" strays (by necessity) far from the source material, both film and story open with West successfully reanimating a human—with dire consequences.

TOP RIGHT: Alternative poster for *Return of the Living Dead* by the American artist Eddie Holly. The famous zombie depicted at top center is fondly known as "Tarman." Created by makeup effects artist Kenny Myers, Tarman was partly a suit (worn by actor Allan Trautman) and partly a puppet head manipulated by Myers's hand.

BOTTOM RIGHT: *Return of the Living Dead 3* art produced by Marc Schoenbach for Gutter Garbs, which sells apparel based on horror movies. As directed by co-producer Brian Yuzna and scripted by John Penney, the film focuses on the zombie Julie (Mindy Clarke), who discovers that pain can help control her brain-food cravings.

JESSE **EISENBERG**   WOODY **HARRELSON**   EMMA **STONE**   ABIGAIL **BRESLIN**

ZOMBIELAND 2

BACK FROM THE DEAD
OCTOBER 11

MY BOYFRIEND'S BACK

a **SEAN S. CUNNINHAM** *production*

written by **DEAN LOREY**   *Directed by* **BOB BALABAN**

SHAUN OF THE DEAD
A ROMANTIC COMEDY. WITH ZOMBIES.

ABOVE LEFT: Alternative poster for *Zombieland: Double Tap* (2019) by the Brazilian designer Neto Ribeiro. This sequel to the 2009 hit expanded the first film's zombie mythology by adding subvariants including "Hawkings," "Ninjas," "Homers," and the nearly indestructible "T-800s."

TOP RIGHT: One-sheet poster (and DVD/Blu Ray cover) for *My Boyfriend's Back* (1993), the original title of which was *Johnny Zombie*. Directed by Bob Balaban and written by Dean Lorey, the film follows the character of Johnny (Andrew Lowery), who returns from the grave as an intelligent zombie but must consume the flesh of the living to keep from decaying.

BOTTOM RIGHT: Alternative poster for *Shaun of the Dead* by the British graphic designer and digital illustrator Doaly. *Shaun's* director, Edgar Wright, has noted that the film's inspiration was the obsession with George Romero's *Dawn of the Dead* that he shared with Simon Pegg, who co-wrote the film with Wright and also plays the title role.

His first feature film, 1987's *Bad Taste*—about aliens harvesting humans for food—was followed by the ultraviolent puppet parody *Meet the Feebles* (1989), but it was his third feature, *Braindead*, that would attain cult status as one of the goriest films ever made.

Set incongruously in the placid suburbia of late 1950s Wellington, New Zealand, *Braindead* follows a young man, Lionel (Timothy Balme), whose domineering mother, Vera (Elizabeth Moody), is bitten by a Sumatran rat-monkey, causing her to die and return as a ravenous zombie who infects most of the surrounding neighborhood. It features a zombie baby, body parts whirling in a blender, Lionel cutting his way out of his mother at one point, and nearly eighty gallons of fake blood. Although it was a box-office flop during its initial release, it garnered critical praise (Peter Rainer in the *Los Angeles Times* quipped, "It makes something like

---

> "I don't think I've got it in me to shoot my flatmate, my mum, and my girlfriend all in the same evening."
>
> Shaun in *Shaun of the Dead* (2004)

Re-Animator seem like a UNESCO documentary about Mother Teresa"), and is now considered a cult classic.

Army of Darkness reunited Sam Raimi and star Bruce Campbell in the latest adventure of hapless hero Ash, who has now been transported to medieval times, where he's caught in between both warring kingdoms and a battle of the living against the dead. The use of the term "zombie" is arguable here, since the resurrected dead—mostly the skeletal soldiers that form the eponymous army—have intelligence, follow orders, and crack jokes, but it eschews the Z-word to refer to its creatures as "deadites." (The *Evil Dead* computer games would explore the mythology of the deadites in detail, explaining that they are demons that first consume a human soul and then take possession of the body, whether living or dead.)

For the next decade or so after *Braindead* and *Army of Darkness*, zombie films thrived in foreign cinemas but nearly vanished from American screens. One of the few interesting Hollywood productions from this period was the first zombie film for children: 1998's animated, direct-to-video feature *Scooby-Doo on Zombie Island*. The film reunites Mystery Inc.—the gang made up of the canine Scooby, Shaggy, Fred, Daphne, and Velma—and for the first time in the *Scooby-Doo* franchise it pits them against real ghosts and zombies on an isolated island deep in the Louisiana bayou. Since the intended audience was primarily kids, the scares are light and gore almost nonexistent, but the zombies are visually effective and the film paved the way for later animated fare like 2012's stop-motion *ParaNorman*, with its story of young Norman, a psychically-gifted boy who can see ghosts and must protect his town from zombies

activated by a witch's curse. In both films, the zombies are finally released from their bodily state to become ghosts that move on to the next world. Directed by Sam Fell and Chris Butler and produced by Laika (the studio behind the popular Neil Gaiman adaptation *Coraline*), *ParaNorman* was nominated for the Academy Award for Best Animated Feature and is also known for including the first openly gay character (the muscled Mitch) in an animated film.

In 2004, zombies exploded back onto the cinema scene with Zack Snyder's remake of *Dawn of the Dead* and a zom-com that achieved international success and acclaim, *Shaun of the Dead*. As written by Simon Pegg and Edgar Wright and directed by Wright, Shaun (Pegg) and Ed (Nick Frost) are two slackers who rescue Shaun's girlfriend (Kate Ashfield), mother (Penelope Wilton), and friends, and take refuge from the zombie hordes in the local pub. Packed with in-jokes referencing everything from Romero films (fans who know how seldom Romero used "zombie" in his work will especially appreciate the scene in which Shaun begs Ed not to use "that word") to popular music, *Shaun* accelerated Wright's career as a director and has gone on to become one of the most beloved entries in the zombie-movie canon.

Zombies eventually received the meta treatment in two features that knowingly and wittily comment on the genre, *Zombieland* (2009) and *The Cabin in the Woods* (2011). Written by Rhett Reese and Paul Wernick and directed by Ruben Fleischer, *Zombieland* starts post-zombie-apocalypse and occasionally stops the action so Columbus (Jesse Eisenberg) can explain (and even diagram) the proper survival methods and zombie data. *The Cabin in the Woods* (directed by Drew Goddard and written by Goddard and Joss Whedon) takes the stereotypical horror trope of a group of college kids trapped in an isolated cabin and dissects the happenings by revealing that there's actually a high-tech group controlling everything. Although we learn that there were any number of creatures the characters could have accidentally chosen (including "deadites"), they recited a few lines from an old book and called up "Zombie Redneck Torture Family."

There's also been a thread of zom-rom-coms—zombie movies that emphasize a romantic element. This subgenre may have begun in 1993 with Bob Balaban's *My Boyfriend's Back*, but the formula proved far more effective with 2013's *Warm Bodies*. Written and directed by Jonathan Levine and based on the novel by Isaac Marion, *Warm Bodies* casts Nicholas Hoult as "R," a zombie who falls in love with the human Julie (Teresa Palmer) after eating her boyfriend's brain.

Over the last decade, zombie movies have mostly veered back to the serious side, thanks to the runaway success of the (decidedly unfunny) television series *The Walking Dead*, although zom-coms still refuse to die. One of the most recent American examples, Jim Jarmusch's *The Dead Don't Die* (2019), opened to less-than-stellar reviews; the *Hollywood Reporter*, for example, called it "a bit deadening."

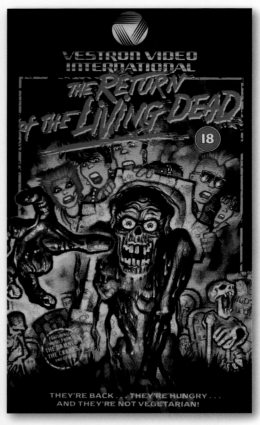

ABOVE LEFT: One-sheet for *The Return of the Living Dead* (1985), featuring artwork by Carl Ramsey (1946–2014), an American artist who lent his unique style to the famous posters for *Beetlejuice* (1988) and *Poltergeist* (1982), among others. He also created the airbrushed cover for Alice Cooper's 1973 album *Billion Dollar Babies*.

TOP RIGHT: Cover artwork from the U.K. home-video release of *The Return of the Living Dead*. Director Dan O'Bannon also penned the screenplay, based on a story by Romero collaborators Rudy Ricci, John A. Russo, and Russell Streiner. The film made just over three times its budget of $4 million and spawned four sequels.

BOTTOM RIGHT: Cover artwork for Shout! Factory's Blu-ray release of *Return of the Living Dead Part II* by Graham Humphreys. Written and directed by Ken Wiederhorn, *Part II* follows on from the first film as a barrel of the zombie-making gas Trioxin falls from a military transport truck and unleashes a second zombie outbreak.

RIGHT: Alternative poster for *The Return of the Living Dead* by the British artist Godmachine. Not only did *The Return of the Living Dead* introduce brain-eating to zombie mythology, it also employs some fast zombies, with writer/director Dan O'Bannon later stating that he wanted to get away from Romero's zombies.

ABOVE LEFT: This advance one-sheet for *Return of the Living Dead Part II* (1988) borrows its "Just when you thought it was safe . . ." tag line from *Jaws II* (1978), and its poster design from director Tom Holland's *Fright Night* (1985).

TOP RIGHT: One-sheet for *Return of the Living Dead 3*. When Brian Yuzna was approached about directing the film, he suggested that the film could be differentiated from other zombie movies by having its main character focus be on a zombie rather than a human.

ABOVE LEFT: Japanese B2 poster for *The Return of the Living Dead*, showing both "Tarman" and another of the film's featured zombies—a talking female half-corpse with twitching backbone who tells the heroes, "I can feel myself rotting."

TOP RIGHT: Italian *duo-foglio* poster for *The Return of the Living Dead*. Dan O'Bannon's name appeared on two genre films released in 1985: this one, which he wrote and directed; and the critically reviled *Lifeforce*, co-written with Don Jakoby and based on Colin Wilson's novel *The Space Vampires*.

BOTTOM RIGHT: French *grande* poster for *The Return of the Living Dead*, featuring art by prolific French movie poster artist Michel Landi, focusing on a stylized version of Linnea Quigley's character "Trash."

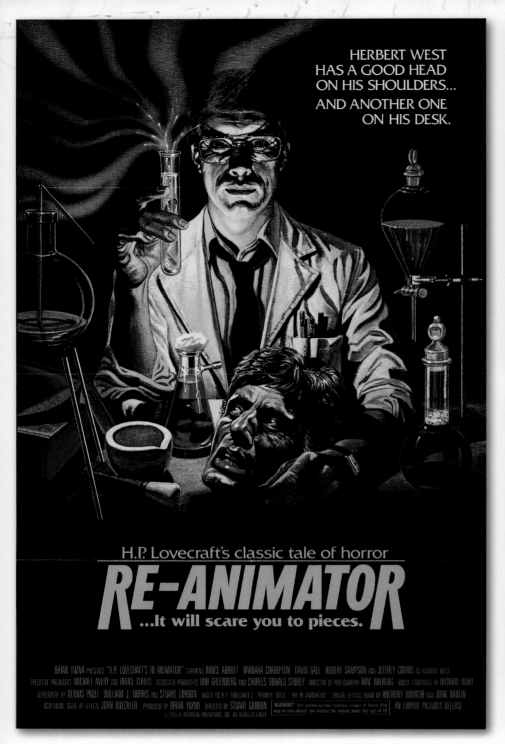

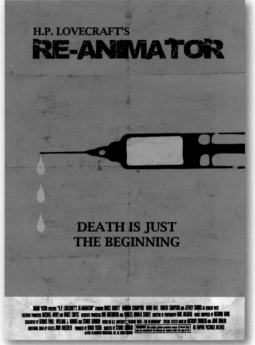

ABOVE LEFT: One-sheet for director Stuart Gordon's *Re-Animator* (1985), which was first released without a rating for fear that its blood and gore effects would earn it an X. Re-cut and re-released in 1986, it received an R rating; most later releases, however, have used the original, uncut version.

TOP RIGHT: French artists Stan and Vince produced this eight-color screen print for Mad Duck Posters in a limited run of 135 copies. It was also made available in a variant with red lettering, two foil variants, and a "VHS" variant with black lettering in a 1980s retro style.

BOTTOM RIGHT: Alternative poster for *Re-Animator* by the American artist J. E. Knight, rendered in the classic, blocky style of the great American poster artist and graphic designer Saul Bass (1920–1996).

OPPOSITE: French *grande* poster for *Re-animator* by the artist Thierry Watorek, showing Jeffrey Combs as Herbert West. Of being cast in the role, Combs would later quip to an interviewer, "God, I had no idea what was to come."

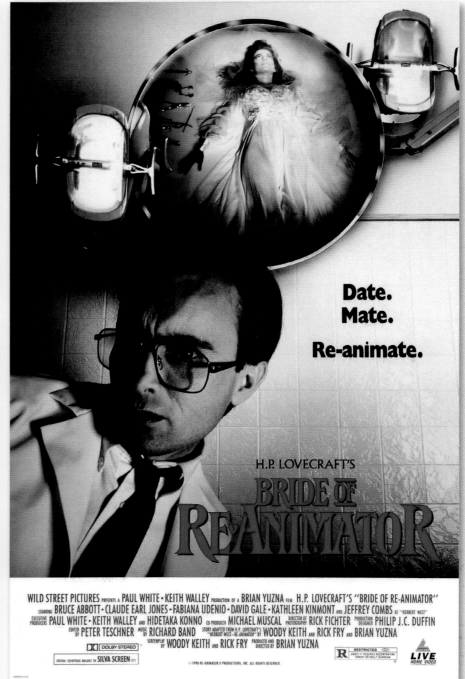

Date.
Mate.
Re-animate.

H.P. LOVECRAFT'S

BRIDE OF REANIMATOR

WILD STREET PICTURES PRESENTS A PAUL WHITE • KEITH WALLEY PRODUCTION OF A BRIAN YUZNA FILM H.P. LOVECRAFT'S "BRIDE OF RE-ANIMATOR" STARRING BRUCE ABBOTT • CLAUDE EARL JONES • FABIANA UDENIO • DAVID GALE • KATHLEEN KINMONT AND JEFFREY COMBS AS "HERBERT WEST" EXECUTIVE PRODUCERS PAUL WHITE • KEITH WALLEY AND HIDETAKA KONNO CO-PRODUCER MICHAEL MUSCAL DIRECTOR OF PHOTOGRAPHY RICK FICHTER PRODUCTION DESIGNER PHILIP J.C. DUFFIN EDITED BY PETER TESCHNER MUSIC BY RICHARD BAND STORY ADAPTED FROM H.P. LOVECRAFT'S "HERBERT WEST—RE-ANIMATOR" BY WOODY KEITH AND RICK FRY AND BRIAN YUZNA SCREENPLAY BY WOODY KEITH AND RICK FRY PRODUCED AND DIRECTED BY BRIAN YUZNA

DOLBY STEREO   ORIGINAL SOUNDTRACK AVAILABLE ON SILVA SCREEN CD'S   ©1990 RE-ANIMATOR II PRODUCTIONS, INC. ALL RIGHTS RESERVED.   R RESTRICTED UNDER 17 REQUIRES ACCOMPANYING PARENT OR ADULT GUARDIAN   LIVE HOME VIDEO

TOP LEFT: *Bride of Re-Animator* art by Graham Humphreys. In this sequel, Dr. Herbert West (Jeffrey Combs) finds that his serum can reanimate body parts—a discovery he uses to craft various strange creatures, like an eyeball attached to four fingers. His friend Cain (Bruce Abbott) calls these experiments "morbid doodling."

BOTTOM LEFT: Limited-edition alternative *Bride of Re-Animator* poster created by the American illustrator and graphic designer Adam Rabalais for Mad Duck Posters, issued in a run of one hundred regular copies and thirteen variant foil editions.

ABOVE RIGHT: Unlike the first film in the series, *Bride of Re-Animator* (1990) was released direct to video. Although it received some praise—mainly for the performance of Jeffrey Combs—most viewers found it to be a pale offspring of its predecessor.

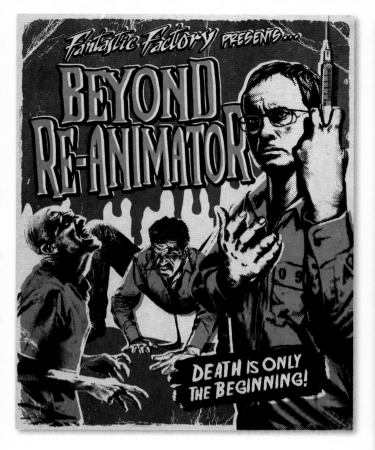

ABOVE LEFT: Designer Thomas Hodge ("The Dude Designs") was brought in by Arrow Video to create branded art for four Brian Yuzna films: *Faust: Love of the Damned* (2000), *Arachnid* (2001), *Beyond Re-Animator* (2003), and *Romasanta: The Werewolf Hunt* (2004). He employed what he called "an alternative pop bubblegum twist on the classic B-movie poster."

ABOVE RIGHT: *Beyond Re-Animator* (2003) was released and is set thirteen years after the events of *Bride of Re-Animator*. This time, Herbert West (Jeffrey Combs) is experimenting from a prison cell and has discovered something called "Nano-Plasmic Energy," which he believes restores life (along with intelligence). Of course, things go wrong.

MAD DOCTORS AND ALIENS: JEFFREY COMBS

"Who's going to believe a talking head? Get a job in a sideshow."

Herbert West in *Re-Animator* (1985)

I n 1981, a young actor named Jeffrey Combs was cast in a horror movie called *Frightmare*. Combs was a native Californian who had pursued acting training at the University of Washington before heading to Los Angeles, where he worked in theater and the occasional small role in a movie. *Frightmare*, his first horror movie, was not a success; the low-budget chiller garnered so-so reviews and little business, and is now notable briefly for being the first horror film featuring the actor who would go on to become the favorite mad doctor of 1980s cinema.

When Combs was cast in *Re-Animator* (after a casting director saw him in a play and suggested he read for Herbert West), he'd never even heard of H. P. Lovecraft, the legendary horror author whose work would provide the basis for a number of Combs's most famous performances. Combs had no idea that West would become an iconic role; at the time he was making the film (which had an 18-day shoot), he believed its low budget would hamper its chances for success. He would go on to play the crazed Dr. West in two more *Re-Animator* films (*Bride of Re-Animator* in 1990 and *Beyond Re-Animator* in 2003). He also played the only-slightly-less-mad scientist Dr. Crawford Tillinghast in the 1986 Lovecraft movie *From Beyond* (also directed by *Re-Animator* director Stuart Gordon and co-starring *Dawn of the Dead*'s Ken Foree), he appeared in the Lovecraft adaptations *The Lurking Fear* (1994) and *The Dunwich Horror* (2009), and he even played the author himself (with considerable prosthetic appliances by John Vulich) in 1993's *Necronomicon*.

Combs's genre work hasn't been confined only to Lovecraft movies. Peter Jackson was such a fan of his work that he cast him as crazed FBI agent Milton Dammers in his 1996 *The Frighteners*, and he worked with Stuart Gordon on *RobotJox* (1990) and *Castle Freak* (1995). He has also plumbed the works of another American horror master: Edgar Allan Poe. In addition to making *The Pit and the Pendulum* (1990), he appeared in the *Masters of Horror* television series episode "The Black Cat," loosely based on the classic short story of the same name (both *The Pit* and "The Black Cat" were directed by Stuart Gordon and written or co-written by Dennis Paoli, who also co-wrote *Re-Animator*). After playing Poe himself in "The Black Cat," Combs reprised the role in a one-man stage show, *Nevermore: An Evening with Edgar Allan Poe* (also directed

by Gordon and written by Paoli). This makes Jeffrey Combs the only actor to have played both Lovecraft and Poe in feature films/television.

Although he has noted that he feels he has been stereotyped as a horror actor, Combs has also appeared in nongenre works, including *Love and a .45* (1994), in which he plays a smalltime mobster called "Dinosaur Bob" (Combs calls this one of his personal favorites); and as the late actor Montgomery Clift in the television movie *Norma Jean and Marilyn* (1996).

His skill at acting under heavy makeup has also made Combs one of the most popular guest actors in the *Star Trek* universe, with appearances in a combined total of forty-five episodes in *Deep Space Nine*, *Voyager*, and *Enterprise*. He

---

When Combs was cast in *Re-animator*, he'd never even heard of H. P. Lovecraft, the legendary horror author whose work would provide the basis for a number of Combs's most famous performances.

---

has also found success in voiceovers (which he's said he enjoys because there's no makeup involved), lending his vocal acting talents to *Transformers: Prime* (fifty-six episodes), *Teenage Mutant Ninja Turtles* (four episodes), *The Avengers: Earth's Mightiest Heroes* (four episodes), *Scooby-Doo! Mystery Incorporated* (two episodes), and many more. His videogame work includes games in the *Star Trek*, *Transformers*, and DC Comics franchises.

More recently, Combs played a World War II Nazi commander in the "Bad Wolf Down" episode of the Shudder TV series *Creepshow* (he was cast by executive producer Greg Nicotero, who provided the makeup effects for *Bride of Re-Animator*), and he will star in the forthcoming crowd-funded feature *Stream*. He is also a popular guest at media and comics conventions, where his many roles in various *Star Trek* and DC franchises have made him a fan favorite. Combs enjoys his following but thinks he's largely unrecognizable to the mass of moviegoers: "Most of the time I'm just a nondescript suburban dad going to the store to get milk."

RIGHT: *Re-Animator* as re-envisioned by the American artist Blake Armstrong.

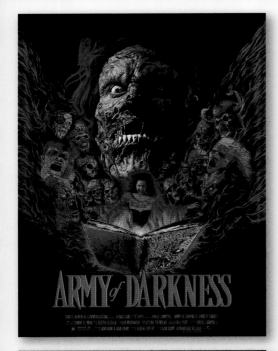

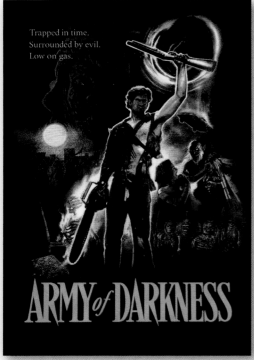

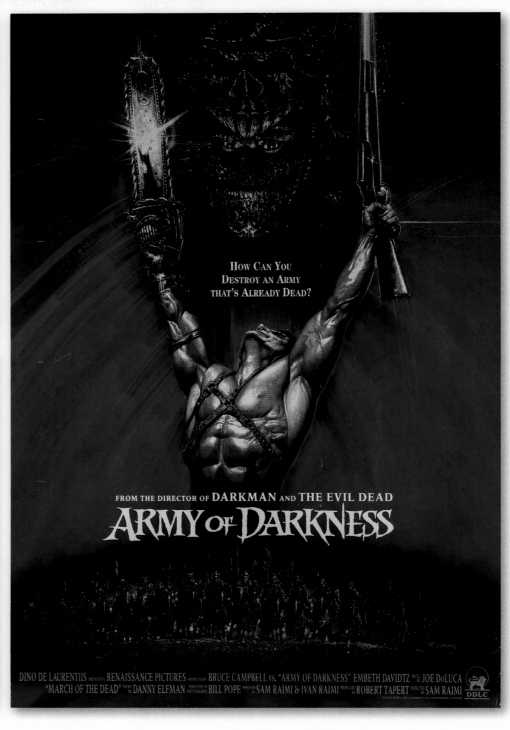

TOP LEFT: "Darkness," a five-color, screen-printed, blacklight poster for *Army of Darkness* by the American artist Mark W. Richards. Officially licensed by Hero Complex Gallery in Los Angeles, it was issued in a limited run of one hundred copies.

BOTTOM LEFT: Cover art for Shout! Factory's DVD release of *Army of Darkness* (1992) by the British artist Paul Shipper. *Army of Darkness* picks up where *Evil Dead II* (1987) ended: the hapless hero Ash (Bruce Campbell) is thrust back into the Middle Ages, where he is caught up in conflict between human armies and "Deadite" forces.

ABOVE RIGHT: International one-sheet for *Army of Darkness*, featuring art by Renato Casaro, who has opted for an extremely buff version of Ash over the more comedic depictions of Bruce Campbell shown on most other *Army of Darkness* posters.

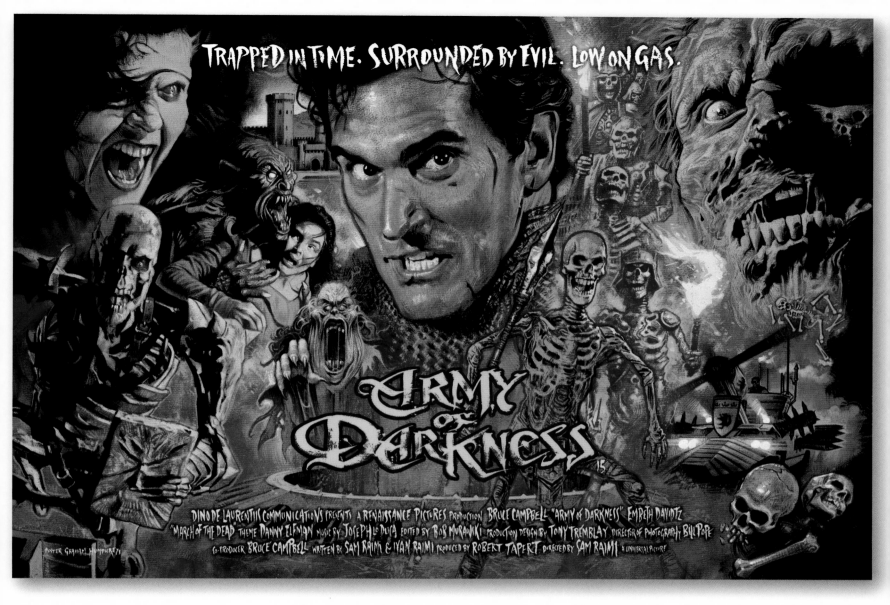

TRAPPED IN TIME. SURROUNDED BY EVIL. LOW ON GAS.

Army of Darkness

DINO DE LAURENTIIS COMMUNICATIONS PRESENTS A RENAISSANCE PICTURES PRODUCTION BRUCE CAMPBELL "ARMY OF DARKNESS" EMBETH DAVIDTZ "MARCH OF THE DEAD" THEME DANNY ELFMAN MUSIC BY JOSEPH LO DUCA EDITED BY BOB MURAWSKI PRODUCTION DESIGN BY TONY TREMBLAY DIRECTOR OF PHOTOGRAPHY BILL POPE CO-PRODUCER BRUCE CAMPBELL WRITTEN BY SAM RAIMI & IVAN RAIMI PRODUCED BY ROBERT TAPERT DIRECTED BY SAM RAIMI A UNIVERSAL PICTURE

ABOVE: *Army of Darkness* art by Graham Humphreys. The film pokes fun at Lovecraft (the grimoire Ash must consult is the *Necronomicon Ex-Mortis*), classic sci-fi (Ash must recite "Klaatu barada nikto," from *The Day the Earth Stood Still*), and consumer culture (he staves off the living dead in his job at S-Mart).

ABOVE LEFT: Italian *quattro-foglio* poster for *Army of Darkness*, featuring artwork by Enzo Sciotti. The skull with eyes is taken from the poster art for *Evil Dead II*.

TOP RIGHT: One-sheet for *Army of Darkness*, featuring artwork by the American artist Michael Hussar. In 2022, Mad Duck Posters celebrated the film's thirtieth anniversary by releasing this poster in several versions, including a foil variant limited to ninety-two copies.

BOTTOM RIGHT: This Japanese B2 poster for *Army of Darkness* takes some of its elements from the American one-sheet but also layers in Campbell's soup cans and some inexplicable toothbrushes, coat hangers, and marine imagery.

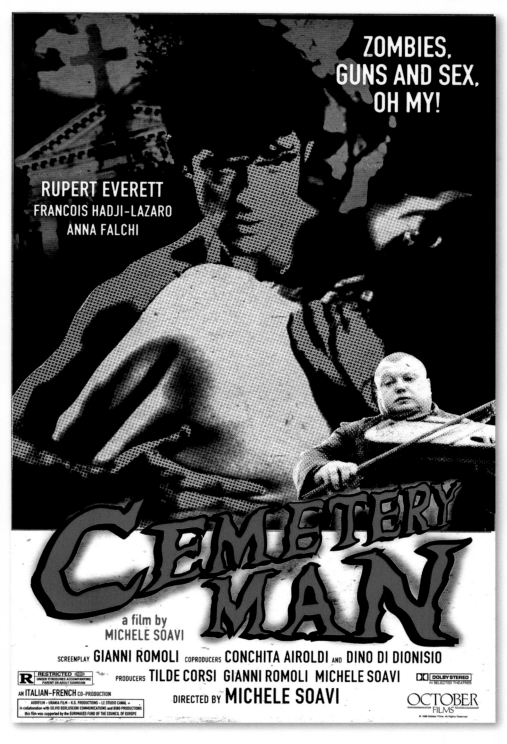

TOP LEFT: Japanese poster and Blu-ray cover for *Cemetery Man* (1994). Directed by Michele Soavi, the film combines horror, comedy, and romance. It was adapted from a novel by Tiziano Sclavi, an Italian writer best known for creating the long-running *Dylan Dog* comic book series.

BOTTOM LEFT: Cover art from the soundtrack to Devon Whitehead's *Cemetery Man / Dellamorte Dellamore*, as released in 2015 by Lunaris Records. The score, by Manuel de Sica, was issued on four different colors of vinyl, including "Gnaghi Vomit" and "Ossuary."

ABOVE RIGHT: One-sheet for *Cemetery Man*. The film's original Italian title, *Dellamorte Dellamore*, is a play on both its lead character's name (Francesco Dellamorte, played by Rupert Everett) and its themes: "*della morte, dell'amore*" is Italian for "about death, about love."

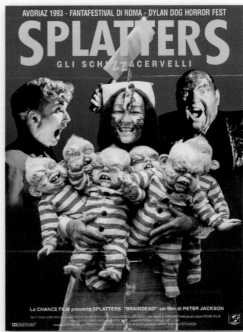

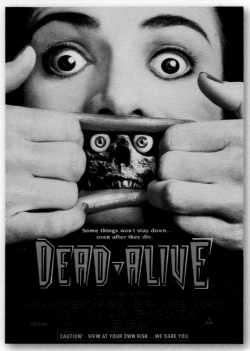

ABOVE LEFT: Screen-printed art based on Peter Jackson's *Dead Alive* by Matt Ryan Tobin, as produced for the Hero Complex Gallery. Also known as *Braindead*, the 1992 production about a zombie outbreak unleashed by a creature called a Sumatran Rat-Monkey has gained a cult following as perhaps the goriest movie ever made.

TOP RIGHT: Italian *duo-foglio* poster for *Braindead*, released here under the title *Splatters*, featuring the infant that's the result of sex between two zombies. In one extended slapstick sequence, hero Lionel (Timothy Balme) tries to take the baby to a local playground, where onlookers watch in horror as he is forced to pummel the pint-sized menace into submission.

BOTTOM RIGHT: One-sheet for *Dead Alive*'s unrated U.S. release. The film was also released in an alternative cut with twelve minutes removed in order to obtain an "R" rating. Cut versions were required in many other countries, too, although the film was banned altogether in some, including South Korea and Singapore.

The Man Who Added the Brains: Dan O'Bannon

In 1974, two USC film students named Dan O'Bannon and John Carpenter pulled together $60,000 to turn a short into a feature film called *Dark Star*, a science-fiction comedy in which O'Bannon plays one of the leads ("Sergeant Pinback"), and hand-crafted special effects so good that he was offered work on Alejandro Jodorowsky's unrealized version of *Dune*. In 1979, a screenplay by O'Bannon and his friend Ronald Shusett called *Alien* was directed by Ridley Scott and went on to become one of the most famous horror/science-fiction films of all time. As a screenwriter, O'Bannon worked on *Heavy Metal* (1981), *Lifeforce* (1985), *Invaders from Mars* (1986), and *Total Recall* (1990). He also directed two films, *The Return of the Living Dead* (1985) and the Lovecraft adaptation *The Resurrected* (1991). O'Bannon died of complications from Crohn's Disease in 2009, at the age of sixty-three.

ABOVE LEFT: Dan O'Bannon on the set of *Return of the Living Dead* (1985). He later noted that he had imbued his film with punk sensibility because he was tired of the preppy kids on display in most of the horror films of the time.

ABOVE RIGHT: After directing *Return of the Living Dead*, Dan O'Bannon made just one other feature film: *The Resurrected* (1991), adapted by Brent V. Friedman (with uncredited work by O'Bannon) from H. P. Lovecraft's novella *The Case of Charles Dexter Ward*. Although Lovecraft fans praised the film, O'Bannon wasn't happy with how Orion Pictures re-cut it. The company dissolved shortly thereafter.

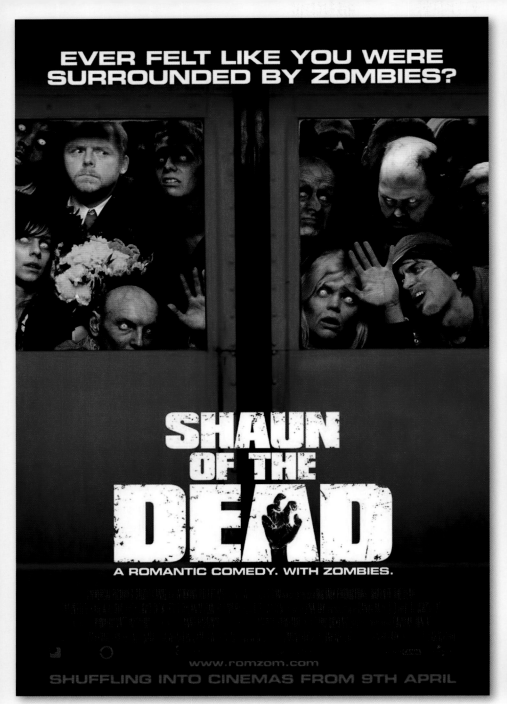

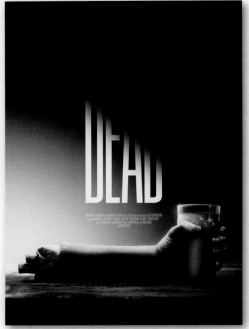

ABOVE LEFT: International advance one-sheet for *Shaun of the Dead* (2004). Prior to *Shaun*, director/co-writer Edgar Wright and star/co-writer Simon Pegg worked together on the British sitcom *Spaced* (1999–2001), about two twentysomethings posing as a couple to rent an apartment in London. The series also co-starred Nick Frost ("Ed" in *Shaun*).

TOP RIGHT: Alternative poster for *Shaun of the Dead* by the artist Daniel Norris, who also created matching art for the other two films in what have become known as Simon Pegg and Edgar Wright's "Three Flavours Cornetto Trilogy." The name derives from the mention of Cornetto ice cream cones in all three films; the other two are *Hot Fuzz* (2007) and *The World's End* (2013).

BOTTOM RIGHT: Alternative poster for *Shaun of the Dead* by the British artist Geraint Williams. Much of the film is set in the Winchester Tavern on London's Archway Road; additional scenes were filmed at the Duke of Albany pub south of the river, which closed down in 2008 and has since been converted into apartments.

TOP LEFT: Alternative poster for *Shaun of the Dead* by the American illustrator and graphic designer Adam Rabalais, who created this piece as the first in a triptych celebrating the "Three Flavours Cornetto Trilogy."

BOTTOM LEFT: Alternative poster for *Shaun of the Dead* by British artist Josh Beamish. Simon Pegg and Edgar Wright have named both *Dawn of the Dead* and the *Resident Evil* videogame as direct inspirations for *Shaun*.

ABOVE RIGHT: *Shaun of the Dead* screen print, produced for Mondo in a limited run of three hundred copies by the American artist Tyler Stout. Stout began his career creating gig posters in the Pacific Northwest; he has since become one of the leading names in the field of alternative movie posters.

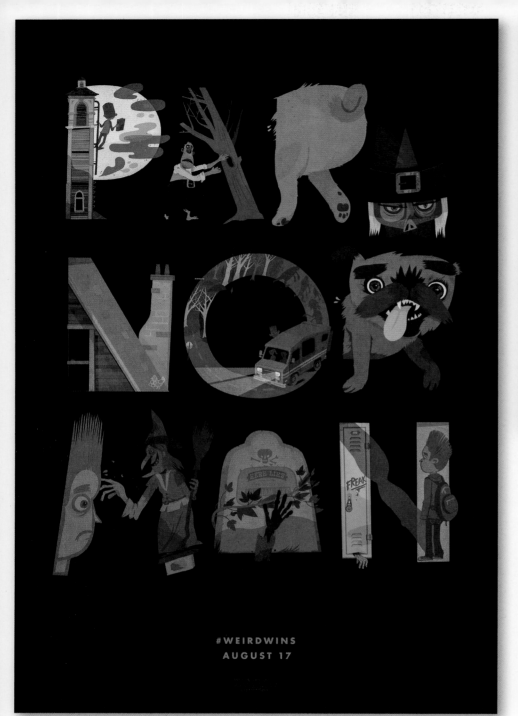

ABOVE LEFT: Advance one-sheet for *ParaNorman* (2012), an animated movie about a psychic boy, Norman (voiced by Kodi Smit-McPhee), who is tasked—by a ghost—with protecting his town from a curse that calls the dead back as zombies.

ABOVE RIGHT: This promotional artwork for *ParaNorman* was used on the back of the DVD box. The film was produced by Laika, a stop-motion animation company that also created an acclaimed adaptation of Neil Gaiman's *Coraline* (2009).

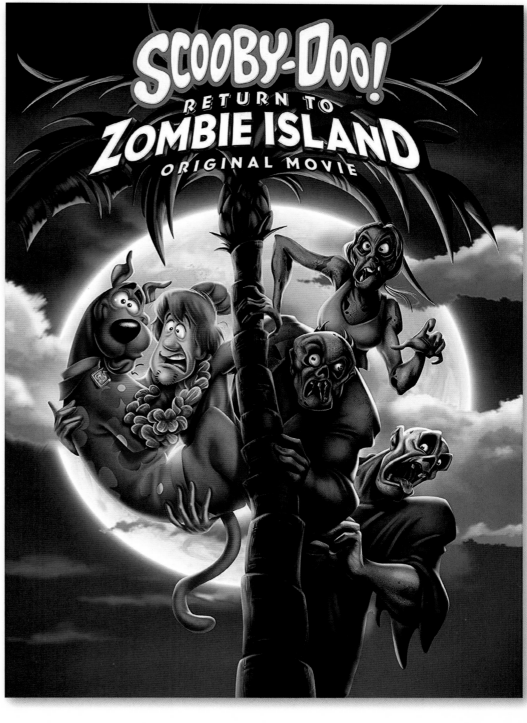

ABOVE LEFT: Video poster for *Scooby-Doo on Zombie Island* (1998), a feature-length entry in the long-running Scooby-Doo franchise. Scooby-Doo's mysteries were typically revealed to be human-perpetrated hoaxes, so this film was notable for plunking the heroes down in the middle of actual supernatural events, including a horde of zombies.

ABOVE RIGHT: *Scooby-Doo!: Return to Zombie Island* was released twenty-one years after its direct-to-video hit predecessor. In addition to featuring yet more zombies, the film also introduces "Mistress of the Dark" Elvira (voiced by Cassandra Peterson).

Crampton and Quigley: The Scream Queens

Where would *Re-Animator* and *The Return of the Living Dead* be without Barbara Crampton and Linnea Quigley, their respective scream queens? Crampton began her acting career in soap operas, but after being cast as Megan Halsey in *Re-Animator* she appeared regularly in horror films, including *Chopping Mall* (1986), *Puppet Master* (1989), *Castle Freak* (1995), *You're Next* (2011), *The Lords of Salem* (2012), *We Are Still Here* (2015), *Little Sister* (2016), and *Jakob's Wife* (2021), which she also developed and produced. She has also appeared in several horror anthology television series, including *Channel Zero: The Dream Door* (2018), *Into the Dark* (2019), and *Creepshow* (2021).

Linnea Quigley had appeared in several horror films, including *Graduation Day* (1981) and *Silent Night, Deadly Night* (1984), prior to being cast as "Trash" in *The Return of the Living Dead*, which confirmed her status as "Queen of the B's." She continued to appear in mostly direct-to-video horror films, including *Sorority Babes in the Slimeball Bowl-O-Rama*, *Nightmare Sisters*, *Hollywood Chainsaw Hookers* (all 1988), and *Blood Church* (1992). She also appeared in *The Guyver* (1991) for *Re-Animator* producer Brian Yuzna, and had occasional small parts in bigger films like *Innocent Blood* (1992).

Quigley is also a musician (she formed an all-female band, the Skirts, in the early '80s), an activist for animal rights, and the author of books including *The Linnea Quigley Bio and Chainsaw Book*, *I'm Screaming as Fast as I Can: My Life in B-Movies*, and *Skin*.

ABOVE LEFT: Cover artwork for *The Linnea Quigley Bio & Chainsaw Book*, which Quigley followed with *I'm Screaming as Fast as I Can*. Both books are now sought-after collectibles.

ABOVE RIGHT: Oil painting by the British artist Rick Melton, showing Crampton in *From Beyond* (1986), produced for the magazine *The Dark Side*. Melton jokes that he takes on "all the low budget, sexploitive horror jobs that decent illustrators pass up."

RIGHT: Portrait of Barbara Crampton as Dr. Katherine McMichaels in *From Beyond* (1986) by Singaporean digital artist Syafiq Shahari. *From Beyond* was the second Lovecraft adaptation Crampton starred in with Jeffrey Combs, with Stuart Gordon again directing and Brian Yuzna producing.

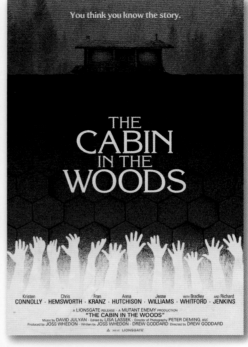

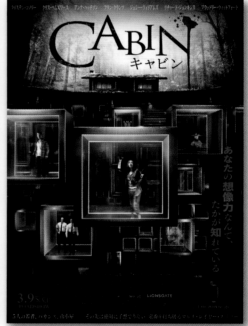

ABOVE LEFT: One-sheet poster for *The Cabin in the Woods* (2011). Joss Whedon, who produced and co-wrote the film with Drew Goddard, who directed it, has called it "a serious critique of what we love and what we don't about horror movies." Whedon and Goddard locked themselves in a hotel room and wrote the script in just three days.

TOP RIGHT: Alternative poster for *The Cabin in the Woods* by Alex Hinojosa. The whiteboard used by the technicians controlling the action in the film lists not just "Zombie Redneck Torture Family" (the creatures inadvertently selected by the unlucky teens) but also "Zombies" and "The Reanimated."

BOTTOM RIGHT: This Japanese poster for *The Cabin in the Woods* plays with the image of the trapped monsters beneath the cabin, as well as the technicians overseeing the mayhem (played by Richard Jenkins and Bradley Whitford). The ballerina with a mouth for a face glimpsed on this poster was makeup effects man David LeRoy Anderson's favorite creature.

RIGHT: Advance one-sheet for *Zombieland* (2009). The horror-comedy's main running gag is a series of rules for surviving a zombie apocalypse, as outlined by lead character Columbus (played by Jesse Eisenberg). They include "Cardio," "Beware of bathrooms," and "Cast iron skillet."

Shaun's Daddy: Edgar Wright

In 1995, a twenty-one-year-old Brit named Edgar Wright wrote and directed his first feature film, *A Fistful of Fingers*, a satirical Western that earned a few decent reviews but quickly vanished. After directing some British television (especially the sitcom *Spaced*, in which Wright first worked with Simon Pegg and Nick Frost), he stepped up to the directing plate again in 2004 with *Shaun of the Dead*; that film was a worldwide hit and earned Wright rave reviews for his wit and kinetic visual style. Co-writing again with Pegg, Wright next directed the police comedy *Hot Fuzz* (2007) and the apocalyptic *The World's End* (2013), both of which also starred Pegg and Frost. His other films as a director are *Scott Pilgrim vs. the World* (2010), *Baby Driver* (2017), the rock documentary *The Sparks Brothers* (2021), and the thriller *Last Night in Soho* (2021). He also contributed a trailer for a nonexistent movie called *Don't* to the anthology *Grindhouse* (2007) and has made a number of commercials. In interviews, Wright has quashed the idea of directing a sequel to *Shaun*: "I find it difficult to cover the same territory again."

ABOVE: *Shaun of the Dead* director and co-writer Edgar Wright, shown here with one of the film's zombies. Not shown here are the heroes, who must pretend to be zombies to make their way through a horde in order to reach their beloved pub, the Winchester Tavern.

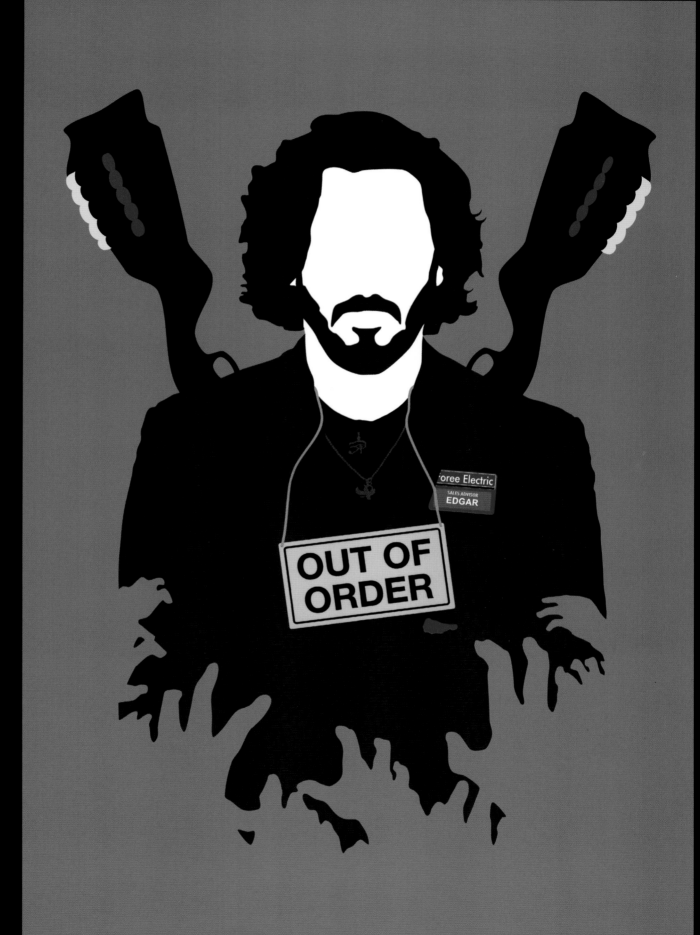

RIGHT: Edgar Wright vector art by Lee Byway (a.k.a. Byway Design), an English graphic designer based in Bristol. Byway says of this piece, "I'm a big fan of Edgar Wright's work and a few years after creating a triptych design based on the main characters in his 'Cornetto Trilogy' films I decided to create another design depicting Edgar Wright with elements and items from each of the three films."

ABOVE LEFT: One-sheet for *Little Monsters* (2019), an Australian comedy/horror film about a teacher, Miss Caroline (Lupita Nyong'o), who must protect her small charges when they're stranded during a field trip to a farm just when the zombie apocalypse happens.

TOP RIGHT: One-sheet for Jim Jarmusch's *The Dead Don't Die* (2019). Despite an impressive cast including Bill Murray, Adam Driver, Tilda Swinton, and Iggy Pop, the film was largely dismissed by critics, who found its humor too deadpan and its horror too light. Jarmusch fared better with his 2013 vampire film *Only Lovers Left Alive*.

BOTTOM RIGHT: Cover art from the DVD release of the Norwegian film *Dead Snow* (2009), directed by Tommy Wirkola, who would also direct its sequel, *Dead Snow 2: Red vs. Dead* (2014). The first film combines the longstanding trope of Nazi zombies with post-Snyder, fast-moving zombies.

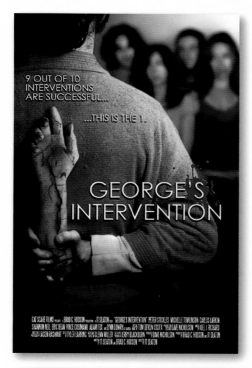

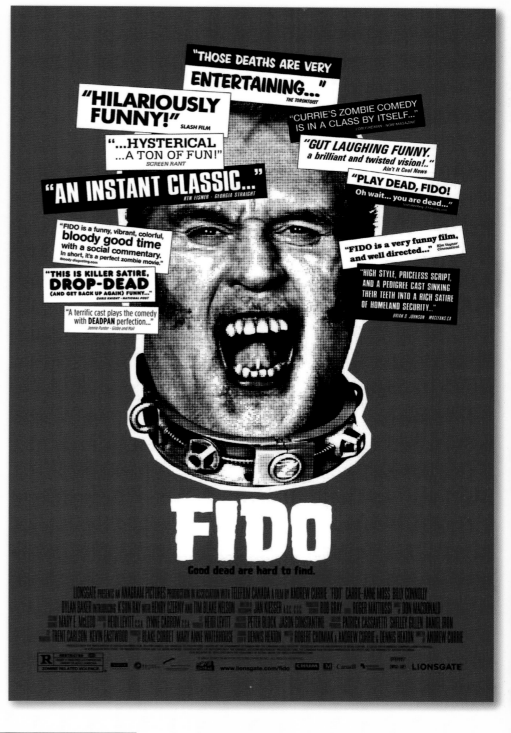

TOP LEFT: One-sheet for *George's Intervention* (a.k.a. *George: A Zombie Intervention*, 2009), an ultra-low-budget comedy/horror film about a postapocalyptic world in which the undead have become an accepted part of society—provided they learn to control their need to consume human flesh.

BOTTOM LEFT: One-sheet for *Zombie Island Massacre* (1984), produced by Troma Entertainment. Founded by Lloyd Kaufman and Michael Herz, Troma specializes in micro-budget horror films that emphasize comedy and outrageous gore, notably the cult favorites *The Toxic Avenger* (1985) and *Class of Nuke 'Em High* (1986).

ABOVE RIGHT: One-sheet for the Canadian horror comedy *Fido* (2006), starring Billy Connolly. The film's setting is a serene suburbia in which zombies can be controlled using special collars and turned into helpful household domestics. Before long, of course, Fido's collar malfunctions . . .

6

THE ZOMBIE AS IP

"IF YOU CAN FIGHT, FIGHT!"

GERRY LANE IN *WORLD WAR Z* (2013)

> "In remaking *Dawn of the Dead*, the only thing we changed was that zombies can kind of move quickly. Otherwise, it's pretty standard: you get bit, and depending on how bad the bite is it might take a while to turn but eventually you will be a zombie."
>
> Zack Snyder, from a 2021 interview with *Esquire*

B y the 1990s, zombies had influenced nearly every media form, from horror literature to music (Michael Jackson's *Thriller* being a prime example) to comics to videogames. Now, the Hollywood snake would begin to eat its own tail as those intellectual properties—all based on or inspired by cinematic zombies—would be adapted back into movies.

On March 30, 1996, two Japanese video game designers, Shinji Mikami and Tokuro Fujiwara, working for a company called Capcom, released a new game called *Resident Evil* (or *Biohazard* in Japan). Built for the PlayStation platform, the game was a significant technological improvement over earlier horror games like Capcom's *Sweet Home*, with greatly improved graphics and sound. The game dropped players into the world of the Umbrella Corporation, which had unleashed zombies in the average American Midwest location Raccoon City; characters were part of the elite STARS (Special Tactics and Rescue Squad) sent out to investigate some gruesome deaths, with players choosing to play as either Chris Redfield or Jill Valentine, both experienced members of the team. (In *Resident Evil 2*, released in 1998, the playable characters are Leon Kennedy, a rookie cop; and Claire Redfield, who is searching for her brother Chris.) The Umbrella Corporation has accidentally unleashed its T-virus, which mutates humans and dogs into violent, powerful zombies. The game was immensely successful, and would be extended and revised over the next quarter-century. It's now credited with inaugurating the survival horror game genre.

In 2002, writer/director Paul W. S. Anderson (who in 1997 helmed the successful videogame adaptation *Mortal Kombat*) wrote a spec script called *The Undead* and offered it as a *Resident Evil* prequel story to Constantin Film, which owned the rights to the videogames; there had been previous unsuccessful attempts at scripts, including one by George A. Romero that was a far more faithful adaptation of the game. Anderson, who wanted to be able to sell *The Undead* as an original story if Constantin passed on it, created a new protagonist, Alice, who did not appear in the games; he set most of the action in an underground laboratory called the Hive, a location he created.

At the beginning of the film, Alice (Milla Jovovich) awakens in a mansion with no memory; she and two men, Spence Parks (James Purefoy) and Matt Addison (Eric Mabius), are captured by a commando group and led beneath the mansion, where a tram takes them deep beneath Raccoon City to the Hive. Along the way, they're told that there's been some sort

Although fans of the videogame complained that *Resident Evil* strayed far from the source, the film was a smash hit and inaugurated what would go on to be one of the most successful horror-movie franchises in history.

of biohazard event and that the team has been sent to shut down the Hive's controlling AI, called Red Queen. As Alice and Spence slowly regain their memories, they realize they were part of the Hive's security team; Matt was an environmental activist seeking evidence to expose the Umbrella Corporation's secret bioweapons research. The team members soon find themselves trapped in the Hive with the powerful zombies created from the release of the T-virus (including zombie dogs and some indefinable creatures), and must fight their way back to the surface, with the resourceful Alice leading the way.

Although fans of the videogame complained that *Resident Evil* strayed far from the source, the film was a smash hit and inaugurated what would go on to be one of the most successful horror-movie franchises in history. Alice (always played by Jovovich) appears in the first six films, discovering that she had been cloned and enhanced and battling against the Umbrella Corporation's zombies in pursuit of an antivirus; she sometimes fights alongside characters from the games, including Jill Valentine (Sienna Guillory), Claire

PREVIOUS SPREAD: "Over the Wall" by the American digital artist Christian Lovel, inspired by *World War Z* (2013). Lovel created this piece by fusing together dozens of stock photos.

ABOVE LEFT: French *grande* poster for *Resident Evil* (2002). The film was a huge hit, earning nearly $104 million worldwide (on a $33 million budget) and inaugurating what would go on to become the second most successful videogame-based movie franchise (behind only *Pokémon*).

TOP RIGHT: The first *Resident Evil* game, released in 1996. Since then, dozens of new installments have appeared and the game has expanded into the realm of virtual reality (*Resident Evil 4* was released in a VR version in 2021), on its way to becoming the bestselling horror game series of all time.

BOTTOM RIGHT: Promotional art for *Resident Evil 2*, a 2019 remake of the original 1998 *Resident Evil 2* videogame. The remake kept the same characters and retained the original story, most of which takes place in the Raccoon City Police Department as it is besieged by creatures unleashed by the T-virus.

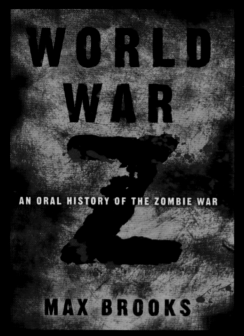

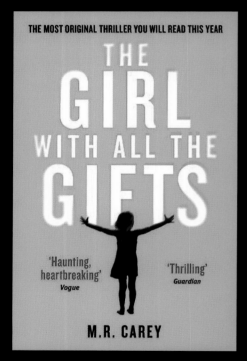

TOP LEFT: Cover art for Max Brooks's *World War Z*, published by Crown in 2006. The book, subtitled *An Oral History of the Zombie War*, was inspired by Studs Terkel's 1984 volume *"The Good War": An Oral History of World War Two*. One of the most successful zombie novels ever published, *World War Z* spent four weeks on the *New York Times* bestseller list.

BOTTOM LEFT: M. R. Carey's acclaimed 2013 novel *The Girl with All the Gifts*. Set twenty years after a fungal infection has turned most of humanity into flesh-eating "hungries," the story centers on a teacher, Helen Justineau, and a brilliant young "hungry" named Melanie, whom Helen protects at all cost. In 2017, Carey published a prequel called *The Boy on the Bridge*.

TOP RIGHT: British quad poster for *Pride and Prejudice and Zombies* (2016), adapted from the bestselling novel by Seth Grahame-Smith and Jane Austen. Natalie Portman was originally slated to play the lead part of Elizabeth Bennet but had to bow out (although she retained a producer credit). Lily James took over, with Burr Steers directing his own screenplay adaptation.

BOTTOM RIGHT: International poster for Robert Rodriguez's *Planet Terror* (2007). Rodriguez first started thinking of doing a zombie movie in the mid-1990s: "I knew zombie movies were gonna come back in a big way—there hadn't been one in about fifteen years or more, and slasher films had run their course."

Redfield (Ali Larter), and Leon Kennedy (Johann Urb). The seventh film, *Welcome to Raccoon City* (2021), tried to reboot the series and stick closer to the games, dispensing with Alice in favor of original game characters. Written and directed by Johannes Roberts, it was a modest financial success but received mostly negative reviews, with critics noting a lack of both substance and scares.

At the same time that the live action *Resident Evil* films were generating substantial profits in theaters, a series of animated films were also produced. Designed to appeal directly to fans of the game, the animated features tie in directly with the games and focus mostly on Leon S. Kennedy, a tough rookie cop first seen in the second game. The animated films (which utilize 3-D computer animation) began in 2008 with *Resident Evil: Degeneration,* and continued with *Resident Evil: Damnation* (2012) and *Resident Evil: Vendetta* (2017). In 2021, a fourth animated feature, *Resident Evil: Infinite Darkness,* was released on Netflix as a four-episode miniseries.

In 2006, Capcom chased the success of *Resident Evil* with another zombie survival horror game, *Dead Rising.* The first game centers on Frank West, a photojournalist trapped inside a Colorado shopping mall during a zombie outbreak.

"They just want to live. Everybody wants that."

Melanie in *The Girl with All the Gifts* (2016)

In 2015, Legendary Pictures released a live action film, *Dead Rising: Watchtower,* set in a fictitious Oregon town where a zombie antiviral drug called Zombrex fails, and the heroes are forced to contend with a zombie outbreak. Directed by Zach Liprovsky, *Dead Rising: Watchtower* was largely panned by critics but was profitable enough to lead to a sequel, *Dead Rising: Endgame* (2016). *Endgame* was released directly to the streaming service Crackle and received slightly better reviews than its predecessor.

Videogames aren't the only intellectual property that has been plumbed for zombie movies. Some of the most successful zombie films of the last decade have been based on books. The Max Brooks bestseller *World War Z* presented a fictitious oral history of a zombie apocalypse and spawned the 2013 blockbuster film of the same name. Directed by Marc Forster, *World War Z* boasted what must surely be the largest ever budget for a zombie film—reported to be somewhere between $190 and $269 million—and brought in more than half-a-billion dollars in box office, thanks in part to the presence of Brad Pitt in the lead role of Gerry Lane, a former UN agent trying to protect his family from the rampaging zombie hordes.

The success of *World War Z* inspired other family drama-zombie mash-ups, including 2015's *Maggie,* with Arnold Schwarzenegger as a father trying to protect his daughter (Abigail Breslin) after she's bitten by a zombie during an outbreak of what the film calls "necroambulism"; and the 2017 Australian film *Cargo,* also about a father trying to save his little girl during a viral pandemic that turns its victims rabid.

The Girl with All the Gifts (2016) also focuses on children, but in a very different way. Based on a novel by M. R. Carey (who also wrote the screenplay), this British entry garnered some of the strongest reviews of any recent horror film. Directed by Colm McCarthy, the story follows a teacher (played by Gemma Arterton) who is involved with a government project to teach a group of hybrid zombie-human children.

Far less serious was the 2016 adaptation of Seth Grahame-Smith's *Pride and Prejudice and Zombies,* a literary mash-up in which flesh-eaters are introduced into the world of Jane Austen. Although the book was a bestseller and the film boasted a budget of $28 million, the adaptation (directed by Burr Steers) died swiftly at the box office.

In 2003, a remake of the 1974 proto-slasher *The Texas Chainsaw Massacre* became a hit, unleashing an era of horror movie remakes. A year later, Zack Snyder's remake of *Dawn of the Dead* dropped and almost instantly inspired a wave of zombie reboots and sequels. Snyder's version kept the idea of a group of survivors holed up in a shopping mall but swapped out Romero's slow-moving walking dead for fast-moving monsters—an idea first explored two years earlier in *28 Days Later,* which, while technically not a zombie film, since its infected aren't dead, nonetheless used many of the tropes of the zombie apocalypse subgenre to great effect. After directing a number of superhero films, Snyder returned to the zombie-action story in 2021 with *Army of the Dead,* an attempt to mash up the zombie and heist film genres.

Dawn of the Dead wasn't the only Romero property to provide fodder for a remake. *Night of the Living Dead* has been remade (aside from the Romero-produced version in 1990) as *Night of the Living Dead 3D* (2006); *Night of the Living Dead: Resurrection* (2012), which replaces Ben with a Final Girl as lone survivor, an idea already explored in Romero's remake; the animated *Night of the Living Dead: Darkest Dawn* (2015); and *Night of the Animated Dead* (2021), a second attempt at rendering the classic tale into animation. Romero's *Day of the Dead* also received a very loose remake in 2008.

The 2007 Robert Rodriguez film *Planet Terror* certainly had one of the odder origin stories: it was originally part of the double feature *Grindhouse,* which paired it with Quentin Tarantino's *Death Proof.* When *Grindhouse* performed badly at the box office, *Planet Terror* was re-edited, extended by fourteen minutes, and released internationally. *Planet Terror* stars Rose McGowan as go-go dancer Cherry Darling, who loses her leg in a zombie attack and eventually replaces it with a machine gun. The film was received well overall by critics and has proved to be a popular DVD and Blu-ray release.

ABOVE LEFT: One-sheet for *Resident Evil* (2002). Milla Jovovich had already been cast as Alice when director Paul W. S. Anderson added Michelle Rodriguez to the cast as Rain. Anderson incurred Jovovich's wrath when he rewrote the script, giving some of Alice's action to Rodriguez's character. They eventually reached a satisfactory compromise.

TOP RIGHT: Alternative poster design for *Resident Evil: Village* by the Australian artist Hyam Cacerez. *Village* was released in 2021 as a follow-up to *Resident Evil 7: Biohazard*. The plot of the game follows military man Ethan Winters as he searches for his kidnapped daughter; he has to negotiate the four rulers of the village, as well as the werewolf-like "Lycans."

BOTTOM RIGHT: Japanese poster for *Resident Evil: The Final Chapter* (2016), the sixth film in the franchise and the last to star Milla Jovovich. It wasn't the final *Resident Evil* feature film, however: 2021's *Resident Evil: Welcome to Raccoon City* attempted to reboot the entire cinematic franchise.

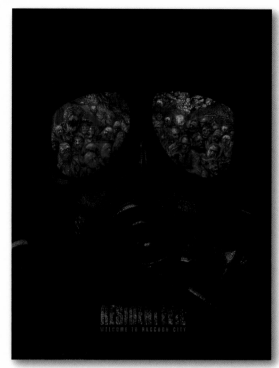

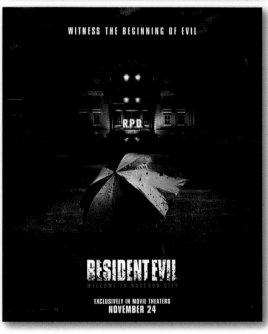

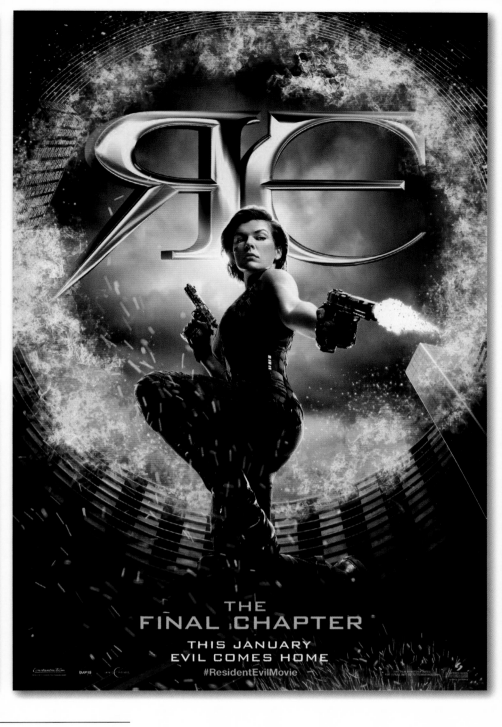

TOP LEFT: "I See Evil," a digital artwork for *Resident Evil: Welcome to Raccoon City* by B4 Abraham, a visual designer currently residing in Dubai. "I wanted to capture the horror of the place in one single image—a simple closeup of the man in the mask reflecting the zombies and creatures, keeping the imagery frightening and bloody without overcrowding the design," he notes.

BOTTOM LEFT: Advance poster for *Welcome to Raccoon City*. A stylized red-and-white umbrella is the logo for the sinister Umbrella Corporation that is a central thread throughout the *Resident Evil* universe; since *Welcome to Raccoon City* was a reboot, making the umbrella a centerpiece let fans know that it would stay true to the original game.

ABOVE RIGHT: One-sheet for *Resident Evil: The Final Chapter* (2016). The plot returns Alice and other survivors of the apocalypse to the Hive (the Umbrella Corporation's underground facility), where they discover that the company has created an airborne antivirus that can rid the world of zombies—but it's up to Alice to stop the company from killing the last humans first.

"A WEAVERESQUE TURN": MILLA JOVOVICH

"A virus escaped. A lot of people died. The trouble was, they didn't stay dead."

Alice in *Resident Evil: Retribution* (2012)

From the time that Sigourney Weaver's Ellen Ripley began kicking ass in 1979's *Alien*, it was perhaps pre-destined that some zombie movie would also feature a no-nonsense woman soldier. That woman arrived in 2002 in the form of Alice, the conflicted security head of the sinister Umbrella Corporation, who ends up having her memory wiped, fighting off hordes of zombies, and being genetically altered herself through the course of the six live action *Resident Evil* films that that center around her.

When it came time to cast Alice, the filmmakers turned to twenty-four-year-old Milla Jovovich, who enthusiastically auditioned because she and her brother were fans of the videogame. Jovovich was born in Ukraine in 1975; her mother was a Russian actress, and the family lived in Moscow for a time before immigrating to the United States when Jovovich was five. She began modeling at nine and studied acting at ten, landing her first role, in the thriller *Two Moon Junction*, when she was twelve. At fifteen, she appeared nude in the film *Return to the Blue Lagoon*, generating considerable controversy.

Her real breakthrough role, however, came after she left the United States for France and was cast by Luc Besson as the alien Leeloo in his science-fiction epic *The Fifth Element* (1997). She married Besson later that year (it was her second marriage), but they divorced two years later. She went on to marry her *Resident Evil* director Paul W. S. Anderson in 2009 (despite accidentally punching him in the eye during one action close-up); they have three children together. Their oldest, Ever Anderson, has also taken up acting; she played the young Natasha Romanoff in the 2021 film *Black Widow*.

For *The Fifth Element*, Jovovich's fight against the brutish alien Mangalores was nominated for the MTV Movie Award for Best Fight, and before launching into *Resident Evil* the actress engaged in studying more fighting skills. Critics took note upon the film's release; although *Resident Evil* received mostly negative notices, Jovovich's performance and skills were lauded: *Variety*'s Scott Foundas praised the film for "immersing viewers in a kinetic onslaught of flesh (namely, that of Milla Jovovich)." In an odd juxtaposition, at the same time that Jovovich was portraying Alice in the *Resident Evil* films, she was one of the world's highest paid models, with close ties to Prada, Versace, and L'Oréal cosmetics.

Jovovich has played two other women protagonists in action/science-fiction films: 2006's *Ultraviolet*, written and directed by Kurt Wimmer, a critical and box-office bomb that Jovovich was openly displeased with; and 2020's *Monster Hunter*, written and directed by Paul W. S. Anderson, and based on another Capcom game. Jovovich has joked about Anderson writing the script for her to star in: "So when he brought me this version and said, 'I wrote this one for you and I think it's the best one I've done,' I was like, 'Are you kidding me? We just closed *Resident Evil*. I've been fighting zombies for the last fifteen years and now you want me to kill monsters?'" Released during the second year

> When it came time to cast Alice, the filmmakers turned to twenty-four-year-old Milla Jovovich, who enthusiastically auditioned because she and her brother were fans of the videogame.

of the COVID-19 pandemic, the film was a box-office dud; although reviewers liked Jovovich's performance, other aspects of the film were not so well reviewed. Anderson and Jovovich had hoped to make a sequel, but that now seems unlikely.

Jovovich has also pursued musical ambitions, releasing two studio albums in the 1990s. In another artistic sideline, she has been involved with fashion design, joining with fellow model Carmen Hawk in 2003 to launch the Jovovich-Hawk clothing line (which ended in 2008).

Jovovich recently appeared in the 2019 reboot of *Hellboy*, playing the main antagonist, the Blood Queen; the Spanish science fiction film *Paradise Hills* (also 2019); and 2018's *Future World*, co-directed by and starring James Franco.

In a 2020 interview for Polygon.com, Jovovich talked about her lifelong love of science fiction: "I remember growing up in the '80s when there were really no female action heroes. Then I watched *Aliens*. I saw Sigourney Weaver going to space and kicking alien butt, and it felt good and inspiring to see a woman doing these things. I had the same feeling with *Terminator* and Linda Hamilton." The interview was appropriately titled, "Milla Jovovich is in the action movie pantheon now."

RESIDENT EVIL: AFTERLIFE

RIGHT: Alternative poster for *Resident Evil: Afterlife* (2010) by the American artist Andre M. Barnett. The fourth of the *Resident Evil* feature films (and the first to be filmed in 3-D), *Afterlife* sets much of its action in a postapocalyptic Los Angeles, where Alice fights both zombies and the Umbrella Corporation as she attempts to rescue survivors.

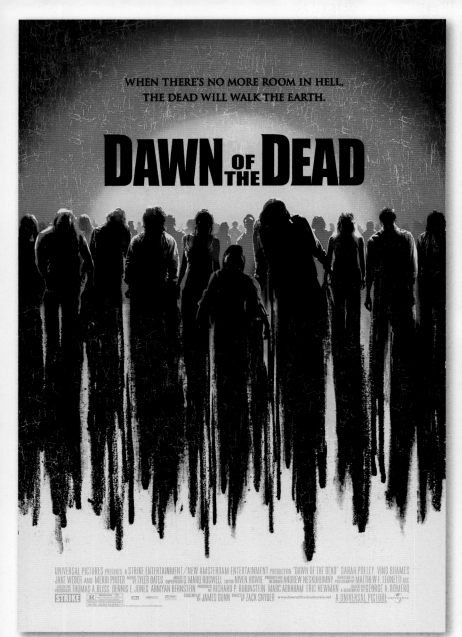

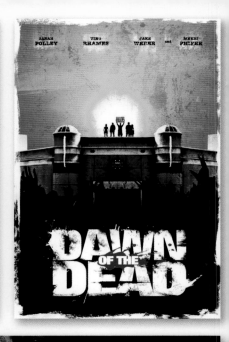

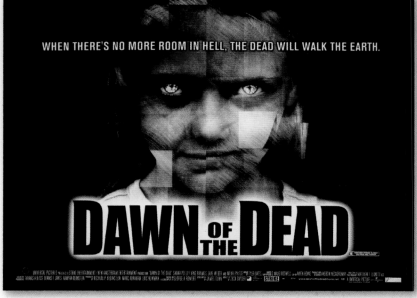

ABOVE LEFT: Advance one-sheet for the 2004 remake of *Dawn of the Dead*. This version's story retains only the central premise of the original film—a group of survivors holed up in a shopping mall during a zombie apocalypse—and creates its own characters and situations, essentially jettisoning Romero's social satire in favor of action.

TOP MIDDLE: Promotional ad for *Dawn of the Dead* (2004). The film marked the directorial debut of Zack Snyder, who would go on to be known for directing numerous comic-book adaptations, including *300* (2006), *Watchmen* (2009), *Man of Steel* (2013), *Batman vs. Superman: Dawn of Justice* (2016), and *Zack Snyder's Justice League* (2021).

TOP RIGHT: Alternative poster for *Dawn of the Dead* (2004) by Hungarian artist Ferenc Konya. The film's zombie effects were supplied by David LeRoy Anderson, who also worked on *The Serpent and the Rainbow* (1988) and *The Cabin in the Woods* (2011), assisted by his wife, Heather Langenkamp, who starred as Nancy in *A Nightmare on Elm Street* (1984).

BOTTOM RIGHT: British quad poster for *Dawn of the Dead* (2004). Richard Rubinstein, who produced Romero's *Dawn of the Dead*, turned down other offers to buy the remake rights, but he was swayed by producers Eric Newman and Marc Abraham because they wanted to make a film with "attitude."

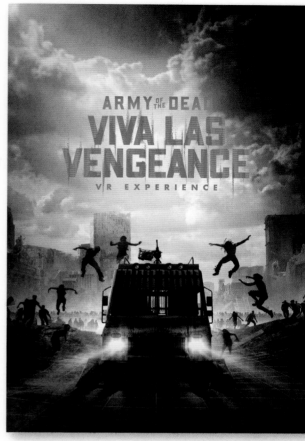

ABOVE LEFT: Promotional ad for *Army of the Dead* (2021). Zack Snyder's "spiritual successor" to his *Dawn of the Dead* combines horror and heist with a plot about a group of mercenaries hired by a Vegas casino owner to battle through the zombie horde that has overrun the city and retrieve $200 million from a secret vault before the city is nuked.

TOP RIGHT: *Army of the Dead: Viva Las Vengeance* is an immersive VR experience that hands guests a gun and a VR headset and takes them for a ride in an armored taco truck through a zombie-infested city. It ties directly into *Army of the Dead*, offering not just the experience but props (including the film's zombie tiger) and of course branded merchandise.

BOTTOM RIGHT: One-sheet for *Army of the Dead*, which had a brief theatrical run in 2021 before taking up residence on Netflix. The film, conceived by Zack Snyder, was first announced in 2007, with Dutch filmmaker Matthijs van Heijningen, Jr. set to direct. It has already spun off a non-zombie prequel, *Army of Thieves* (2021).

The Re-Dawning: Zack Snyder

American film director Zack Snyder may be most well-known for his work on movies set within the DC Comics franchise, including *Watchmen* (2009), *Man of Steel* (2013) and *Justice League* (2017), so it's perhaps easy to forget that he started not with superheroes but zombies. In 2004, Snyder's first film was the remake of George Romero's *Dawn of the Dead*; he had previously directed television commercials and was excited by the possibility of "re-envisioning" Romero's classic. He opted to update his zombies by making them fast—a decision that paid off handsomely, because *Dawn of the Dead* was a smash hit. In 2021, Snyder made a second zombie movie, *Army of the Dead,* which launched in selected theaters and on Netflix, where it became one of the streaming service's most-watched originals. There are now several *Army of the Dead* spin-off and sequel projects in development.

ABOVE: Zack Snyder at work on *Army of the Dead*. Snyder, whom Variety once called "one of the most divisive filmmakers of the twenty-first century," ended up directing, co-writing, co-producing, and shooting the film.

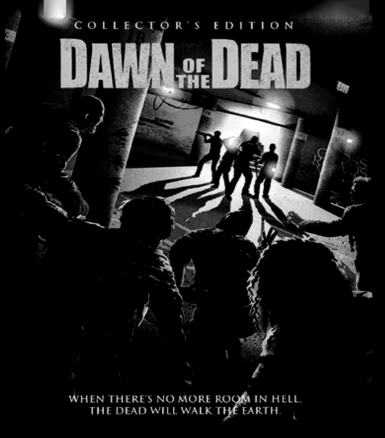

TOP LEFT: Slipcase cover for Shout! Factory's Blu-ray Collector's Edition release of *Dawn of the Dead*, featuring the work of the French artist Nathanael Marsh. *Dawn of the Dead* was a big box-office hit, grossing over $100 million worldwide and leading to a plethora of zombie movie remakes and knockoffs.

BOTTOM LEFT: A promotional still of *Dawn of the Dead*'s fast zombies in action. Although both Dan O'Bannon (in 1985's *Return of the Living Dead*) and Danny Boyle (in 2002's *28 Days Later*) could lay claim to having used fast zombies before *Dawn of the Dead*, there's no question that Snyder's film popularized them.

ABOVE RIGHT: International one-sheet for *Dawn of the Dead*. The film launched two careers behind the camera: in addition to marking the debut of Zack Snyder, it was also the breakthrough screenplay by James Gunn, who would go on to write and direct *Slither* (2006), *Guardians of the Galaxy* (2014), and *The Suicide Squad* (2021).

TOP LEFT: Cover art for the first *Dead Rising* videogame, created by Keiji Inafune and released by Capcom in 2006. The game follows photojournalist Frank West as he finds himself trapped in a shopping mall during a zombie outbreak in the fictitious town of Willamette, Colorado. The series has since been extended through five full games plus various expansions and remakes.

BOTTOM LEFT: Cover art from the soundtrack to *Dead Rising 3*. This installment centers on mechanic Nick Ramos as he tries to survive a zombie infestation in the fictitious town of Los Perdidos, California. The zombies in *Dead Rising* are generally less dangerous, singly, than those in *Resident Evil*, but there are many more of them for players to deal with.

ABOVE RIGHT: Poster for the feature film *Dead Rising: Endgame*. The videogame franchise has spun off three feature films: *Zombrex: Dead Rising Sun* (2010), *Dead Rising: Watchtower* (2015), and *Dead Rising: Endgame* (2016). The first of the three was a Japanese production; the last two were English-language releases and were made available via the free streaming service Crackle.

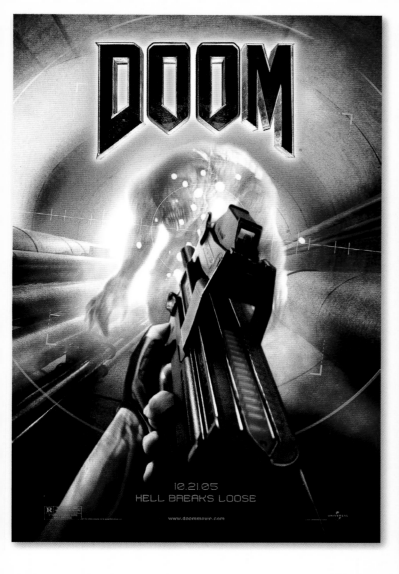

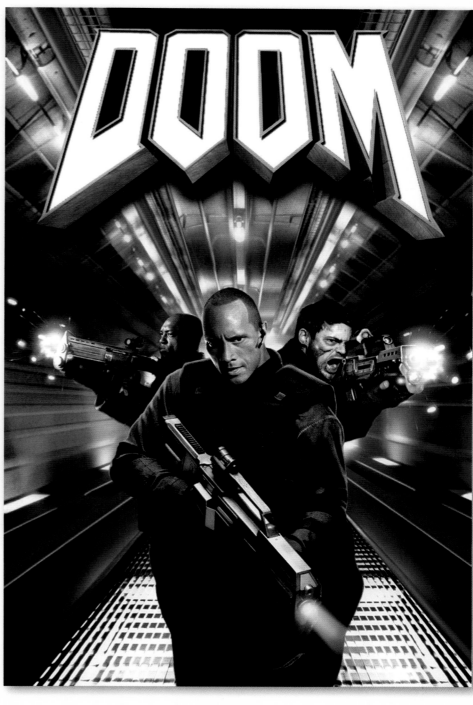

ABOVE LEFT: Bus-shelter poster for the feature film version of *Doom* (2005). The influential videogame was first released in 1993 by id Software, and was an early pioneer in first person shooter games. Players inhabit the point of view of an unnamed Marine dealing with a horde of demons and undead monsters.

ABOVE RIGHT: Cover art from the DVD release of *Doom* (2005). Despite a cast that includes action star Dwayne "The Rock" Johnson (center) and Karl Urban (right), *Doom* lived up to its name at the box office. A second film, *Doom: Annihilation*, was released direct to video in 2019, but it was disowned by id Software.

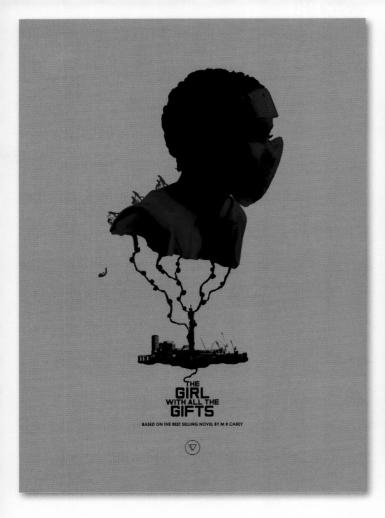

ABOVE LEFT: Alternative poster design for *The Girl with All the Gifts* (2016) by Lewis Dowsett. Mike Carey, who wrote both the original novel and the screenplay, said that he wanted to explore "science zombies," as compared to "supernatural zombies." The novel was based on Carey's short story "Ighigenia in Aulis" (2013).

ABOVE RIGHT: Advance one-sheet poster for *The Girl with All the Gifts*. Although the film underperformed at the box office, it garnered both critical praise and awards, winning "Best Horror Feature" at the Austin Fantastic Fest and "Best Non-U.S. Release" from the Online Film Critics Society.

TOP LEFT: Japanese *chirashi* poster for *28 Days Later* focusing on the protagonist, Jim (Cillian Murphy), who has just awakened from a coma to find the world in turmoil. Danny Boyle and Alex Garland, the director and writer of the first film, have reportedly discussed producing a third film in the series.

BOTTOM LEFT: German poster for *28 Weeks Later*, the 2007 sequel to *28 Days Later*. With director Juan Carlos Fresnadillo taking over from Danny Boyle, this second film in the series is set in a London slowly recovering from the devastation wrought by "Rage," as the infected begin to die of starvation.

ABOVE RIGHT: One-sheet poster for Danny Boyle's breakout hit *28 Days Later* (2002). Scripted by Alex Garland, the story focuses on the character of Jim (Cillian Murphy), who awakens from twenty-eight days in a coma to find that the world has been devastated by a virus called "Rage" that turns the afflicted into mindless maniacs.

Living on Planet Terror: Robert Rodriguez

Robert Rodriguez has tackled more genres than most filmmakers: action, horror, children's adventure, and comic-book adaptations. He first came onto the scene with *El Mariachi*, a stylish "neo-western" he made, aged twenty-three, for $7,000. The idea of doing a zombie movie first came to him when he was directing *The Faculty* (1998); at the time, zombie movies had largely vanished, but Rodriguez intuited that they'd be making a big comeback. He wrote half the script, ran into a stumbling block, and put it away, only to pull it out when he and Quentin Tarantino started talking about doing an anthology movie called *Grindhouse*. One of the last elements he added was Cherry's machine-gun leg, because he wanted the poster to have a powerful, '70s-style image. Rodriguez once described *Planet Terror* as the movie that John Carpenter and George Romero might have made if they'd ever teamed up.

ABOVE: Robert Rodriguez behind the camera on the set of *Planet Terror*. In addition to writing, directing, and co-producing the film, renaissance man Rodriguez also shot it, co-edited it, and scored it.

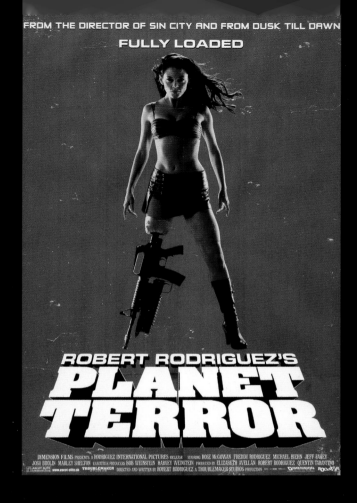

ABOVE LEFT: The heroine in *Planet Terror*, Cherry Darling (Rose McGowan), replaces the leg she loses to zombies with an assault rifle. Asked if he worried about having the idea stolen before his movie came out, writer/director Robert Rodriguez said, "No. I thought that even if somebody did hear about the idea and made their own machine gun leg movie, it would be more sleek. Ours was gonna be really raw."

ABOVE RIGHT: Alternative poster for Rodriguez's *From Dusk Till Dawn* (1996) by Chris Barnes. As well as featuring stars George Clooney (top left), Salma Hayek (center), and Quentin Tarantino (top right), this image also includes Tom Savini (lower right) in his role as "Sex Machine."

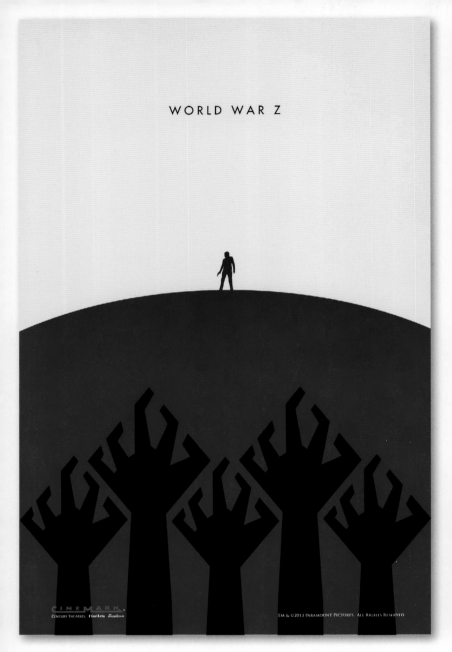

WORLD WAR Z

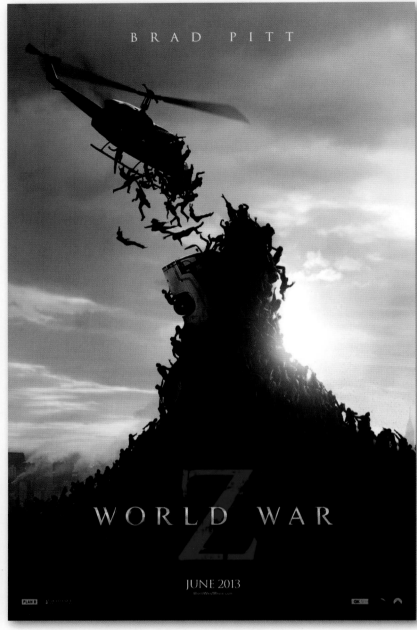

BRAD PITT

WORLD WAR Z

JUNE 2013

ABOVE LEFT: Cinemark exclusive mini-poster for *World War Z* featuring artwork by Matt Ferguson. George Romero was not a fan of the film version of *World War Z*, as he believed zombie stories are more successful on a smaller, more intimate scale.

ABOVE RIGHT: One-sheet for *World War Z*. The film's zombies aren't just fast, they can also pile on top of each other to crest walls. They're also attracted by sound and can be repelled by sickness (although the film never explains why the dead would have to worry about illness). In one early draft, they were fought off with shovel-like weapons called "lobos"— short for "lobotomizers."

OPPOSITE: This painting by the Barcelona-based artist David Benzal illustrates the moment in *World War Z* when Gerry Lane (Brad Pitt) confronts a teeth-chattering zombie portrayed by Michael Jenn.

Zombie Masters: KNB FX Group

Although the KNB FX Group is probably now most recognized for creating the zombies for the hit television series *The Walking Dead*, the company was making the dead walk long before that series debuted in 2010. Founded in 1988 by makeup effects wizards Robert Kurtzman, Greg Nicotero, and Howard Berger, KNB can trace its zombie lineage back to George Romero's *Day of the Dead* (1985), when Berger and Nicotero both worked under Tom Savini. (Nicotero also has a small acting role in the film as "Private Johnson.") Just prior to forming KNB, all three worked on *Evil Dead II* (1987); since then, they've loaned their expertise to *Army of Darkness, Land of the Dead, Diary of the Dead, Planet Terror*, and dozens of other films and television series. They received an Academy Award for their work on *The Chronicles of Narnia: The Lion, the Witch and the Wardrobe* (2006).

TOP LEFT: KNB FX Group, Inc. co-founder Greg Nicotero with some of the company's zombie creations. Born in Pittsburgh, Nicotero got his start on Romero's *Day of the Dead*; since then, he has moved on to directing, with thirty-seven episodes of *The Walking Dead* to his name. He also occasionally plays a "walker" in the show.

BOTTOM LEFT: Gas-station attendant turned zombie ringleader Big Daddy (Eugene Clark) wields a severed head in a chilling moment from the fourth film in Romero's *Living Dead* series, *Land of the Dead* (2005).

ABOVE RIGHT: "Who's laughing now?" Ash Williams (Bruce Campbell) comes under attack by his own zombified severed hand in a scene from *Evil Dead II*. KNB's Howard Berger handled the special effects makeup for Campbell's character in the film.

RIGHT: Promotional poster for AMC's television series *The Walking Dead* (2010–2022). Based on the graphic novels written by Robert Kirkman and drawn by Tony Moore and Charlie Adlard, the series was developed by Frank Darabont and proved to be nothing less than a cultural phenomenon.

THE WALKING DEAD

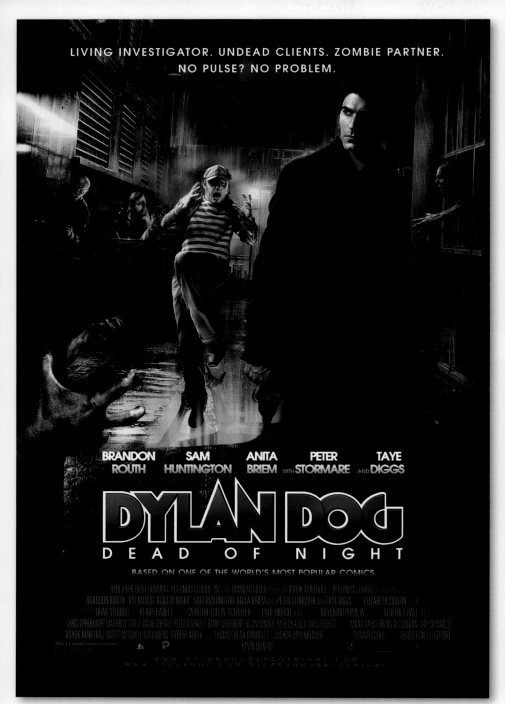

LIVING INVESTIGATOR. UNDEAD CLIENTS. ZOMBIE PARTNER.
NO PULSE? NO PROBLEM.

BRANDON   SAM   ANITA   PETER   TAYE
ROUTH   HUNTINGTON BRIEM WITH STORMARE AND DIGGS

DYLAN DOG
DEAD OF NIGHT

BASED ON ONE OF THE WORLD'S MOST POPULAR COMICS.

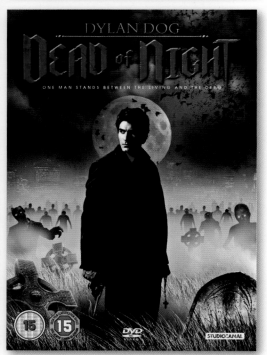

ABOVE LEFT: Although it has direct ties to 1994's *Dellamorte Dellamore* (a.k.a. *Cemetery Man*) via the character Francesco Dellamorte, the first official *Dylan Dog* movie did not appear until 2011, with Brandon Routh taking on the role. The film bombed with audiences and critics, ruling out the possibility of more.

TOP RIGHT: The Italian comic book series *Dylan Dog* debuted in 1986. Created by Tiziano Sclavi, the first issue was titled "L'alba dei morti viventi," or "Dawn of the Living Dead," and was an instant bestseller. The original artist, Claudio Villa, based the taciturn eponymous character on actor Rupert Everett, who would fittingly go on to star in the film adaptation of Sclavi's *Dellamorte Dellamore*.

BOTTOM RIGHT: Cover art from the U.K. DVD release of *Dylan Dog: Dead of Night*, focusing on Brandon Routh as the laconic title character. The film includes vampires, werewolves, demons—and zombies, who here are intelligent and who attend "zombie support groups."

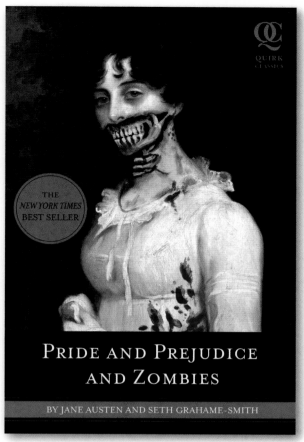

PRIDE AND PREJUDICE AND ZOMBIES

BY JANE AUSTEN AND SETH GRAHAME-SMITH

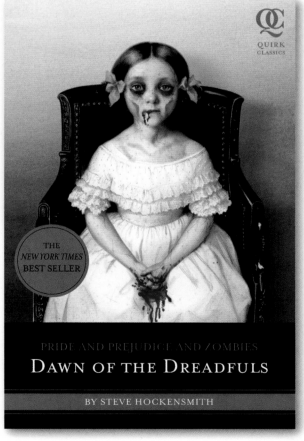

PRIDE AND PREJUDICE AND ZOMBIES

DAWN OF THE DREADFULS

BY STEVE HOCKENSMITH

ABOVE LEFT: Advance one-sheet for *Pride and Prejudice and Zombies*. The film had a troubled history, going through numerous directors before it settled on Burr Steers, who had previously directed the features *Igby Goes Down* (2002), *17 Again* (2009), and *Charlie St. Cloud* (2010). Many critics felt that, while the film had its moments, it quickly ran out of steam.

TOP RIGHT: The initial concept for the 2009 novel *Pride and Prejudice and Zombies* was first suggested by Quirk Books editor Jason Rekulak to author Seth Grahame-Smith, whose job it was then to mix zombie action directly into Jane Austen's literary classic.

BOTTOM RIGHT: *Pride and Prejudice and Zombies* was successful enough to spawn a prequel, *Dawn of the Dreadfuls* (2007), which details how heroine Elizabeth Bennet learned the skills necessary to become a seasoned zombie hunter. Steve Hockensmith was brought in to write the book because Seth Grahame-Smith was busy at the time writing *Abraham Lincoln, Vampire Hunter*.

7
ZOMBIES AROUND THE WORLD

"YOU . . . YOU'RE INFECTED."

SEOK-WOO IN *TRAIN TO BUSAN* (2016)

> "We've always had talented filmmakers. And we've made horror comedies before . . .
> I just happened to be the guy that grew up loving zombie films."
>
> Alejandro Brugués, in a 2011 interview with *Miami New Times*

Zombies began as a component of Afro-Caribbean Vodou, but after they were remade into mindless flesh-eaters in 1968 (with thanks to reviewers who used the Z-word that George Romero didn't in *Night of the Living Dead*), they shambled past American pop culture and spread around the world. Just as America exported other forms of artistic expression in the past (jazz music, comic books, Halloween), the modern cannibalistic zombies soon truly walked the earth.

Even before Lucio Fulci claimed the zombie genre for himself in the late 1970s, Italy was a prime breeding ground for the undead. The great Mario Bava (whose earlier films like *Black Sunday*, *Black Sabbath*, and *Planet of the Vampires* are now considered classics) directed 1972's *Baron Blood* (*Gli orrori del castello di Norimberga*) about a young American, Peter Kleist (Antonio Cantafora), visiting his ancestral castle to research his ancestor, Baron von Kleist, who was known for his sadism and whose victims rise to wreak vengeance. Andrea Bianchi's *Burial Ground* (*Le notti del terrore*, 1981) follows a group of wealthy vacationers who are forced to endure a zombie siege in an isolated villa; while it offers some inventive makeup (notably one zombie whose face is covered with live maggots) and some social commentary (the decadence of the very rich), it's most remembered now for its disturbing scenes of a woman breastfeeding her teenage son, who is actually played by a small adult.

Cult director Pupi Avati's *Zeder* (also known as *Revenge of the Dead*, 1983) combines zombies with the popular Italian *giallo* style. The plot concerns a writer (played by Gabriele Lavia, who also made several films with Italian maestro Dario Argento) who receives a typewriter that offers up strange messages that lead him into a mystery centering on "K-zones"—ancient historical sites scattered around the world that can return the dead to life. The film is atmospheric and eerie, and the ending—as the writer performs the ultimate test of a K-zone—is genuinely shocking.

The success of Lucio Fulci's 1979 *Zombi 2* (*Zombi* was the Italian title for Romero's *Dawn of the Dead*) engendered a series of unrelated films that bore related titles. *Zombi 3* (1988), codirected by Fulci and Bruno Mattei, is set in the Philippines and concerns a leaked government experiment that resurrects the dead; *Zombi 4: After Death* (1988), directed by Claudio Fragasso, returns to voodoo and an isolated island; and *Zombi 5: Killing Birds* (1989), directed by Aristide Massaccesi and Claudio Lattanzi, takes place in Louisiana and features both zombies and . . . well, killing birds. Another Italian horror series began in 1985 with the Dario Argento–produced, Lamberto Bava–directed *Demons* (*Dèmoni*), about demonic creatures that possess dead bodies and return to life as violent, goo-spewing monsters.

Spain produced several early zombie entries, including *Let Sleeping Corpses Lie* (*No profanar el sueño de los muertos*, also known as *The Living Dead at Manchester Morgue*, 1974), in which the dead are called back to life by experimental farming equipment designed to kill insects. However, a more recent Spanish film made a bigger impact: 2007's *Rec*, directed by Jaume Balagueró and Paco Plaza. Considered by many to be one of the best "found footage" films ever made, *Rec* follows a news crew into an apartment building where a viral outbreak has led to an infestation of zombies. It also inaugurated a franchise with the final entry, *Rec 4: Apocalypse*, released in 2014.

Spanish horror icon Paul Naschy tackled zombies in several films, most notably *Vengeance of the Zombies* (*La rebelión de las muertas*), made in 1972, Naschy's most prolific year, but not released internationally until 1974, in which he appears as a heroic Indian fakir, a mutilated voodoo master, and the Devil; and *The Hanging Woman* (*La

Even before Lucio Fulci claimed the zombie genre for himself in the late 1970s, Italy was a prime breeding ground for the undead.

orgia de los muertos*, also 1972), in which he has a supporting role as a gravedigger.

The 1970s French filmmaker Jean Rollin specialized in dreamy, erotic-tinged horror films, and he tackled zombies in two of them: *The Grapes of Death* (*Les raisins de la mort*, 1978) and *The Living Dead Girl* (*La morte vivante*, 1982). Later French zombie films include *La Horde* (2009), in which cops join forces with criminals to fight off a zombie invasion of Paris; and *The Night Eats the World* (*La nuit a dévoré le monde*, 2018), based on a popular novel by Pit Agarmen, about a single man (played by Norwegian actor Anders Danielsen Lie) fending for himself in a large apartment building during a zombie apocalypse.

Great Britain and Ireland have been making zombie films since the 1960s (principally the excellent Hammer production *The Plague of the Zombies*). More recent releases include 2008's *Colin*, written and directed by Marc Price on a budget of £45 (around $70 at the time); the eponymous character is zombified in the film's opening minutes, and the film is told from his point of view. The cleverly titled *Boy Eats Girl* (2005) is an Irish zom-rom-com that posits snake venom as a cure to the zombie virus.

PREVIOUS SPREAD: Cover art for Death Waltz Recording Co.'s release of Giuliano Sorgini's soundtrack to *The Living Dead at Manchester Morgue*. The wailing screams heard in the music were provided by the film's director, Jorge Grau. The art is by British artist Luke Insect, who calls his style "oddball surrealism and psychedelic pop art."

FUIR.
SE CACHER.

MAIS NE JAMAIS CESSER DE FILMER.

[●REC]

UN FILM DE
JAUME BALAGUERÓ & PACO PLAZA

PRIX DU PUBLIC · PRIX DU JURY
FESTIVAL DE GÉRARDMER 2008 · FESTIVAL DE SITGES 2007

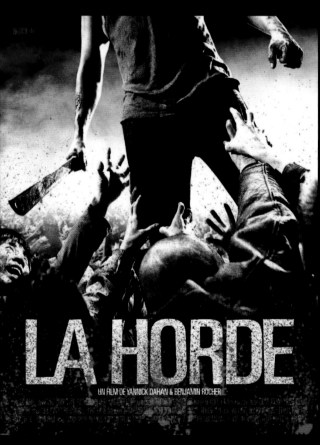

ABOVE LEFT: French poster for *Rec* (2007), a Spanish found footage-zombie movie that premiered within a few months of George Romero's similarly styled *Diary of the Dead*. Directed and written by Jaume Balagueró and Paco Plaza (with Luis A. Berdejo also contributing to the script), *Rec* is one of the most acclaimed zombie films of the last twenty years.

TOP RIGHT: Cover art from the DVD release of Andrea Bianchi's *Burial Ground* (a.k.a. *The Nights of Terror*, 1981) by the American artist Wes Benscoter, centered on wealthy Evelyn (Mariangela Giordano, credited here as Maria Angela Giordan) as she protectively embraces her son Michael (the twenty-five-year-old Pietro Barzocchini, here named as Peter Bark).

BOTTOM RIGHT: French poster for *La Horde* (*The Horde*, 2009). Directed by Benjamin Rocher and Yannick Dahan, this French film finds a group of cops tangling with a gang of drug dealers when a zombie outbreak happens, forcing them to work together.

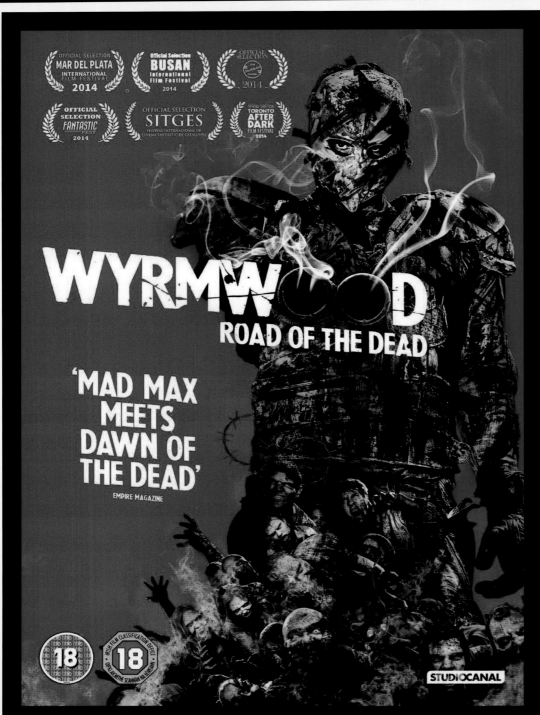

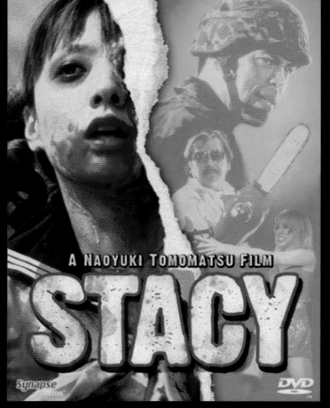

ABOVE LEFT: Cover art from the British DVD release of the Australian film *Wyrmwood: Road of the Dead* (also known as simply *Wyrmwood*, 2014), directed by Kiah Roache-Turner. In *Wyrmwood*, the zombie apocalypse is caused by a meteor shower; hero Barry (Jay Gallagher) survives because he's wearing a gas mask.

TOP RIGHT: One-sheet for the Canadian film *Pontypool* (2008), directed by Bruce McDonald and based on the novel *Pontypool Changes Everything* by Tony Burgess, who also wrote the screenplay. The film is set in a radio station during the outbreak of a disease that's spread by language and causes victims to try to consume each other.

BOTTOM RIGHT: DVD cover artwork for Naoyuki Tomomatsu's *Stacy* (a.k.a. *Stacy: Attack of the Schoolgirl Zombies*, 2001). In this Japanese zom-com, only teenage girls are affected by a zombie outbreak; once they contract the virus, they experience a period of "Near Death Happiness" (or NDH), followed by death and then resurrection as flesh-eaters.

One of the most extreme zombie movies of the last decade is also the first Belgian zombie film: *Yummy* (2019), directed by Lars Damoiseaux and based on a 2016 short called "Patient Zero." *Yummy* is set in a large, busy hospital that specializes in plastic surgery, and the extensive gore effects involve bags of human fat, a legless woman trailing blood, a surgically enhanced penis, entrails used as a climbing rope, and more.

The Middle East has produced several zombie movies, most notably the Israeli *JeruZalem* (2015), which combines zombies, a gateway to hell, demons, possession, and the End of Days; and the Bahraini *Dead Sands* (2013), about a group of strangers uniting to fend off a zombie attack.

In India, where the Bollywood musical has reigned supreme for decades, filmmakers started to tentatively venture into zombie territory with *Go Goa Gone* (2013), which combines comedy, action, and horror; however, the film was a failure financially and critically, and as a result Indian zombie films remain few and far between.

The Nigerian film industry (often called "Nollywood") has been burgeoning since the 2010s and has produced one acclaimed zombie film, *Ojuju* (2014). Directed by C. J. "Fiery" Obasi, it is set in a Nigerian slum where tainted water (a real problem in the country) has led to a zombie outbreak.

"Don't stop shooting!"

Director Higurashi in *One Cut of the Dead* (2017)

During the 1990s, Japanese filmmakers developed their own form of high-octane, blood-drenched horror movies, which led to zombies being thrown in some genuinely fresh new directions. Movies like *Battle Girl: The Living Dead in Tokyo Bay* (1991), *Wild Zero* (1999), *Versus* (2000), and *Helldriver* (2010) were cheap, fast, and washed in scarlet. Possibly the most unusual of this crop is *Stacy: Attack of the Schoolgirl Zombies* (2001), in which the infection is contracted only by teenage girls who experience "NDH" (Near Death Happiness) before dying and becoming flesh-eating "Stacys." More recently, Shin'ichirō Ueda's film-within-a-film zom-com *One Cut of the Dead* (2017) went on to become one of the most wildly successful independent films of all time.

Hong Kong filmmakers made a few early curiosities, like the 1976 horror-martial arts mash-up *Black Magic 2 (Vengeance of the Zombies)*, before producing one certified classic in Wilson Yip's *Bio-Zombie* (1998), a variant of the "survivors trapped in a shopping mall" that has young gangster wannabees Woody Invincible (Jordan Chan) and Crazy Bee (Sam Lee) stuck in a labyrinthine downtown mall during a zombie outbreak.

South Korea's film industry has exploded since the 1990s—as Hong Kong's has receded—and in 2016 came the international hit *Train to Busan* (directed by Yeon Sang-ho), which takes the formula of a father (Gong Yoo) trying to protect his daughter (Kim Su-an) from rampaging zombies and sets its action almost entirely in a speeding train. Its success led to an animated prequel, *Seoul Station* (also 2016), and a live-action sequel, *Peninsula* (2020).

The Filipino *Trip Ubusan: The Lolas vs. Zombies* (2017) follows the three Lolas—played by comics Jose Manalo, Wally Bayola, and Paolo Ballesteros, reprising roles they'd made popular on a daytime talk show—as they fight off zombies created by infected meat.

As might be expected, Australian filmmakers have occasionally combined zombies with their most successful cinematic export—*Mad Max*–style action—in movies like *Wyrmwood* (2014) and *Wyrmwood: Apocalypse* (2021), while other entries like *Undead* (2003) and *Cargo* (2017) take advantage of the sprawling Australian landscape. *Little Monsters* (2019)—written and directed by Abe Forsythe and starring Lupita Nyong'o as a sweet, naïve teacher who finds herself defending her young students from zombies during a field trip to a nature reserve—focuses more on the resourceful teacher's attempts to protect her small charges than action or vistas.

New Zealand has produced mainly comedic zombie movies, beginning with Peter Jackson's neo-classic *Braindead* (1992) and continuing on through *Black Sheep* (2006), in which a virus is spread by undead, carnivorous livestock; *I Survived a Zombie Holocaust* (2014), like Japan's *One Cut of the Dead*, is centered on a movie crew shooting a zombie movie who find themselves confronting the real thing.

Some of the most unusual, thoughtful zombie movies have come from Canada. Like *28 Days Later*, *Pontypool* (2008)—directed by Bruce McDonald and written by Tony Burgess, based on his novel *Pontypool Changes Everything*—is technically not a zombie movie, since its infected aren't dead, but its scenes of infected chewing off body parts often earns it a slot in zombie movie lists. *Ravenous* (*Les Affamés*, 2017) is a French-language movie that infuses social commentary with a story of survival, while 2019's *Blood Quantum*, written and directed by the late Jeff Barnaby, is set on the Red Crow reservation, and posits that indigenous peoples are immune to the zombie virus (Barnaby was a native Mi'kmaq).

Although Mexico has produced surprisingly few zombie movies (aside from those involving wrestling stars like Santo), others have emerged from elsewhere in Central and Latin America and received considerable acclaim. The Venezuelan *Infection* (*Infección*, 2019) is an award-winner that uses fast zombies and social allegory, while Argentina's *Plaga Zombie* (1997) was successful enough to lead to three follow-ups, *Zona mutante* (2001) and *Revolución tóxica* (2012), and *American invasion* (2021). But the biggest Spanish-language international breakout hit was *Juan of the Dead* (*Juan de los Muertos*), written and directed by Alejandro Brugués. The film follows *Shaun of the Dead*'s lead in making Juan (Alexis Díaz de Villegas) a perennial loser who starts one of the most original businesses in horror cinema: a zombie-slaying company whose slogan is "Juan of the Dead, we kill your beloved ones."

ABOVE LEFT: One-sheet for Mario Bava's *Baron Blood* (1972). The film's first American showing took place in Philadelphia, where it was previewed alongside the Jim Brown action film *Slaughter*. Although most reviews were lukewarm, critics praised its atmosphere and setting. It was shot at the picturesque Austrian castle Burg Kreuzenstein.

TOP RIGHT: Italian *duo-foglio* poster for *Le notti del terrore* (a.k.a. *Burial Ground*, 1981), in which zombies are brought to life when an archaeologist enters an old crypt and unleashes a terrifying curse. The zombies are heavily decayed, but they use tools as they attempt to gain entrance to the lavish villa where the wealthy guests are cowering.

BOTTOM RIGHT: One-sheet for the 1985 American release of the Italian *Burial Ground*. Although the film was not officially classified as a "video nasty," twenty-five minutes were cut from the original British home video release (and then restored when it was re-released in 2004).

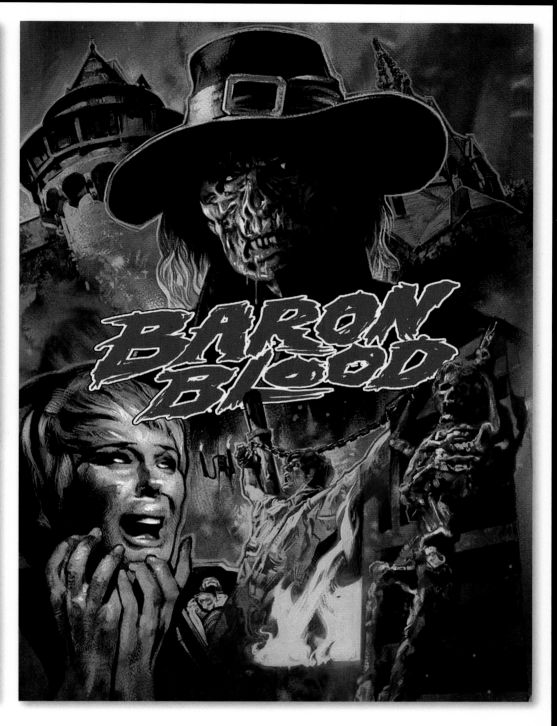

ABOVE LEFT: Italian *locandina* for *Baron Blood*. The film's original Italian title, *Gli orrori del castello di Norimberga*, translates to *The Horrors of Nuremberg Castle*. Star Elke Sommer would go on to make *Lisa and the Devil* (1973) with Mario Bava, widely considered to be one of Italian director's best films.

ABOVE RIGHT: Cover artwork for the 2013 Arrow Blu-ray release of *Baron Blood* by Graham Humphreys. In addition to the usual extras, this release includes three different versions of the film; the American International Pictures' version not only recut the film but replaced Stelvio Cipriani's score with a new one by Les Baxter.

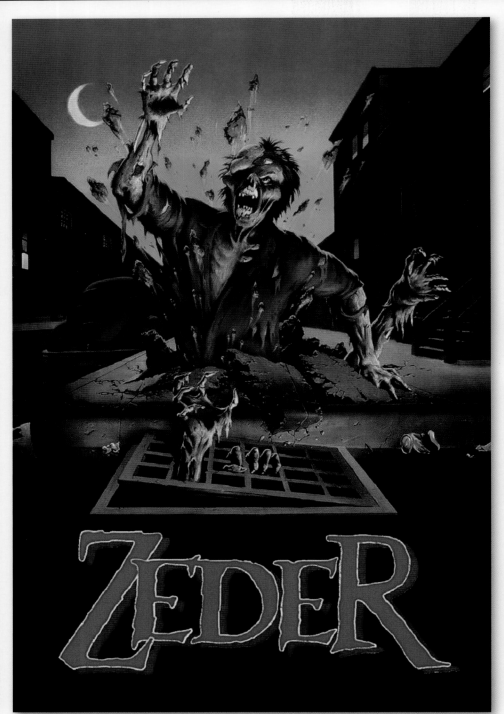

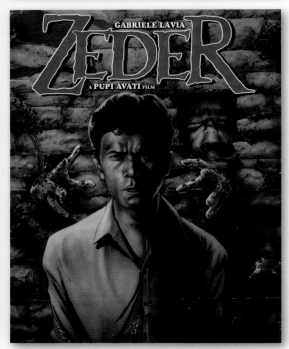

ABOVE LEFT: VHS artwork for Pupi Avati's 1983 thriller *Zeder*, also known as *Revenge of the Dead*. Although he is not as well known as some other Italian horror filmmakers, Avati has built a cult reputation for making dense, smart thrillers like *The House with Laughing Windows* (1976) and *The Arcane Enchanter* (1996).

TOP RIGHT: DVD cover artwork by Graham Humphreys for 88 Films' British release of *Zeder*. The toothless man shown in much of the film's promotional art is Don Luigi Costa (Carlo Schincaglia), a former priest who renounces his vows after contracting an incurable disease and has himself buried in a "K-zone" so he can return after death.

BOTTOM RIGHT: Orbit DVD's slipcover artwork for *Zeder*, as created by the American artist Nathan Thomas Milliner. Milliner has chosen to capture a scene from the movie's climax, wherein hero Stefano (Gabriele Lavia) leaps into a pit while crossing the mysterious K-zone, unaware of the fate he narrowly escapes.

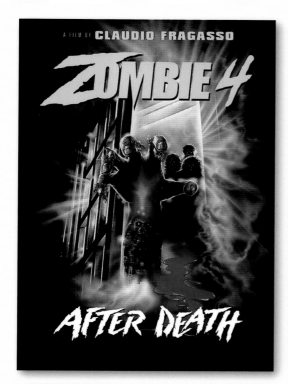

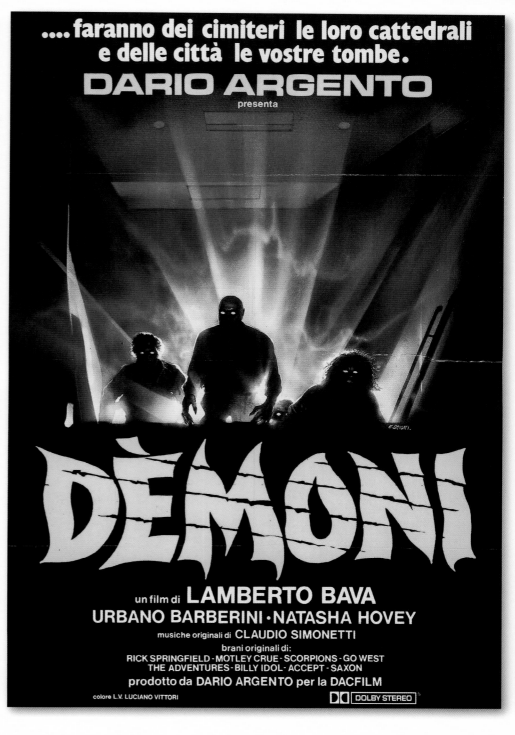

TOP LEFT: Promotional artwork for *Zombi 4: After Death* (1988), officially the fourth film to follow after George Romero's *Dawn of the Dead* was released in Europe as *Zombie*. *Zombi 4: After Death* is now chiefly notable for featuring the first performance by porn star Jeff Stryker in a non-porn movie.

BOTTOM LEFT: French poster for the Italian film *Zombi 5: Killing Birds*, initially released in France in 1988 under the title *L'attaque des morts-vivants* (*Attack of the Living Dead*). The film, which stars American actor Robert Vaughn, is set in Louisiana and combines zombies, bloodthirsty birds, and human killers.

ABOVE RIGHT: Italian *duo-foglio* poster for *Demons* (1985), showcasing the work of Italian artist Enzo Sciotti. The film was directed by Lamberto Bava, produced by Dario Argento, co-written by frequent Fulci collaborator Dardano Sacchetti, and has a score by Goblin co-founder Claudio Simonetti.

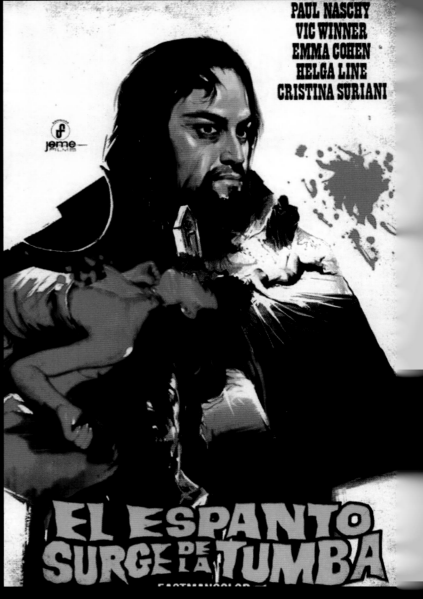

The Spanish Lon Chaney: Paul Naschy

Born Jacinto Molina Álvarez in 1934, Spanish horror star Paul Naschy is most famous for the series of movies he made about the tragic werewolf Count Waldemar Daninsky (there are twelve in all, although the films are unrelated in terms of plot), but he played nearly every other kind of monster, too, including vampires, black magicians, and even the Devil. After landing small roles in a few films, in 1968 he wrote *Frankenstein's Bloody Terror*, the first Waldemar Daninsky film, and took on the part when Lon Chaney, Jr. turned down the lycanthropic lead. He made his directorial debut with 1977's *Inquisition* (which he also wrote and starred in), and continued acting until his death in 2009 aged seventy-five., Naschy also appeared in many non-horror films during his career, but he nonetheless titled his 1997 autobiography *Memoirs of a Wolfman*. He was inducted into the Fangoria Hall of Fame in 2000.

ABOVE LEFT: Spanish poster for *The Fury of the Wolfman* (1970), the fourth of Naschy's twelve films about werewolf Waldemar Daninsky. This one—which suggests that Daninsky received the werewolf curse after being bitten by a yeti in Tibet—finds the title character trapped by a sadistic female mad scientist, Dr. Ellmann (Perla Cristal).

ABOVE RIGHT: Spanish poster for *El espanto surge de la tumba* (*Horror Rises from the Tomb*, 1972), starring Naschy as both resurrected warlock Alaric de Marnac and his modern-day descendent Hugh de Marnac. The warlock has sworn to wreak revenge on the descendants of those who executed him, and he does so by killing and zombifying them.

ABOVE LEFT: International poster for *Vengeance of the Zombies* (*La rebelión de las muertas*, 1972), featuring the work of Italian poster artist Mario Piovano of Studio Paradiso. Starring Naschy and directed by frequent collaborator León Klimovsky, this one involves an evil mystic named Katanka creating an entourage of female zombies.

ABOVE RIGHT: "Waldemar and the Vampire Women," a digital artwork by British illustrator Jolyon Yates. "Spanish horror is haunted by the Civil War," Yates said of this piece, "so the monumental ruins of Belchite are the background and Francisco Goya nightmare critters are in the air."

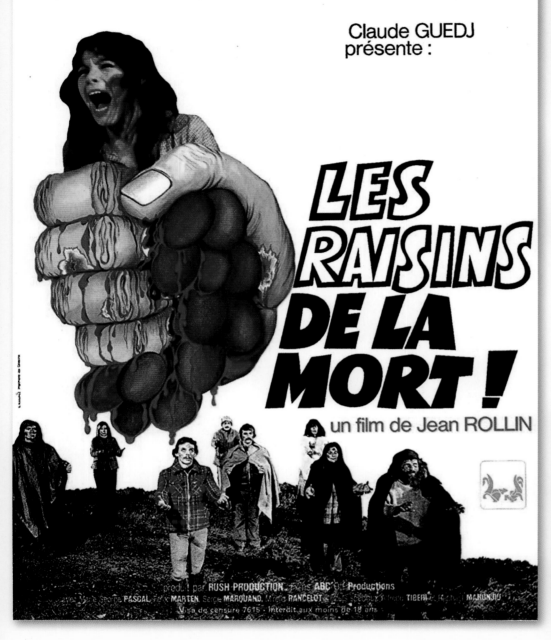

ABOVE LEFT: French poster for Jean Rollin's *Les raisins de la mort* (*The Grapes of Death*, 1978), in which zombies are created from a pesticide manufactured for use in a vineyard. The gore is relatively light (and the zombie makeup somewhat primitive), but since this is a Jean Rollin film, the cast is attractive, and at least one woman is dressed in a flimsy white gown.

TOP RIGHT: French poster for *La nuit erotique des morts vivants* (*Erotic Nights of the Living Dead*, 1980), which centers on traditional Caribbean voodoo zombies. It was written and directed by Joe D'Amato, who shot a second film, *Porno Holocaust*, at the same time, with the same cast, and in the same location (Santo Domingo) as this one.

BOTTOM RIGHT: Spanish poster for *La rebelión de las muertas* (*Vengeance of the Zombies*, 1972), featuring artwork by famed Spanish poster artist Francisco Fernandez Zarza-Pérez, who provided the art for a number of posters for Naschy's films and signed his work "Jano."

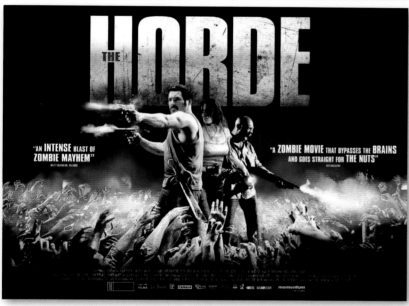

TOP LEFT: Belgian poster for the French film *La revanche des mortes vivantes* (*Revenge of the Living Dead Girls*, 1987). The zombies here are awakened by toxic waste dumped by a sleazy chemical company owner and his secretary. Though the film features some heavily sexualized gore, the special effects are infrequent and unconvincing.

TOP MIDDLE: DVD cover artwork for *Les revenants* (*They Came Back* or *The Returned*, 2004), in which the dead return as seemingly placid zombies, leaving the living to puzzle over what to do with them. Directed by Robin Campillo, it led to both French and American television series (*Les Revenants*, 2012–2015, and *The Returned*, 2015).

BOTTOM LEFT: British quad poster for the French thriller *The Horde* (2009). Like many zombie movies, this one takes place in a high-rise, but here the action starts at the top and works its way down as both cops and thugs battle to escape the building.

ABOVE RIGHT: DVD cover for the British release of the French film *The Night Eats the World* (2018), directed by Dominique Rocher. Based on a novel of the same name by Pit Agarmen, it spends much of its time on the character of Sam (Anders Danielsen Lie), who finds himself the last living resident of a Paris apartment complex after a zombie uprising.

ABOVE LEFT: Spanish poster for *La orgia de los muertos* (a.k.a. *The Hanging Woman*, 1972), featuring the work of the Spanish movie poster artist Jose Montalban. Paul Naschy was not originally involved in the film, but when director/co-writer José Luis Merino begged him to take on the small part of gravedigger Igor, Naschy agreed—and rewrote the script to expand his character's part.

ABOVE RIGHT: Cover artwork from the Spanish VHS release of Jess Franco's *Una virgin en casa de los muertos vivientes* (*A Virgin Among the Living Dead*, 1987), which includes zombie footage shot by French director Jean Rollin.

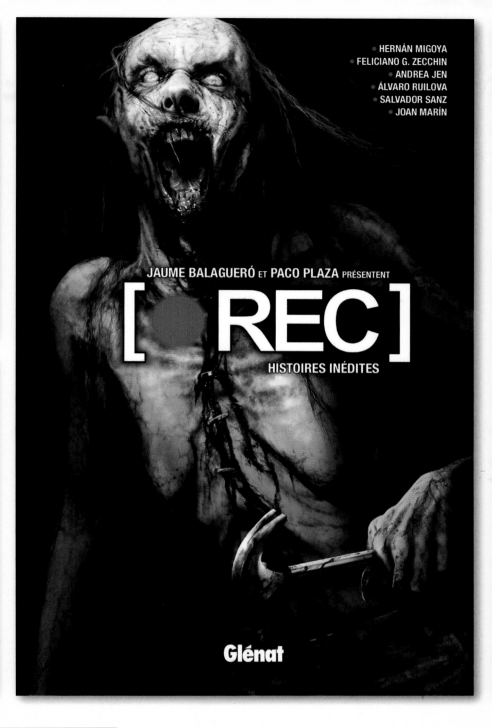

TOP LEFT: French *grande* poster for *Let Sleeping Corpses Lie* (a.k.a. *The Living Dead at Manchester Morgue*, 1974), featuring artwork by the French artist Constantin Belinsky (1904–1999). Despite the mention of Manchester Morgue in the alternate title, the film was a Spanish/Italian co-production; a few exteriors were shot in the UK, but it was primarily filmed in Italy.

BOTTOM LEFT: One-sheet for *Ladronas de almas* (*Soul Robber*, 2015). Directed by Juan Antonio de la Riva and set during the Mexican Civil War (1857–1860), the film takes place mostly in a half-ruined hacienda as a group of insurgents descend upon it, hoping for easy pickings—but instead find that the women living there have developed a unique defensive strategy involving zombies.

ABOVE RIGHT: French cover for *Rec: Historias ineditas*, a Spanish-language comic released in 2017, featuring artwork by the Uruguayan-born British artist Alejandro Colucci. The image is based on the film's character Niña Medeiros. In addition to the comic, the first *Rec* film also led to three sequels: *Rec 2* (2009); *Rec 3: Genesis* (2012); and *Rec 4: Apocalypse* (2014).

THE QUEEN OF CULT: EIHI SHIINA

"Some people seem to think that I'm scary, but I'm not a scary person."

Eihi Shiina during a live Q&A after a 2011 screening of *Helldriver*

Most western moviegoers know Eihi Shiina from her breakout role as the chilling, vengeful Asami in Takashi Miike's *Audition* (1999), but her numerous credits position her as a horror icon. She started as a model, getting her first major job (for Benetton) at the age of nineteen, but she segued into acting in 1998 with the film *Open House*. When she received a call the following year to meet Takashi Miike, she didn't realise that their casual conversation was an audition, but the next day he asked her to star in his film. Adapted from Ryu Murakami's novel of the same name, *Audition*—about a widowed middle-aged man who holds fake auditions to find a new girlfriend and then finds that his pick, Asami, is not what she seems—shook up male privilege all over the world and established Shiina as a breakout star.

Her next appearance in a genre film came in 2003, when she appeared in the manga adaptation *Sky High* (which also served as a prequel to a television series), playing the Guardian of the Gate that leads to the afterlife; the film was directed by Ryûhei Kitamura, whose *Versus* (2000) helped re-popularize zombies in Japanese cinema (and who the *Hollywood Reporter* once called "a guru of gore effects"). In 2008, she reaffirmed her status as a horror-movie star with her cool, charismatic performance in Yoshihiro Nishimura's *Tokyo Gore Police*, in which she plays Ruka, a specialist in taking out mutated monsters called "Engineers." That film began a collaboration with Nishimura that continued with 2009's *Vampire Girl vs. Frankenstein Girl*; now in her thirties, Shiina was technically too old to play a teenage protagonist, so instead she played a mother.

Shiina's best performance in a zombie movie was in Nishimura's *Helldriver* (2010), in which she (again) plays the heroine's mother. *Helldriver* is crazed even by splatter movie standards; Shiina's character, Rikka, begins the film trying to murder her daughter Kika (Yumiko Hara), before both are put into cocoons by an alien substance. When they awaken a year later, zombies have taken over Japan's northern half, Rikka has become their queen, and it's up to Kika (who now has a chainsaw sword in place of a right arm)

to venture across the devastated land to destroy her mother. The film's gore is plentiful, and the zombie makeup is well done (these zombies each sport a Y-shaped appendage growing from their foreheads that must be cut off to kill them). Shiina's performance is equally—and delightfully—extreme; as a reviewer at the website *Asian Movie Pulse* put it, "Shiina's presence . . . is as cult as always."

Helldriver is also notable for its main production company: Sushi Typhoon was founded in 2010 (as part of Japanese cinema giant Nikkatsu) by a number of Japanese filmmakers, among them Nishimura and Takashi Miike, with the goal of producing low-budget genre pictures;

Helldriver is crazed even by splatter movie standards; Shiina's character, Rikka, begins the film trying to murder her daughter before both are put into cocoons by an alien substance.

---

although it produced only a handful of films, several—including *Helldriver* and the same year's *Mutant Girls Squad* (directed by Nishimura with Noboru Iguchi and Tak Sakaguchi)—have garnered cult status.

Shiina also appeared in Naoya Tashiro's *Use the Eyeballs!* (2015) and Nishimura's *Meatball Machine Kodoku* (2017), and she has worked on non-horror films with renowned Japanese filmmakers Shinji Aoyama (*Eureka*, 2000) and Takeshi Kitano (*Outrage*, 2010).

She recently decided to take a break from acting in order to focus on pursuing other forms of art: in 1998, she released a book of photographs and poems called *No Filter, Only Eyes*, and she has subsequently decided to focus on photography again. She is currently showing her work (mainly floral images) on her social media accounts, although she has also noted that she would be happy to return to the roles of Asami Yamazaki or Ruka, if *Audition 2* or *Tokyo Gore Police 2*, respectively, are ever made.

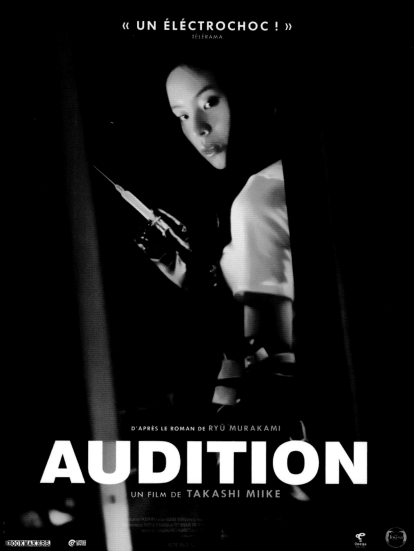

ABOVE LEFT: DVD cover art for *Tokyo Gore Police*, in which Eihi Shiina plays the cool, implacable Ruka. The film, directed by makeup-effects expert Yoshihiro Nishimura, was aptly described by V. A. Musetto of the *New York Post* as "quite possibly the goriest, craziest, most eye-blowing, chunk-spewing, head-exploding sci-fi movie of all time."

ABOVE RIGHT: French poster for Takashi Miike's *Audition* (1999), featuring Eihi Shiina as Asami, who seeks revenge against a lonely businessman, Aoyama, after he stages a fake audition for a new romantic partner.

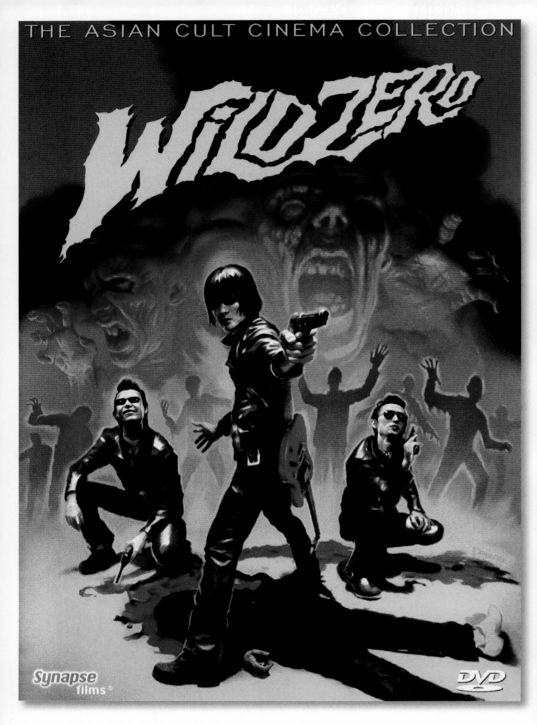

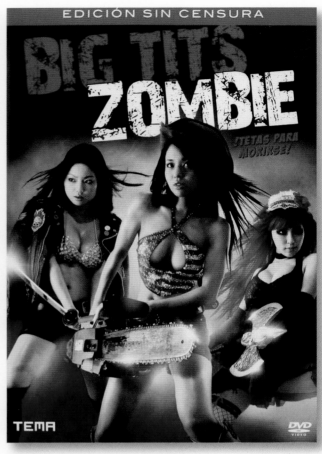

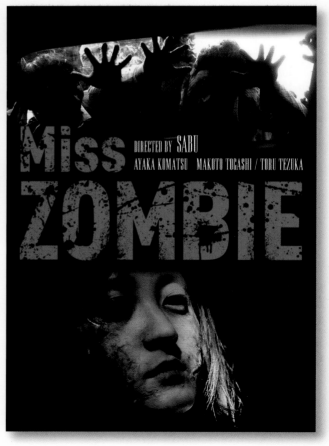

ABOVE LEFT: DVD cover for *Wild Zero* (1999), directed by Tetsuro Takeuchi and starring the real Japanese garage rock band Guitar Wolf, who are forced to put music aside to fight zombies after a strange meteorite crashes into Japan. Ads for the film's Blu-ray release note that it was "inspired by Romero and the Ramones."

TOP RIGHT: DVD cover art for the Japanese film *Big Tits Zombie* (2010), the full title of which translates literally to *Big Tits Dragon: Hot Spring Zombie vs. Stripper 5*. The film focuses on two exotic dancers who are hired to work at a spa resort, where they discover a medieval grimoire and recite a spell that unleashes zombies. Gore and bare breasts ensue.

BOTTOM RIGHT: DVD cover artwork for the Japanese *Miss Zombie* (2017), directed by Sabu. Set in a future where zombies have been domesticated and are sold as slaves to the wealthy, the eponymous character slowly regains her self-awareness and physical agility, even as the family and local townsfolk shower her with abuse and cruelty.

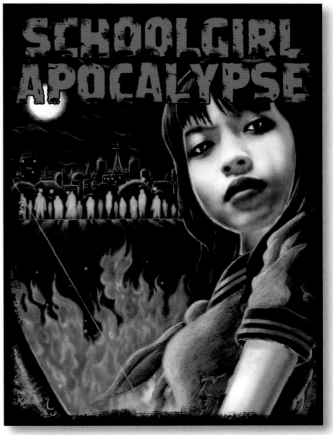

ABOVE LEFT: Japanese poster for *Zombie Ass: Toilet of the Dead* (2011), directed by Noboru Iguchi. Yes, it really is a movie about a group of kids who go camping and face zombies that emerge from the outhouse.

TOP RIGHT: Japanese poster for *School-Live!* (2019), a live-action feature based on a long-running manga series of the same name about a group of friends surviving a zombie holocaust at a girls' high school (previously adapted as a 2015 anime). The feature film stars members of the popular Japanese girl band Last Idol.

BOTTOM RIGHT: Cover art by Ken Crane for John Cairns's novelization of his film *Schoolgirl Apocalypse* (2011). Sakura (played by Higarino) is a sixteen-year-old who survives the first wave of a zombie outbreak that only affects men; she escapes her village and meets Aoi (Mai Tsujimoto), a sociopath whose deadly skills soon turn against Sakura.

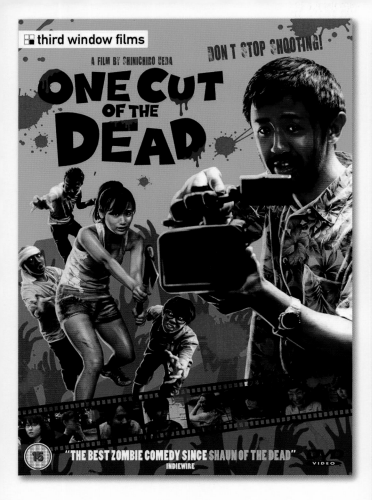

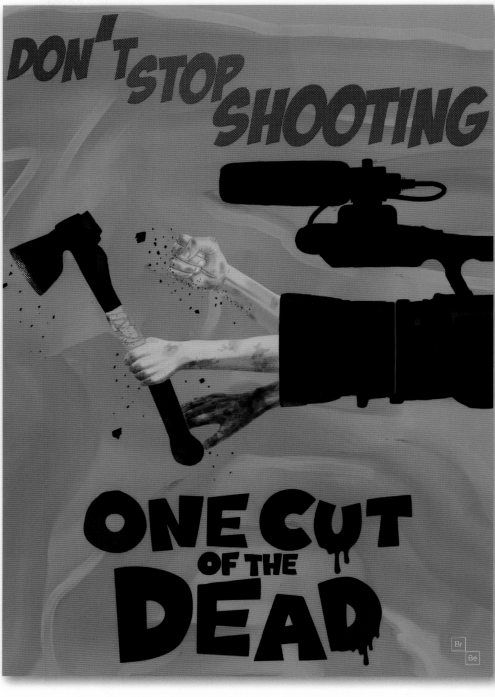

ABOVE LEFT: British DVD cover artwork for writer and director Shin'ichirō Ueda's *One Cut of the Dead* (2017). The first thirty-seven minutes of the film were completed in one single take, as a crazed director (Takayuki Hamatsu) bullies his actors during the shooting of a zombie film in an isolated water-treatment facility, and then as the cast and crew must confront real zombies. Just as the film seems to be ending, it begins again, revealing the truth behind the production.

ABOVE RIGHT: Alternative poster for *One Cut of the Dead* by the Indian artist Gokul Gautham. Ueda's debut feature, *One Cut of the Dead* was shot over eight days, with a cast of mostly unknowns, on a budget of roughly $25,000. It went on to earn more than $50 million worldwide. *One Cut of the Dead* is easily the funniest, smartest, and most surprising zombie movie of the last decade; at the time of writing it has a rare 100 percent "Certified Fresh" rating at the review-aggregate website Rotten Tomatoes.

ABOVE LEFT: Wilson Yip's *Bio-Zombie* (1998) cast actors Jordan Chan and Sam Lee as Woody Invincible and Crazy Bee, two likable, hapless, wannabee thugs who are trapped in a Hong Kong mall during a zombie outbreak. Featuring game-style graphics of Woody Invincible and Crazy Bee as they prepare for battle against the zombies, the film beat *Zombieland* (2009) and *The Cabin in the Woods* (2011) to the punch as the first "meta" zombie film.

ABOVE RIGHT: Cover art for the French Blu-ray release of *Bio-Zombie*, with artwork by Ilan Sheady of Uncle Frank Productions. *Bio-Zombie* melds two popular Hong Kong movie genres into one: triad crime dramas, as popularized by the *Young and Dangerous* series (featuring *Bio-Zombie* star Jordan Chan), and low-budget, localized horror movies. The film's main setting is a sprawling shopping complex that's a maze of tiny phone stores and eateries.

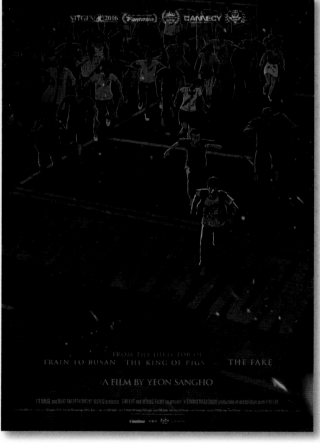

ABOVE LEFT: Alternative digital poster design for *Train to Busan* (2016) by Portuguese artist Edgar Ascensão, who says of this striking image, "A horde of zombies works in a way like carriages on a train. A virus that spreads one after the other, forming this unstoppable force. An idea of hands in single file creates the metaphor." *Train to Busan* was the highest-grossing film of 2016 in South Korea.

TOP RIGHT: Poster for the Filipino film *Trip Ubusan: The Lolas vs. Zombies* (2017), which stars male comics Jose Manalo, Wally Bayola, and Paolo Ballesteros as the three flamboyant Lola sisters, who fight off a zombie outbreak with the help of a little girl, Marcy (Ryzza Mae Dizon), who has an encyclopedic knowledge of zombies. The film's title is also a play on *Train to Busan*.

BOTTOM RIGHT: The success of *Train to Busan* led to the release of an animated prequel, *Seoul Station* (2016), and a live-action follow-up, *Peninsula* (2020). An English-language remake called *The Last Train to New York* has also been announced. A 2022 survey at *Paste* magazine of "The 50 Best Zombie Movies of All Time" placed *Train to Busan* at #14.

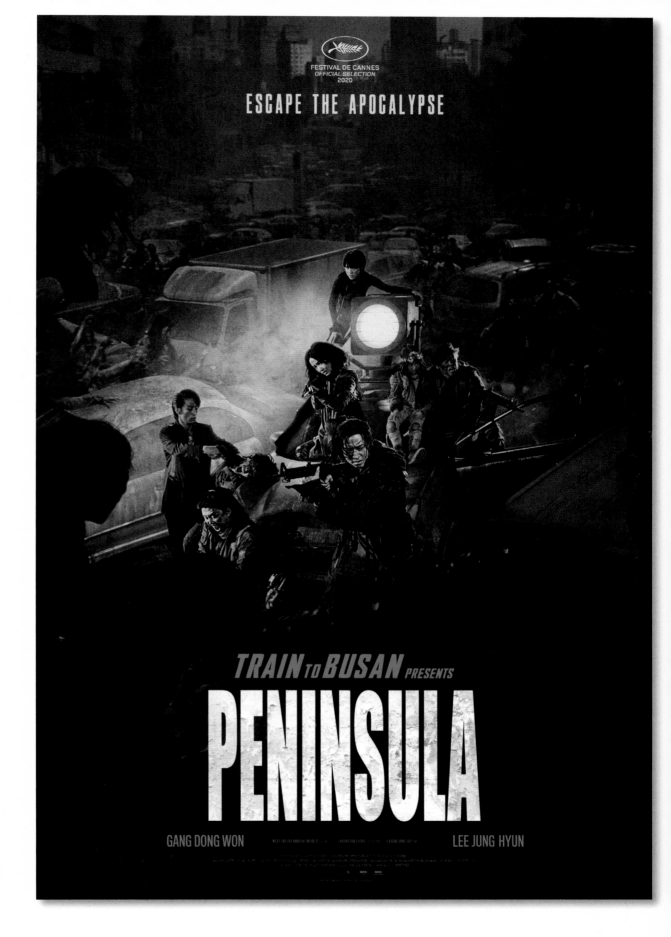

RIGHT: One-sheet for *Peninsula* (2020). Whereas *Train to Busan* focused on a father's attempt to protect his daughter aboard a speeding train full of zombies, *Peninsula* is similar to Zack Snyder's *Army of the Dead* (released in 2021), since both follow a team hired to make their way through a zombie-infested territory to retrieve a fortune.

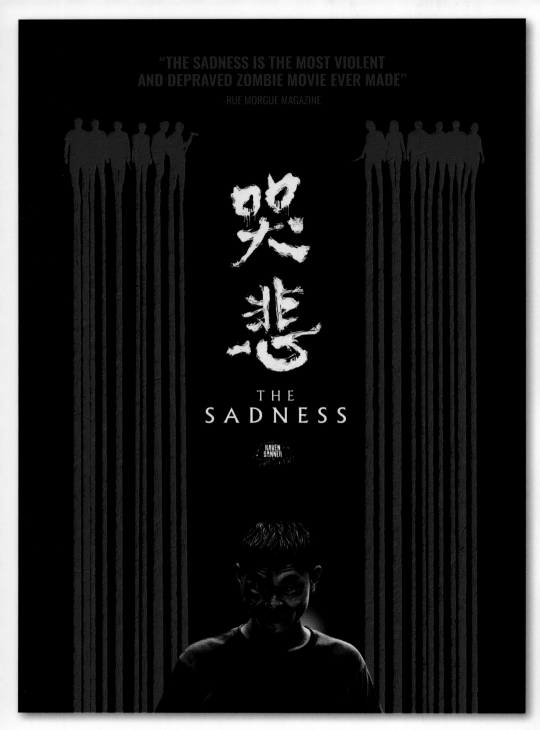

"THE SADNESS IS THE MOST VIOLENT
AND DEPRAVED ZOMBIE MOVIE EVER MADE"
-RUE MORGUE MAGAZINE

哭悲

THE
SADNESS

ABOVE LEFT: Promotional ad for *The Sadness* (2021), a Taiwanese film akin to *28 Days Later* in which the victims of the "Alvin" virus don't die but become aggressive and bloodthirsty. Unrelentingly violent and misanthropic, *The Sadness* won a "New Flesh" award for first features at the 2021 Fantasia International Film Festival.

TOP RIGHT: Chinese poster for *Black Magic Part II* (1976), one of the few horror films released by the Hong Kong–based Shaw Brothers, who are known mainly for their martial-arts films. The film stars Lo Lieh and Ti Lung as the evil magician and the hero; its zombies—corpses brought back to life and controlled by the sorcerer—are more acrobatic than most.

BOTTOM RIGHT: Chinese poster for another horror entry from the Shaw Brothers, *Bewitched* (1981). A man is arrested for murdering his daughter, but claims he was possessed; a detective (Melvin Wong Gam-Sam) investigating the crime heads to Thailand, where he finds himself embroiled in supernatural terrors.

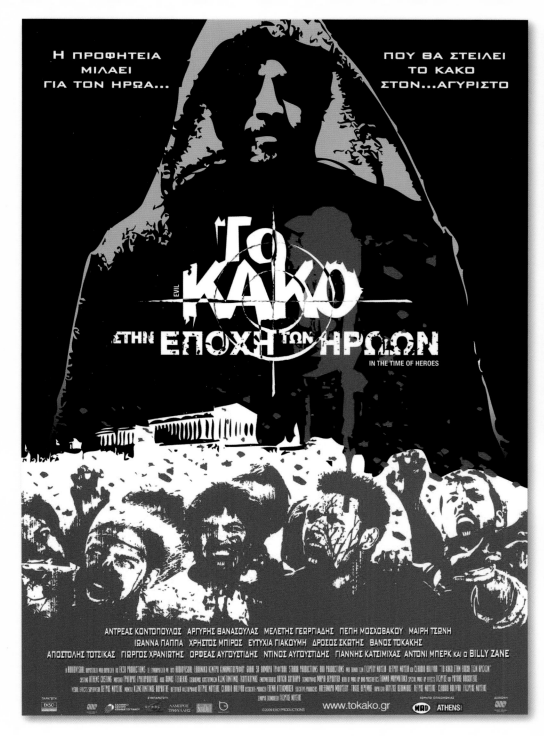

ABOVE LEFT: Poster art for the Greek film *Evil: In the Time of Heroes* (*To Kako 2*, 2009), directed by Yorgos Noussias and co-starring American actor Billy Zane. A sequel to 2005's *Evil*, which followed the events surrounding a zombie uprising in modern-day Athens, this entry includes scenes set in the country's classical past.

TOP RIGHT: One-sheet for the Filipino film *Block Z* (2020), directed by Mikhail Red, about a group of students trapped in their university during a zombie outbreak. These zombies are vulnerable not just to headshots but also to water.

BOTTOM RIGHT: Promotional ad for *Hsien of the Dead* (2012). Billed as "Singapore's first zombie movie," the film employs considerable slapstick comedy as it follows four survivors attempting to flee an apocalypse of the undead. Note that the pronunciation of the name Hsien is very similar to "Shaun."

ABOVE LEFT: One-sheet for *ABCs of Death 2* (2014), the follow-up to 2012's *ABCs of Death*. Each film includes twenty-six shorts by different filmmakers, each taking on a different letter of the alphabet. In "E is for Equilibrium," Brugués offers up a tale of two castaways on a deserted island whose lives take a grim turn when a woman washes up on the beach.

ABOVE RIGHT: One-sheet for *Nightmare Cinema* (2018), an anthology film featuring shorts by Brugués, Joe Dante, Mick Garris, Ryûhei Kitamura, and David Slade (with a wraparound by Garris). Brugués' entry, "The Thing in the Woods," starts where most slasher movies end, as a blood-covered woman confronts a maniac called "The Welder."

Unhinged: Alejandro Brugués

Argentine filmmaker Alejandro Brugués didn't start off with zombies—his first feature was the 2007 drama *Personal Belongings*—but he achieved international renown for *Juan of the Dead* (2011). He followed that breakout hit with 2014's "E Is for Equilibrium," from the anthology feature *ABCs of Death 2*, and in 2018 he wrote and directed "The Thing in the Woods," part of the anthology film *Nightmare Cinema*, whose other segments were directed by Joe Dante and Mick Garris. Brugués has since directed shorts for other horror film and television anthologies, including *From Dusk Till Dawn: The Series* and *50 States of Fright*. His latest credits are *The Inheritance*, a thriller for Netflix (Brugués noted that working on this film "unhinged" him), and the film adaptation of Gabino Iglesias's novel *The Devil Takes You Home*.

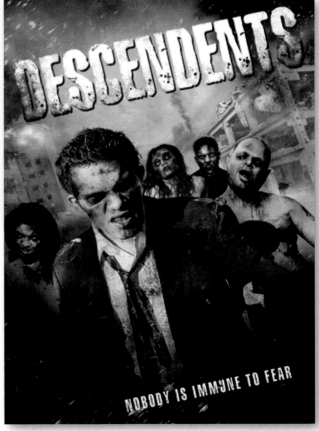

ABOVE LEFT: Spanish-language poster for *Juan de los muertos* (*Juan of the Dead*), Alejandro Brugués's 2010 hit. The film is often praised for its political angle and social commentary, although in a 2011 interview with *Miami New Times*, the director noted, "There is a lot of subtext in the film . . . but that's very open to interpretation."

TOP RIGHT: One-sheet for *Plaga-Zombie: American Invasion* (2021), the fourth film in the Argentinian series that started in 1997 with *Plaga Zombie*. This comedy/horror/sci-fi hybrid is set in a small American town where four unlikely heroes fight off both zombies and an alien invasion.

BOTTOM RIGHT: Promotional ad for *Descendents* (2008), billed as the first Chilean zombie movie, although it was shot in English. Director Jorge Olguín scored a hit with his 2002 vampire film *Eternal Blood* (*Sangre Eterna*), but *Descendents*—which follows a child trying to make her way through a zombie-infested wilderness—received poor reviews.

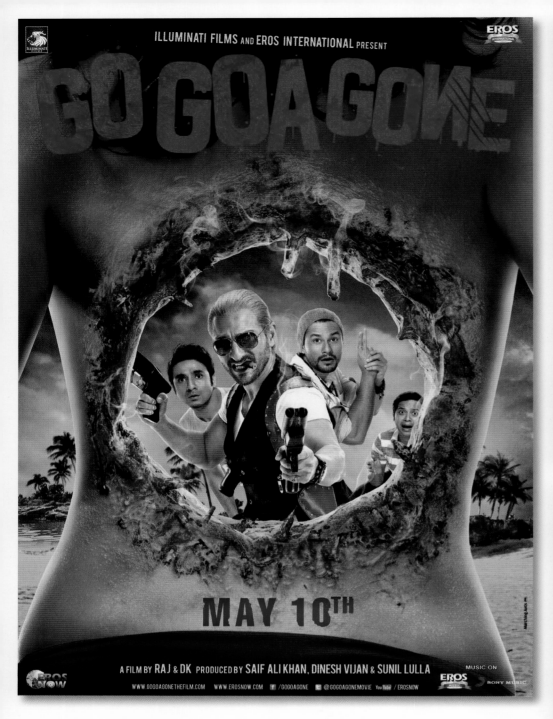

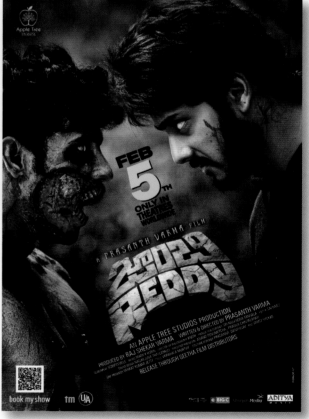

ABOVE LEFT: One-sheet for the Hindi-language *Go Goa Gone* (2013), which calls itself the first Indian zombie movie. It follows several friends who travel to the coastal state of Goa for a vacation but instead find themselves trapped on an isolated island with zombies created by a new Russian drug called D2RF; fortunately, the zombies can be rendered immobile by throwing cocaine at them.

TOP RIGHT: One-sheet for *Miruthan* (2016), a Tamil-language film from India. The title translates to *AnimalMan.* After zombies are created by a toxic waste spill, a traffic officer (Jayim Ravi) fighting his way through the zombie outbreak discovers that the woman he's in love with (Lakshmi Menon) is immune to the zombie virus, so he becomes devoted to protecting her to save humanity.

BOTTOM RIGHT: One-sheet for *Zombie Reddy* (2021), the first zombie film in India's Telugu language. After zombies attack a wedding party in an outlying village, the heroes stumble on a lab hidden away in the jungle and learn that the outbreak was caused by a failed COVID vaccine. The title is a play on the fact that "Reddy" is the name of a dominant caste in South India.

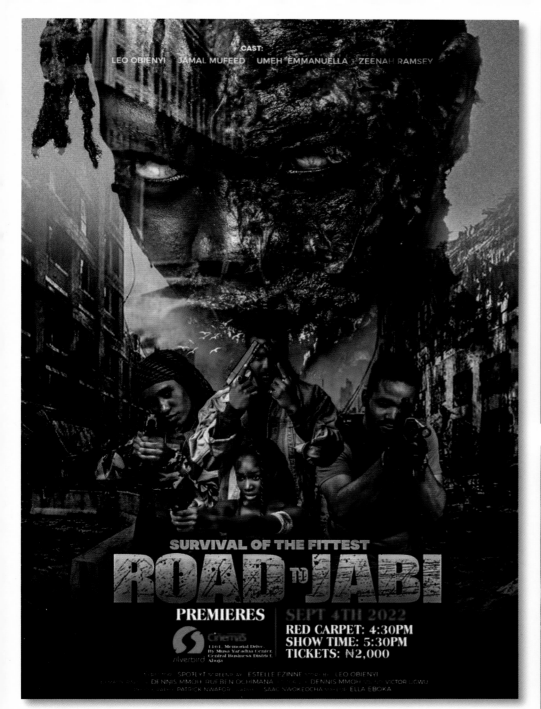

ABOVE LEFT: Poster for the premiere of *Road to Jabi* (2022), a Nigerian zombie film. The film, directed by Ogegbo Omotola Sulaiman (a.k.a. Spotlyt) runs to just thirty minutes, but it garnered a strong following after its premiere at the Silverbird Cinema in Abuja. The plot follows a group of survivors trying to escape a zombie apocalypse by making it to a secure military base.

TOP RIGHT: Poster for *Zombie* (2022), Egypt's first zombie film. This zom-com centers on a singer and his band who must confront zombies in an isolated area. Director Amr Salah specializes in genre comedies: his last film, *Dedo* (2021), was a comedy about a group of robbers who get miniaturized by their scientist target.

BOTTOM RIGHT: Poster art for *Zombie* (2019), a zom-com from India. *Zombie* received comparisons to *Miruthan*, since both are Tamil-language zombie films, but whereas *Miruthan* is a serious thriller, this one is played for laughs. The film received poor reviews, however; *Indian Express*, for example, called it "an utterly shoddy film that is best forgotten."

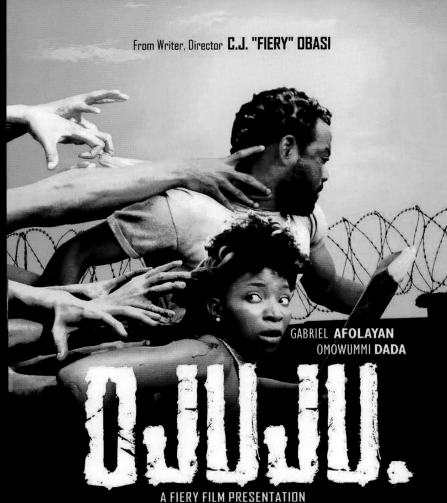

From Writer, Director **C.J. "FIERY" OBASI**

GABRIEL **AFOLAYAN**
OMOWUMMI **DADA**

OJUJU.

A FIERY FILM PRESENTATION

ALSO STARRING KELECHI UDEGBE, CHIDOZIE NZERIBE, BRUTUS RICHARD, MEG OTANWA, YVONNE ENAKHENA, JUMOKE AYADI, PAUL UTOMI, TOMMY OYEWOLE, AND INTRODUCING KELECHI JOSEPH, WITH GUEST APPEARANCE FROM KLINT O' DRUNK
C.J. "FIERY" OBASI WRITER, DIRECTOR, EDITOR OGE UWGU PRODUCER TUNJI AKINSEHINWA DIRECTOR OF PHOTOGRAPHY
VICTOR AKPAN PRODUCTION MANAGER/ART DIRECTOR FRANK EKWE ASSISTANT DIRECTOR MURI SABILU PRODUCTION MANAGER
LAWRENCE ADAMA SECOND CAMERA FUNKE OLOWU SPECIAL MAKE-UP FX SUNDAY ADESUGBA SOUND RECORDIST
DAYO THOMPSON SOUND EDITING/MIXING BEATOVEN AND WACHE POLLEN ORIGINAL SCORES DAVID JONES DAVID ORIGINAL THEMES

www.facebook.com/ojujuthemovie
@ojujumovie
www.ojuju.afieryfilm.com

FIERY FILM

www.facebook.com/fieryfilm
www.afieryfilm.com

Fiery: C. J. Obasi

Growing up in the small town of Owerri, Nigeria, C. J. "Fiery" Obasi always enjoyed horror and science fiction, but he didn't make the decision to become a filmmaker until 2012. He formed a production company called Fiery Film Company, and in 2014 released his first feature, the zombie thriller *Ojuju*, which screened all over the world. His second feature, the crime film *O-Town*, followed in 2015; in 2018, he released the short *Hello, Rain*, based on the short story "Hello, Moto" by author Nnedi Okorafor. His latest feature film is *Mami Wata*, which he describes as "a female-driven revenge thriller based on the Mermaid folklore of West Africa."

ABOVE LEFT: Portrait of C. J. Obasi, director of *Ojuju*. The *Hollywood Reporter* has said of the film and its maker, "*Ojuju* overcomes its technical limitations with well-drawn characters and pungently compelling situations. It certainly indicates that its talented filmmaker . . . is eminently capable of moving on to bigger and better things."

ABOVE RIGHT: One-sheet for Obasi's *Ojuju* (2014), which was showcased at the Brooklyn Academy of Music's New Voices in Black Cinema. In a review at *Twitch Film*, Todd Brown noted that the film's obvious budget restraints "place a stronger emphasis on the characters and neighborhood. Which is absolutely fine, really, given that these elements all play to Obasi's strengths as a director."

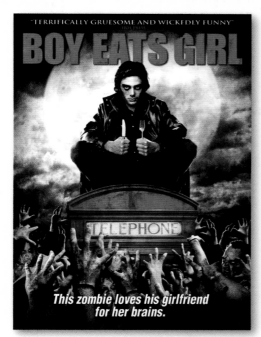

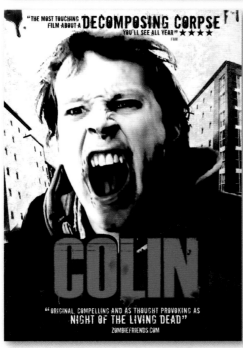

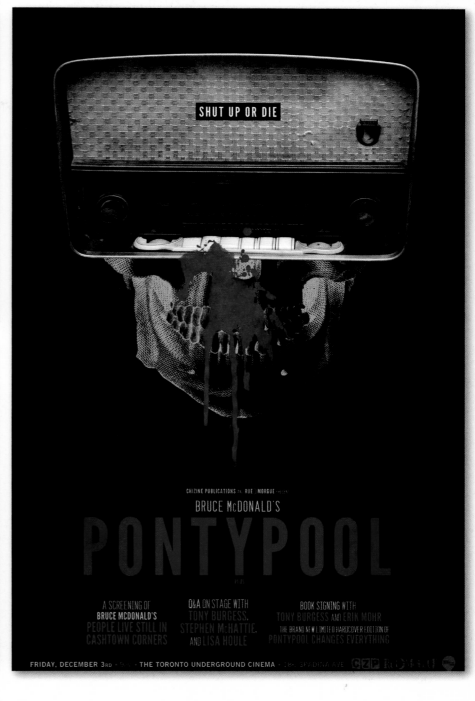

TOP LEFT: Cover artwork for the DVD release of Irish zombie film *Boy Eats Girl* (2005). After Grace (Deirdre O'Kane) accidentally kills her teenage son Nathan (David Leon), she uses a voodoo spell from a book she has found to bring him back to life. Unfortunately, he soon begins biting his friends, who in turn become zombies.

BOTTOM LEFT: DVD cover art for the British film-festival hit *Colin* (2008), which was reportedly shot by filmmaker Marc Price on his camcorder on a budget of £45. It follows the eponymous zombie through an apocalypse in London and is told from the zombie's point-of-view. It played at numerous film festivals before being released on DVD in 2010.

ABOVE RIGHT: Poster advertising a screening of *Pontypool* at the late Toronto Underground Cinema. *Pontypool* was adapted from the second novel in Tony Burgess's trilogy *The Bewdley Mayhem*; the other two books are the short-story collection *The Hellmouths of Bewdley* and *Caesarea*, about a contagious form of insomnia with dreadful side effects.

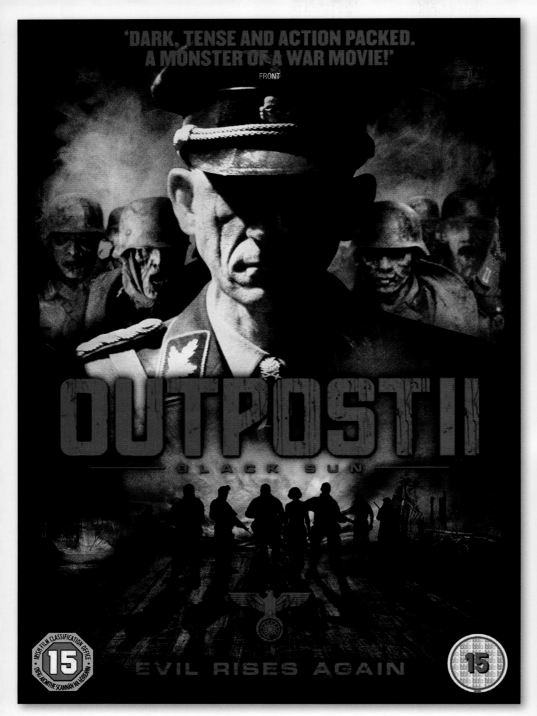

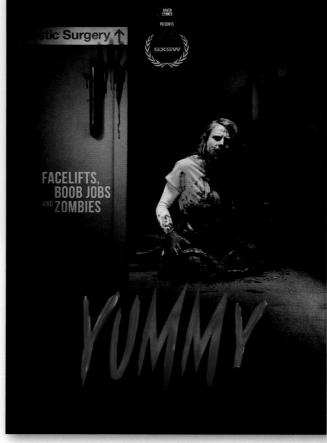

ABOVE LEFT: Cover artwork for the DVD release of the British film *Outpost II* (also known as *Outpost: Black Sun*, 2012), a sequel to 2008's *Outpost*. A prequel called *Outpost: Rise of the Spetsnaz* followed in 2013. All three films center on soldiers who discover that the Nazis had found the secret for reanimating the dead.

TOP RIGHT: One-sheet for *The Dead* (2010), a British zombie film set in Africa, written and directed by brothers Howard J. and Jon Ford. The plot focuses on an American engineer (played by Rob Freeman) who joins forces with a local soldier (Prince David Osei) to escape a zombie outbreak.

BOTTOM RIGHT: Promotional ad for the Belgian splatterfest *Yummy* (2019), directed by Lars Damoiseaux. When the film's chances at theatrical release in the U.S. were sidelined by the COVID pandemic, it was acquired by the streaming service Shudder.

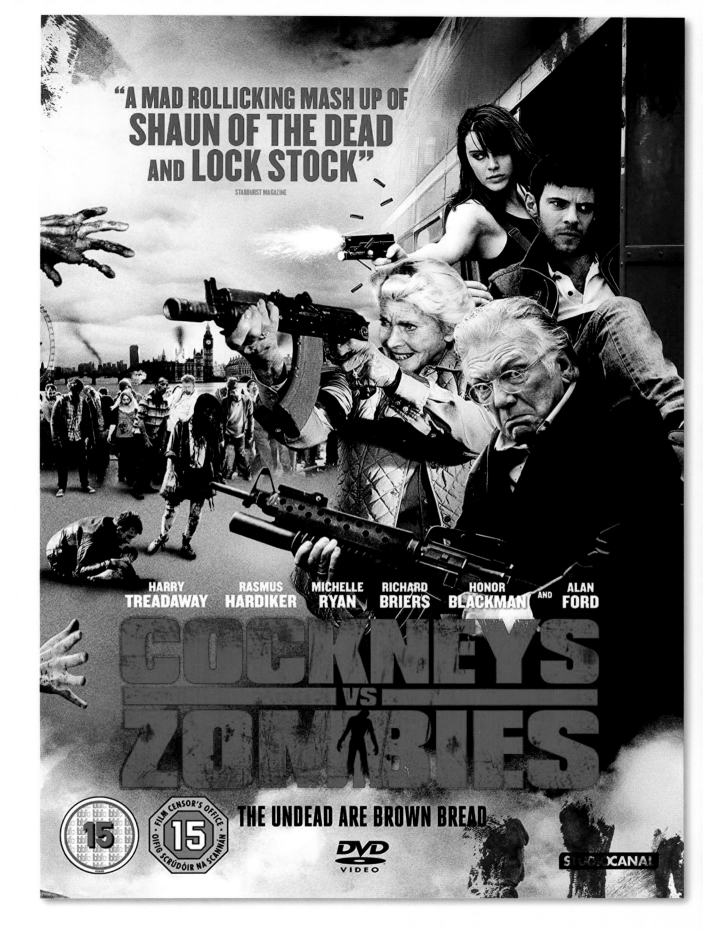

RIGHT: cover artwork for *Cockneys vs. Zombies* (2012), about an attempt by a group of cockneys to rescue the residents of a retirement home during a zombie uprising. It marks the final film appearance by Honor Blackman, best known as "Pussy Galore" in *Goldfinger* (1964).

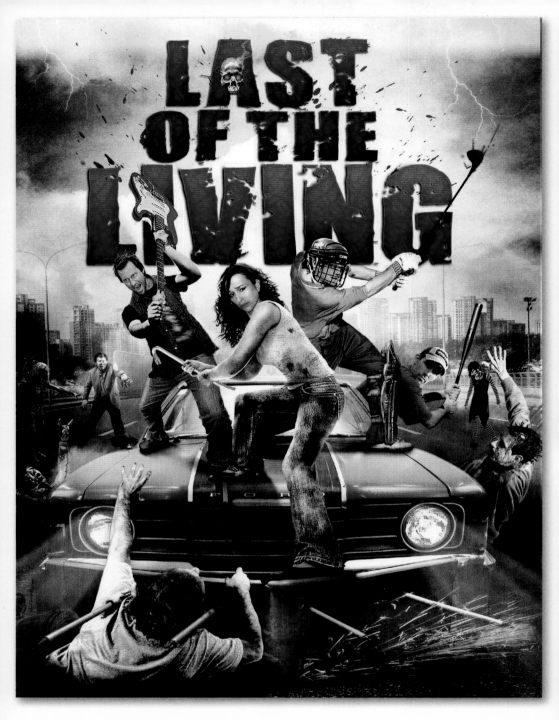

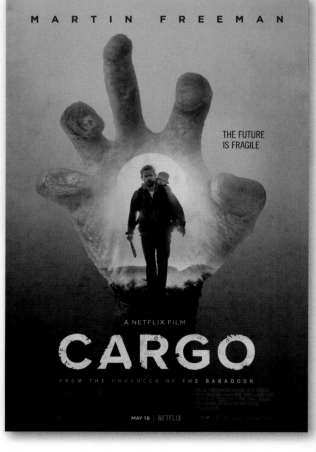

ABOVE LEFT: DVD cover art for *Last of the Living* (2009), a New Zealand zom-com about three slackers who might just be the last surviving humans after a zombie apocalypse . . . until they stumble on a hot female survivor who may hold the cure to the zombie infection. It's up to them, then, to save both the woman and humanity.

TOP RIGHT: One sheet for the French-language Canadian film *Brain Freeze* (2021), a zom-com set in an exclusive Montreal gated community, where an experimental material used to melt snow from the golf course has trickled into the water supply and is zombifying the residents.

BOTTOM RIGHT: Advance one-sheet for the Australian film *Cargo* (2017), about an infected man, Andy (Martin Freeman), trying to lead his wife and child to safety through the outback during a zombie apocalypse—until he turns. After his wife is killed, Andy is aided by aborigines, who assist him in caring for his child.

ABOVE: British quad poster for *Death Warmed Up* (1984), a New Zealand thriller about a man, Michael Tucker (Michael Hurst), who as a child was subjected to cruel experiments and forced to kill his parents by Dr. Howell (Gary Day). Now an adult, Michael tries to seek vengeance against the mad doctor, only to run up against his army of mind-controlled zombies.

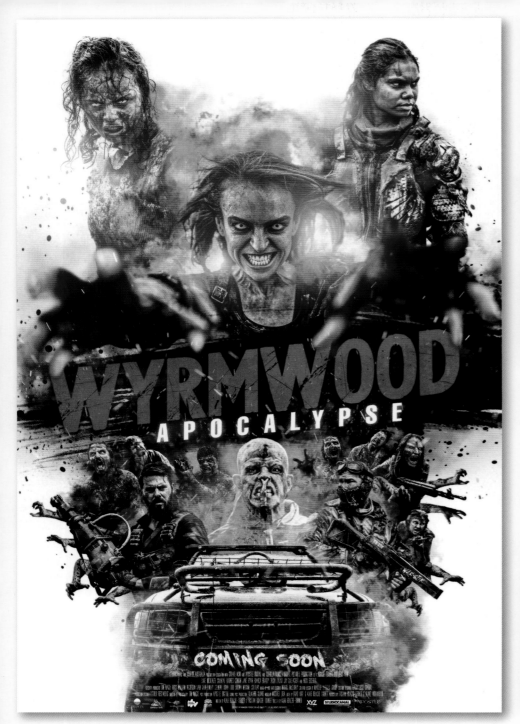

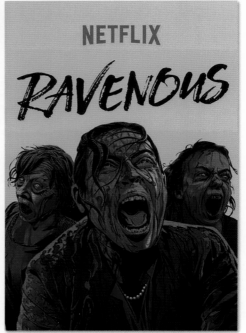

ABOVE LEFT: One-sheet for *Wyrmwood: Apocalypse* (2021), the follow-up to the Australian action thriller *Wyrmwood* (2014). This time, the story is centered on Rhys (Luke McKenzie), a tough soldier in the military's employ who ends up taking off with some human insurgents. Critics praised the film's gleeful gore and hyperkinetic style.

TOP RIGHT: One-sheet for the Canadian film *Blood Quantum* (2019), set on the Red Crow Indian Reservation near Quebec during a zombie apocalypse. Writer/director Jeff Barnaby was a member of the Mi'kmaq tribe who tragically died of cancer in 2022 at the age of forty-six.

BOTTOM RIGHT: Promotional ad for *Ravenous* (a.k.a. *Les Affamés*, 2017), a French-language Canadian thriller that depends on eerie atmosphere as much as gore. Set in a remote village in a heavily wooded area, the film follows a group trying to escape from zombies who are fast and can work together to take down their human victims.

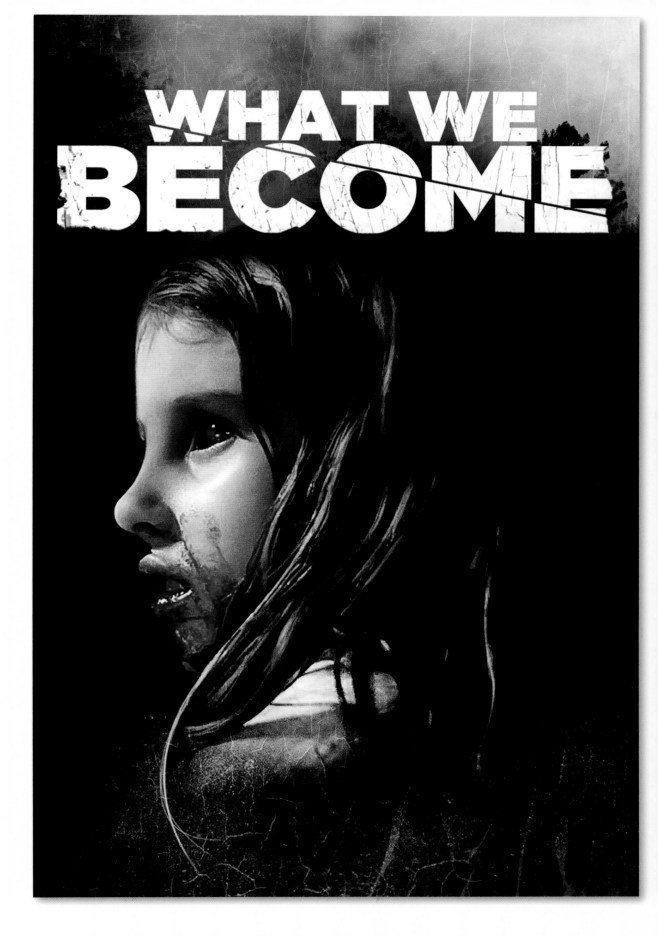

RIGHT: Promotional ad for the Danish film *What We Become* (a.k.a. *Sorgenfri*, 2015), directed by Bo Mikkelson, about a family trying to flee their small town after a zombie uprising. The film spends as much time on examining the effects of distrust and paranoia on the family as it does on gunplay and gore.

CONCLUSION

> "Without George A. Romero, there is no *Walking Dead*. His inspiration cannot be overstated. He started it all, so many others followed."
>
> Robert Kirkman, tweet from July 17, 2017 (the day after Romero's death)

Less than three years after George Romero passed away, the world locked itself down in the face of a global pandemic. A virus that could kill or leave those infected with long-term health issues caused economic freefall, healthcare panic, and out-and-out rebellion among some who refused to trust government or science.

The fact that zombies were missing from this viral outbreak was almost surprising.

Romero's infected, reanimated dead have become so ubiquitous in the twenty-first century that many of us, as we crouched anxiously in our homes during the height of the Coronavirus rampage, made jokes about zombies. We may even have secretly envied the heroes in zombie stories who have the clear target of destroying their enemies' brains; we felt helpless against something we couldn't even *sense*, let alone clearly fight.

Zombies are their own virus, and they have infected nearly every aspect of our modern life. Turn on your television and you may come across *The Walking Dead* (2010–2022), based on Robert Kirkman's long-running comic book series of the same name, or one of its various spin-offs. A Korean historical zombie series called *The Kingdom* (2019) shook up Netflix viewers, and the postmodern oddity *Z-Nation* (2014–2018) has its own cult following.

Horror literature has certainly fueled the popularity of the shambling corpses. In 1989, influential horror authors and editors John Skipp and Craig Spector released a tribute anthology to Romero's zombies called *Book of the Dead*, launching a literary resurrection that continued on through two follow-up anthologies, *Still Dead* (1992) and *Mondo Zombie* (edited only by Skipp, 2006). Other influential zombie fiction included Brian Keene's *The Rising* (2003), Max Brooks's *World War Z* (2006), John Joseph Adams's anthology *The Living Dead* (2008), Jonathan Maberry's *Patient Zero* (2009), Carrie Ryan's *The Forest of Hands and Teeth* (2009), Mira Grant's *Feed* (2010), Stephen Jones's six-volume *Zombie Apocalypse!* series (beginning in 2010), Colson Whitehead's *Zone One* (2011), M. R. Carey's *The Girl with All the Gifts* (2014), and finally back to George A. Romero, whose unfinished novel *The Living Dead* was completed by author Daniel Kraus and published in 2020. There are cultural studies of zombies (Roger Luckhurst's *Zombies: A Cultural History*, 2015), zombie poetry books (Ryan Mecum's *Zombie Haiku*, 2008), and there's even a cookbook called *The Art of Eating Through the Zombie Apocalypse* (2014). There are zombie graphic novels and comics—Marvel has created a popular subfranchise by zombifying its superheroes—and Jonathan Maberry's young adult zombie series *Rot and Ruin*, which began in 2010, has been adapted into a "webtoon"—a comic designed to be read on a phone.

Zombies have also spread throughout the visual arts as well, with zombie tattoos, T-shirts, games, and art prints. Sprint, Toshiba, LG, Honda, and H&R Block are just a few of the companies who have employed zombies in their commercials. For kids, there are zombie/army-men play sets, Lego figures, and dolls. There are zombie hot sauces, beers, and gummy candy (Zomboogers, anyone?). There are zombie board games, dozens of zombie video games, zombie

---

> "Years Before COVID-19, Zombies Helped Prepare One Hospital System for the Real Pandemic"
>
> Title of a 2021 episode of the podcast *Scientific American 60-Second Science*

---

fortune telling cards, and even a cute bestselling game, *Plants vs. Zombies*.

Of course, zombies have become an essential part of Halloween, the yearly festival of fear. There are zombie-themed haunted attractions, or—if you prefer to stay home and engage in DIY scares—zombie animatronics that can walk, crawl, and shudder. Looking to put on a zombie-themed Halloween party? Don't forget the brain-shaped Jell-O mold or the recipes for edible fingers and eyeballs from nearly every seasonal party guide.

Curiously, George Romero often tried to deny the deeper meaning of zombies in interviews ("They've always been a cigar"). With all due respect to the memory of the artist who created this most modern of monsters, this is a cigar that has infiltrated the mass consciousness, lodged there, spread throughout the culture, and shows no sign of slowing down. Whether it's because they represent our deepest fears of conformity or contamination, or our repressed desires to be able to kill all threats with a blow to the head, these rotting flesh-eaters speak to us.

Zombies rule.

ABOVE LEFT: Poster by Graham Humphreys for Weekend of the Dead 2020. The event, billed as "Europe's Biggest Romero Convention" and held in Manchester, England, has run every year since 2015. It offers fans the chance to interact with actors and crewmembers from Romero's films and purchase collectibles.

TOP RIGHT: "Pinball," a White Zombie concert poster designed by the artist Bill Wood in which a classic pinball-machine design has been meshed with occult references to promote a performance by the metal band named after the first zombie movie.

BOTTOM RIGHT: Smart Lab's "The Inhuman Squishy Zombie." Intended for children aged eight and up, the package contains a book that "makes the science of contagions a lesson in zombie-based fun!" and a "zombie model with posable arms, removable flesh, squishy intestines, spleen, heart, lungs and brain."

AFTERWORD
FINAL THOUGHTS ON ZOMBIES AND ART

Daniel Kraus

Having seen *Night of the Living Dead* at around age five, and roughly every year thereafter, I can make a specific biographical statement. The film inspired my interest not only in horror but in the arts as a whole, as well as a general preference: slow zombies for me, every time.

Not that I haven't enjoyed a fast zombie movie now and then. *28 Days Later, Train to Busan, Rec*—you can make a good argument for *Evil Dead*, too. But these movies, I would argue, are doing something entirely different from the flicks in the Romero mold. So much so that they deserve a differentiated name. Zoombies, perhaps?

I don't crack open this grand old message-board debate for kicks. I'd argue this debate has raged for as long as it has precisely because (whether all debaters can articulate it or not) speed is everything when talking zombies.

As anyone who grew up in the VHS era can tell you, perhaps no box cover was scarier than that of Lucio Fulci's *Zombi 2* (or *Zombie*, depending on which version your store carried): a straight-on photo of the nastiest snaggle-toothed, maggot-eyed zombie ever seen, emblazoned with the brilliantly blunt tagline "WE ARE GOING TO EAT YOU!"

The package dared me, puny adolescent, to rent it. I did not do so until I was of drinking age.

What is vital about the cover of *Zombi 2* is that the zombie isn't doing anything. It's not attacking. Not even looming. If not for the tagline, it might simply be a corpse. The message was clear to me, even as a kid: the zombie threat wasn't only slow, it was *slowness itself*; it was patience, inevitability; it was, if you'll allow me to go big here, God.

It would be another couple decades before I learned that the word *zombie* derives from *nzambi*, which roughly translates to "God" in various African traditions. So it was there at the origin, a recognition that the zombie cannot be defeated no more than death can be defeated.

Zombies don't *cause* death. They *are* death. It doesn't matter how you try to protect yourself. It could be inside *Night of the Living Dead*'s farmhouse, *Dawn of the Dead*'s shopping mall, *Day of the Dead*'s military bunker; it could be inside hyperbaric chambers or cryogenics pods; it could be within the spiritual fortifications of religion. It does not matter. Zombies will wait you out. You have to come out sometime.

You can stretch this metaphor indefinitely. A single zombie is like finding a worrisome mole or a lump in your breast: it might mean the end, but you've still got a fighting chance. A horde of zombies is like old age: the gig is up, and all those undead shamblers might as well be all the people you knew who died before you, eager to welcome you into the biggest (if least popular) club in the world.

This is why, for me, exemplars of zombie cinema have always been those willing to lean into this spirit of unavoidable doom: Romero's six-film zombie cycle, Tourneur's *I Walked with a Zombie* (1943), Ragona and Salkow's *The Last Man on Earth* (1964), Clark's *Deathdream* (1972), Maslansky's *Sugar Hill* (1974), Fulci's *Zombi 2* (1979) and *The Beyond* (1981), Parkinson's *I, Zombie: The*

Zombies don't *cause* death. They *are* death. It doesn't matter how you try to protect yourself. Zombies will wait you out. You have to come out sometime.

Chronicles of Pain (1998), Sarmiento's *Deadgirl* (2008), Gardner's *The Battery* (2012), England's *Contracted* (2013), Hobson's *Maggie* (2015), and Bonello's *Zombi Child* (2019).

As this book illustrates, the canniest of poster artists know how to tap into this doom—the awareness of which, after all, is what makes us human. The pure terror of Mrs. Cooper's face on the front of so many *Night of the Living Dead* posters; the zombie head like the rising sun—what a powerful, thoughtful image!—on the original *Dawn of the Dead* poster; the thousand-yard (if eyeless) stare of the aforementioned *Zombi 2*.

These images, included in this book, first stared out at us from ramshackle theater lobbies and video rental shelves, waiting with a zombie's patience for us to slow down—way down—and build up the guts to watch the movies, thereby looking into the face of death, the corporeal facts of our decomposition and the ultimate irrelevance of our existence. In this way, zombie films are the cinema subgenre that tells us more about ourselves than any other.

That is a high art indeed.

RIGHT: One-sheet poster for *Dawn of the Dead* (1978). There is also a variant with the title logo in green. Since *Dawn*'s extraordinary violence and gore would have earned it an "X" rating from the MPAA, Romero and producer Richard Rubinstein did something virtually unheard of: they released the film without a rating. To mitigate this, they went with a "soft" look for the poster, based on a production crew T-shirt designed by artist Lanny Powers.

ACKNOWLEDGMENTS

Thanks first to the scholars and experts whose work I drew from in researching this book: Robert Cremer, Chris Fujiwara, Paul R. Gagne, Steve Haberman, Zora Neale Hurston, Lee Karr, Arthur Lennig, Tim Lucas, Roger Luckhurst, Kim Newman, Gary D. Rhodes, George A. Romero, William C. Seabrook, J. P. Telotte, Stephen Thrower, and Tom Weaver. A considerable debt of gratitude is owed to Ben Rubin of the George A. Romero Archival Collection at the University of Pittsburgh; Ben not only plumbed the depths of the collection to find some wonderful images, he also provided insight into Romero and his films.

Thanks to Will Steeds and Laura Ward at Elephant Book Company for believing in me, to Donald Maass for business advice, to my editor Tom Seabrook for bringing it all together, to layout artist supreme Paul Palmer-Edwards, and to Sally Claxton for making sure the pictures worked. Thanks to my Iliad Bookshop family and the writing friends who keep me going (and the non-writing friends, too—extra shout-out to Kevin Cazares), and of course to my partner-in-all-crimes Ricky Grove. HUGE thanks to all of the artists whose incredible work brought this book to (undead) life.

One individual, though, deserves special recognition—in fact, this book is dedicated to him: Stephen Jones. It's not enough to simply say that *The Art of the Zombie Movie* would not exist without him (although it's true); my entire writing career would not exist without him. Thank you, Steve.

ART CREDITS

AUTHOR BIOS

Lisa Morton is a screenwriter, author of nonfiction books, and prose writer whose work was described by the American Library Association's *Readers' Advisory Guide to Horror* as "consistently dark, unsettling, and frightening." She is a six-time winner of the Bram Stoker Award®, the author of four novels (including *Zombie Apocalypse!: Washington Deceased*) and over 150 short stories, and a world-class Halloween and paranormal expert. Her other books include *Ghosts: A Haunted History, Calling the Spirits: A History of Seances, Trick or Treat: A History of Halloween, The Halloween Encyclopedia,* and *The Cinema of Tsui Hark,* and she also contributed to Stephen Jones's acclaimed *The Art of Horror.* Lisa lives in Los Angeles and online at www.lisamorton.com.

With forty books published internationally and nineteen feature movies in worldwide distribution, **John A. Russo** has been called a "living legend" and "just a nice guy who likes to scare people." He began his career by coauthoring the screenplay for the classic horror film *Night of the Living Dead,* and went on to write and direct several other horror films, including *Midnight* and *Santa Claws.* His three books on moviemaking have become bibles of independent production; one of them, *Scare Tactics,* won a national award for Superior Nonfiction. His novels include *The Awakening* and *Dealey Plaza.*

Daniel Kraus is a *New York Times* bestselling author. His collaboration with legendary filmmaker George A. Romero, *The Living Dead,* was acclaimed by the *New York Times* and the *Washington Post.* With Guillermo del Toro, he coauthored *The Shape of Water,* based on the same idea the two created for the Oscar-winning film. Also with del Toro, Kraus coauthored *Trollhunters,* which was adapted into the Emmy-winning Netflix series. Kraus's *The Death and Life of Zebulon Finch* was named one of *Entertainment Weekly's* Top 10 Books of the Year. Kraus is a three-time Bram Stoker Award finalist. Visit him at danielkraus.com.